Raising a
Responsible Child

Raising a Responsible Child

HOW PARENTS CAN AVOID INDULGING TOO MUCH AND RESCUING TOO OFTEN

Elizabeth M. Ellis, Ph.D.

A CITADEL PRESS BOOK
Published by Carol Publishing Group

To James, Andrew and Sarah

A Citadel Press Book
Published by Carol Publishing Group
Citadel Press is a registered trademark of Carol Communications, Inc.
Editorial, sales and distribution, rights and permissions inquiries
should be addressed to Carol Publishing Group, 120 Enterprise Avenue,
Secaucus, N.J. 07094

In Canada: Canadian Manda Group, One Atlantic Avenue, Suite 105,
Toronto, Ontario, M6K 3E7

Carol Publishing Group books may be purchased in bulk at special discounts
for sales promotion, fund-raising, or educational purposes. Special editions
can be created to specifications. For details, contact Special Sales Department,
120 Enterprise Avenue, Secaucus, N.J. 07094.

Manufactured in the United States of America
10 9 8 7 6 5 4 3 2 1

Ellis, Elizabeth M.
    Raising a responsible child : how parents can avoid indulging too
much and rescuing too often / Elizabeth M. Ellis.
        p. cm.
    "A Citadel Press book."
    Originally published: 1995
    Includes bibliographical references and index.
    ISBN 0–8065–1824–3 (pb)
    1 Child rearing.   2. Child psychology.   3. Parent and child.
4. Parental overprotection.   5. Responsibility.   I. Title.
[HQ769.E5645   1996]
849′.1—dc20   96–24000
                                                            CIP

Contents

Author to Reader

As I write this, I am reminded of two young men I recently saw in my practice. One was a twenty-three-year-old man, Pete, who was seriously depressed about himself and his future. He had withdrawn from his college courses yet another time, feeling unable to face the pressure of exams and term papers. In five years of attempts at college, he had managed to complete less than two years' worth of credits. He had decided to join the military to try to make a success of his life, but his parents were opposed.

His mother said she would miss him if he were far away. "We've always been very close," she said. His father was worried that if Pete got into trouble in the military, he wouldn't be able to be there to help Pete out. His father admitted, "I guess we've done too much for Pete over the years," but insisted on paying for his treatment and for vocational testing to make sure the military was the right choice for him. Pete just wanted to get away as soon as possible, as he felt terrible taking any more of his parents' money.

The following day, I saw Joe, aged eighteen, a freshman at a major technical university in town. Joe had been hit with incapacitating waves of anxiety and panic about three weeks into his first quarter at school. These attacks of anxiety had become so severe that he had ended up in the emergency room of the local hospital. He could not open up, and we had not been able to determine just what was the source of this anxiety. After the third visit, I suggested Joe go to his family doctor down the street and consult with him about some medication. Joe gave me a bewildered look and shuffled slowly out the door.

Later that evening, his mother called to discuss the situation. When I described his bewildered look, she explained that he probably seemed that way because he had never called a professional, made an appointment for himself, or called an employer about his work schedule. She had always done those things for him. In fact, she had always washed his laundry, made sure his athletic uniforms were ready for practices and games, had his car checked out, and paid his bills. As she went on, I began to see why Joe was so anxious. He was having to make decisions on his own for perhaps the first time in his life.

While Pete and Joe have different clinical diagnoses, they have much in common. Both come from very loving families. In fact, both sets of parents are competent, informed people who are devoted to their children. Yet they are typical of a growing trend that I have seen over a span of seventeen years in private practice. They are parents who do too much for their children and set too few limits. Determined to give them all the advantages they didn't have growing up in the fifties and sixties, these parents protect their children from stresses whenever possible and rescue them from the consequences of their behavior.

These children grow into "underdeveloped" children and adolescents, and even young adults. They are dependent on others to make decisions for them; they have low self-esteem; they are typically underachievers in school; they have poor coping skills when faced with the problems of everyday life. They cope by withdrawing from tough situations, becoming anxious, depressed, and even suicidal. Often they vent their frustration on others and blame them for their troubles. They have a difficult time growing up and becoming responsible, capable, and confident adults. Joe's parents agreed to turn over more decision-making to Joe and to support his choices. They also encouraged him to stay in school and not drop out, even though he had expressed a wish to do so. After Joe finished his quarter with passing grades, his anxiety level began to subside to manageable levels. Pete went on to join the navy, against his parents' wishes. When I last heard from his dad, he said that, though he himself was depressed and missed Pete a lot, Pete was doing well as far as he knew.

While parenting styles are thought to shift over time, the growing trend in the United States over the past forty years has clearly been a trend toward greater permissiveness and greater warmth toward children, coupled with an increased closeness between parents and children. These three elements make up a parenting style that psychologists call "overindulgent." For the most part, this trend has had tremendously positive results for children. Gone are the days when food was withheld from babies in order to keep them on rigid schedules and children were routinely struck with hickory sticks. Sayings such as "Spare the rod and spoil the child," and "Children are better seen than heard," are now considered a neglectful at best, if not abusive, and rightfully so. Our culture now prizes children, is eager to hear what they have to say, and values love along with discipline.

Yet this trend toward overindulgent parenting has had its negative repercussions as well. Studies show that alcohol abuse by teens is a growing national problem. There are more suicides, especially and surprisingly among teens in middle-class suburbs. Antisocial behaviors, such as shoplifting, vandalism, and sexual assault, are also on the rise among well-off teens. These problems are reflected in increased numbers of teens in psychiatric hospitals and in the juvenile courts.

As a clinical psychologist, I come face to face with these families on a daily basis. Some are parents of problem children as young as two and three years of age; yet others are concerned about their son or daughter in his or her late twenties. Most are concerned parents who have tried to do a good job at parenting yet are shocked and dismayed at the level and type of behavior problems their children are having. They come in seeking help for their youngsters but also seeking answers to their questions. It is for these families that this book was written.

This book began as a series of articles published in our clinic newsletter. We have built a private practice in suburban Atlanta over the last twelve years and we send out a newsletter on family issues to over eight hundred people in the community who work with children and families. I was surprised at the strong response in the community to the series titled "Overindulgent Families and Underdeveloped Children."

One high school principal asked to reprint the article in his own newsletter which goes out to all the parents in the school. I met with his staff over lunch and listened to their concerns. They spoke about meting out consequences to the students, only to see the parents make great efforts to rescue their children from those consequences. They were frustrated with parents who did too much for their children and with parents who were willing to call the school to make up false excuses for them when they failed to show up for final exams. They saw a general overconcern on the part of parents with making their child "happy."

One day-care center director said the article really hit home. Jeanette Beck, with thirty-four years in the day-care business, manages a staff of thirty-two who care for 184 kids. She saw a growing problem over the years with parents who do too much for their children and give them too many things, primarily out of guilt. They feel guilty because they are divorced, because they do not have custody, or because they are working and have to put the child in day care, or because they have to work late.

Katherine Leviakos, an elementary school counselor for thirty-one years, met with me in the library of her school. She was particularly interested in the topic and asked me to talk to the parents who attended the PTA. She voiced her concerns about the lack of consistency in the home, about responsibilities in the home that were vague at best, and about "rescuers"—parents who protect their children from the unpleasant consequences of the children's actions. She saw a particular problem with fourth graders, in that fourth grade represents a big advance in terms of the amount of homework and individual responsibility required of students. She had had a significant number of "criers" in the fourth grade, more than any other grade, who just couldn't keep up. They had difficulty concentrating, following directions, solving problems, keeping up with assignments. They appeared to have a learning disorder, when in fact they simply weren't prepared.

Angela Crowell, an administrator at Parkwood High School, also called my office and asked permission to reprint the articles in her newsletter to parents. In charge of students with problems of frequent absences and excessive tardiness, she expressed grave concerns about parents who seemed overly allied with their son or daughter—parents who not only made excuses for their children but even blamed the school administrators for their problems. She said that many of these same parents seemed to set no limits for their teenagers, reserving hotel rooms for them on prom night and allowing keg parties in their homes. They saw themselves as powerless to stop their teens' reckless behavior and felt that at best, all they could do was monitor it.

In writing this book, I hope to give insight to parents about themselves: why they parent the way they do and what it is about their style of operating that is not working. I also hope to give them a clear analysis of their children's problems and a brief overview of relevant child psychology research to help explain why their children are having problems. Because most books are long on analysis and short on solutions, I have tried to offer more in the way of guidance than background and development.

This is not meant to be a "parent-bashing" book. Given the climate and complexity of today's society, most parents deserve medals for their efforts—for having the courage to bring a child into this uncertain world and for making the commitment and sacrifices necessary to be a caring parent in a "me first" society. As a psychologist and as a parent, I always try to be mindful of the fact that my influence over my child is not that powerful. Yes, that's right, not that powerful. While Freud thought the parent shaped the child and that the child was shaped by the age of six, we now know that those premises are false. Children's behavior, attitudes, accomplishments, and values are shaped equally by three factors: (1) by their innate, inborn temperament, (2) by the community and culture in which they live, and (3) by the family.

We write books for parents not because parents are to blame for children's problems but because this is the one variable among the three that we can change. Parents can't change their child's temperament or their culture, but they can change what they do in the home. I write this book for overindulgent parents because they are exceptionally qualified as agents of change with their children. They are loving, warm, involved, and highly motivated. They are already striving to be good parents. It is hoped that with the skills they learn in this book, they can be even better mothers and fathers.

Raising a
Responsible Child

1 The Historical Background of Today's Overindulgent Parenting Style

While we hear much in the media about how our society has changed dramatically—from an agricultural nation to an industrialized one, and now evolving into a high-speed, electronic and computerized culture—few have paid much attention to the fact that our attitudes and values about how to raise children have changed dramatically, too. When we were an agricultural society, we had children for two primary reasons: to provide cheap labor to work the farm and to care for us in our old age. They also stood to inherit the land and thus to maintain and expand the family assets. Because we needed several farmhands, cooks, and seamstresses, we had large families of six or eight or even ten children. And since our children often died before the age of four, we could not afford to become as sentimentally attached to them as we are today.

We can still see this pattern today in other parts of the world. In less developed agricultural societies, children begin to contribute to the economic well-being of the family by the age of six or seven. By the age of twleve, they bring in enough income and labor to equal the family's expenditure on them in terms of food and clothing and shelter. By the age of fifteen, these adolescents are primary caretakers and breadwinners for their families.

Our transition to an industrialized nation, which began in earnest after the Civil War, changed a great many factors in the American family. Families moved to the towns and cities so that fathers could go to work in the factories and mills. Children were not needed as farmhands and household workers or heirs to the land, and thus the birthrate began to go down. New developments in birth control enabled us to limit the size of our families. Our health improved, and many early-childhood illnesses were brought under control. When we began to have only two, three, or four children, who often lived past early childhood, we tended to form deeper emotional bonds with them.

As we saw our children growing up in the cities and taking jobs there, education became more important. It was apparent that a higher level of reading and math skills would be needed for jobs in the cities, and laws were passed making it mandatory that children stay in school until the age of sixteen. The first kindergartens were established at this time. While in some states the exploitation of child labor was not abolished till the 1920s, by the early 1900s the publication of photographs of children as young as seven working long shifts in mills and factories brought a storm of criticism that led to widespread reforms.

In a span of time as short as fifty years, we underwent a revolution. We began to see children as innocent, fragile, dependent on us, and in need of our nurturance and guidance. We viewed childhood as a time of protection from the adult world of harsh demands and exploitation. It was to be a prolonged time of development and growth, of play and experimentation, of dependency upon the family. We, in turn, saw our role not as breeders of workers but as instillers of culture. We were to educate these few children we were having, to impart our values and wisdom to them and give them the skills they would need to be productive citizens. Children were cherished as individuals in their own right, with their own thoughts, feelings, and needs.

It was not until around the turn of the century that authors began to write books just for children, that furniture, clothing, and toys were mass-produced for children only. No longer an economic investment, children, in fact, became more of an economic drain on the family. We began to have children not for economic but for emotional reasons. We have children to hold a marriage together, to fulfill ourselves, to "complete our family," to feel loved and needed.

It was against this background of dramatic changes in our view of children and our role as parents that Benjamin Spock entered the child-care scene with his classic *Baby and Child Care* in 1945. Up to that time, there still existed a widespread belief that the oppressive control of children was a good thing. The federal agency that gave advice to mothers on health and childrearing, the Children's Bureau, still advocated that mothers feed babies and put them to bed on a precise, minute-by-minute schedule, regardless of their age or emotional state. Some professionals held that failure to follow a strict routine would upset the household, irritate or "spoil" the baby, or bring about some vaguely defined dire consequences.

Spock's message was one whose time had come—that children know innately what they need, and that most parents know instinctively how to care for them, so let's let go of this obsessive preoccupation with strict control of the child's bodily functions. While Spock is sometimes linked with the shift in our views of parenting toward a climate of permissiveness, the first edition of his child-care manual simply brought together some of the progressive thinkers of his day. One line of thought came from early pioneers in education such as John Dewey and William Kilpatrick, who established that a child learns better and faster if she is developmentally "ready" to learn and that there is great individual variation in the readiness to learn. Thus, it is pointless to stress early walking, early toilet training, or early self-help skills. Rather, it is better to wait for the child to demonstrate to us that she is ready and then seize the moment.

These views were bolstered by the writings of Sigmund Freud, which were held in high esteem in the 1930s and 1940s. Freud formed his beliefs about the nature of some kinds of mental illness by listening to people who had grown up in Victorian Austria, a society that was very prim and proper with regard to expressions of sexuality and aggression. He viewed neuroses as having their origin in the pressure that mothers placed on children to suppress their sexual and aggressive impulses. Many interpreted his writings to mean that firm efforts to establish potty training or to stop children from having tantrums or fighting might make them neurotic as adults. While we know now that this is not true, Freud's ideas were influential in shaping our cultural attitudes for a good fifty years, and there are still some strong adherents of Freud even to this day.

Spock was also influenced by the early studies done on delinquents and criminals in the 1920s. Researchers found that the majority of them had suffered as much from a lack of love and from excessive punishment as from a lack of discipline. These results seemed to fall in line with what Freud was saying at the time. Lastly, Spock was influenced by the studies of Dr. Preston McLendon and Ms. Frances Simsarian, published in 1942, on feeding schedules for babies. They revealed to many exhausted and relieved mothers that babies did just as well if not better on "self-demand" schedules, remaining healthy, happy, and free of disease.

The confluence of Freudian thinking and the dissemination of beliefs about child psychology into the mass culture, through such popular books as *Baby and Child Care,* have given rise in the last forty years to a phenomenon in our culture that I call the "over-psychologizing" of childhood stresses and the overvaluation of maternal love. While our mothers, even as late as the 1950s, may have bragged about how soon they were able to force their children to walk, be potty-trained, or drink from a cup, mothers today would view this strong push to achieve mastery of self-help skills, which the child may not be ready for, as not simply misguided but downright harmful and abusive.

The trend over the last few decades has been one of delaying transitions to new developmental stages as long as the child wishes. Mothers at malls now brag about having breastfed a child until she was two years old and having let potty training go until she was "ready" at three and a half.

Somehow there has come to be a hidden assumption in our culture that the transition from one developmental stage to another is traumatic for children and is out of the realm of normal experience. We have acquired this massive national anxiety as parents that if we make a mistake—if the transition is difficult, is frustrating, or done too early—our children will be emotionally scarred for life. Freud was a big believer in psychological determinism: that all adult behavior is shaped by the forces acting on children in their early years. And so our culture has become imbued with the belief that children are fragile, and that parents, more specifically mothers, are so powerful, that they alone are responsible for molding and shaping children and are responsible for all adult mental maladjustment.

A friend of mine recently confided that she had decided not to have a second child because she just couldn't go through breastfeeding again. She nursed her first child every two hours for ten months and was so exhausted that she was delirious half the time. This same friend was still going through potty training when her son was three and a half. It was embarrassing for him to go out in diapers, but she felt compelled to stress to him that she didn't mind one way or the other whether he learned to use the potty. It was totally up to him to do it when he was "ready."

But of course, this was a lie. She wanted very much to be through with diapers but felt it would scar him emotionally if she let her feelings be known. She asked me once if it would put undue pressure on him if she rewarded him by giving him a treat for using the potty.

The overpsychologizing of childhood stresses has great implications for us today as parents. We, as a culture, have become afraid to set firm expectations for children to mature and to become independent. Rather than see developmental milestones as opportunities for children to grow, we have come to see them as minefields with the potential to harm children. We see transitions to the next stage of development not as events to be celebrated but almost as traumas to be avoided. In this book's preface, we saw Pete, who wanted to join the military at twenty-three to make his way in the world, but his father was concerned that the military base might be too far away for him to get to Pete easily if he "should get into trouble." He could not applaud his son's courage for wanting to move on to his next phase in becoming a man. Instead, he was overly concerned that Pete might not be "ready" to be so far from home.

In our modern, post-Freudian culture, not only have the normal stresses of childhood been pathologized but the antidote to all unhappiness and mental illness consists of the liberal application of parental love, particularly maternal love. This has become a belief so entrenched in all levels of our society that it is almost heresy to challenge it. Jerome Kagan, perhaps America's most eminent child psychologist, has written that current Western society attributes a power to maternal love that is greater than that in any period of our history or in any other part of the world. It is a power that is equaled in other societies only by the power they invest in spirits, sorcery, sin, God, or witchcraft.

We have come to define maternal love in our culture as the frequent display of physical affection, verbal expressions of love and acceptance, and the making of great financial and material sacrifices for the child. I use the word "define" here because individuals in other societies perceive themselves to have been loved even though they had very few of these things. Love is defined differently in their culture, just as parental roles are defined differently from one society to another. For example, Japanese fathers often use harsh physical punishment, stern anger, and a complete absence of affection and play with their children, but their children perceive themselves to be loved because they view their fathers as trying to teach them behaviors that will keep them out of trouble.

As parents, we have come to believe that our primary role is to "give love" to our children so that they will be happy and healthy adults. I believe that this emphasis on "love" has supplanted to a large degree the other roles we once had as parents: to impart knowledge, to instill the values of our culture, to continue the faith, rituals, and religious observances, and to create productive citizens to run the community. Whereas the giving of love to our children is important, we have invested it with far too much power. Kagan writes, "A mother's love for the child is treated as a mysterious force which, if sprinkled plentifully over young children, guarantees salvation." Psychologists have known for years that large doses of maternal love do not guarantee emotional salvation, yet this knowledge has not yet been disseminated to the larger society.

All these changes bring us to the current American scene in the 1990s, where love predominates and limits are a thing of the past. Our families are even smaller than they were at the turn of the century— one or two children has become the norm. With the divorce rate skyrocketing in the seventies and eighties, we have shrunk even more, to perhaps one parent with one or two children becoming a common unit.

We do not live in large, extended families where several adult women care for the children. No longer are our children wet-nursed by strangers, put in the field to work at seven, or sent to boarding schools or apprenticeship programs at ten as they were in the 1700s and 1800s. We live in very small families now, isolated from the extended family. We form very intense bonds with our children. Our children stay at home longer than ever and may be with us until they are in their early twenties.

I have continued to be amazed by the numbers of children who still sleep with parents, especially a single parent, at the age of eight, ten, even fourteen. Our small family units are increasingly turned inward, as we band together for security in large, urban areas. We have become a mobile society: We live in communities we did not grow up in, have no extended family nearby, and have no church ties. We may not even know our neighbors. We are reluctant to let our children play down the street or even in the front yard unsupervised, for fear of violent crime. We feel we must fill the role of playmate to our children. Often alone ourselves and overly stressed, we turn to our children as companions and confidants as well.

These bonds are very deep, and they have become more and more focused on the giving of love unceasingly, with the goal of bringing about "happiness" in our children. Because we now also have children in order to meet our own emotional needs, we often parent in a way that meets our own needs more than the child's needs. We seek to produce this elusive thing called "happiness" in our children and, more recently, "self-esteem." The current cultural myth holds that if we simply give enough love to our children, we will bring about happiness and self-esteem: Yet it doesn't seem to be working. Researchers have known for thirty years now that giving children affection and "I love you's" does not necessarily bring about self-esteem, yet this information remains hidden from the general public.

Along with these trends, another set of changes occurring in the American family has intensified our guilt as parents. Mothers have gone back to work, parents have been divorced and remarried, and people work longer hours at their jobs. Mothers feel guilty about working and not being there when the children come home from school. They feel guilty about initiating divorce—an event that leads to the loss of a full-time father for their children. Fathers feel guilty for being part-time dads. They feel guilty for remarrying, knowing their children are living with an unhappy mother. Remarried parents feel guilty about bringing a new person into the home whom the children may resent. Often their remarriage brings stepsiblings into the home, then half siblings, all of whom may make their first children feel displaced. Overwhelmed with guilt, we seek to do better by our children by providing more "love" as we see it, which often includes a relaxing of limits, a focus on having fun together, and the offering of more material privileges.

As our family size has been shrinking, our affluence has been increasing, not just in the United States but in all industrialized Western countries. The amount of financial resources that we can and do spend on just one child today is tremendous compared to other cultures and to other periods in our history. It is estimated that the cost today to bear a child and to raise her to maturity, including putting her through college, is about $200,000. Not only is this a tremendous outlay, but it is one that is never recouped. Recall in the beginning of this chapter it was stated that in more primitive cultures, children began to return the investment in their upkeep by about the age of twelve.

Our increased affluence and the cost of rearing children today has many far-reaching implications. On the positive side, we can truly feel good about the fact that our children want for so little. They will not have to be ashamed of their shabby clothing, crooked teeth, or the poor haircut done by Mom in the family kitchen.

On the other hand, it has promoted a kind of narcissistic entitlement that is new and to some degree frightening. A comfortable lifestyle, with all the amenities featured in advertisements, has come to be seen as a birthright by children of today. School-aged children expect to have stylish clothing and hairstyles, to have their own television and VCRs, and the latest Nintendo games. Teenagers in large urban areas and their surrounding suburbs have come to expect designer clothes, a private phone line, and a late model car on their sixteenth birthday. These goods are not viewed as privileges to be earned or acquired but as things that are automatically provided to the children of the middle class. We cannot blame our children for this. We, as parents, have come to believe that it is our duty to offer a very comfortable lifestyle to our children. We see it as our obligation to them to provide a life that is free of need.

This increased affluence, and with it a sense of entitlement, has had very damaging effects on children's self-esteem in our society today. In less industrialized cultures, children are valued from the age of seven because of the labor that they provide for their families. Even girls as young as four and five care for toddlers while their mothers work in the fields. Children are given levels of responsibility at an early age that help them to feel that they are important people, that the success of the family unit and of the community as a whole depends on them.

Our children have few opportunities to feel that they contribute to the economic well-being or the day-to-day functioning of the family. While they enjoy affluence and the privileges it provides and have come to feel entitled to it, many feel the hollowness that comes with it. When money is tight, they realize that they are an economic burden to their families. Many teenagers desperately want a part-time job so they can feel they are making a financial contribution to their upkeep. Yet so often parents deny them this opportunity, stating, "I'd just as soon give him the money. I want him to enjoy being a child as long as he can."

Our children today are dependent on us emotionally and financially until they are eighteen, twenty-one, or even twenty-five. While this prolonged dependency has been a luxury enjoyed by children and sometimes adults as well, it has had serious ramifications for postponing the development of the capacity in our children to function independently. Our children arrive at new developmental stages in their lives ill equipped to handle them. Ultimately, they come to adulthood with no road map of how to get through the twists and turns that lie ahead.

Kagan has written that for many middle-class families today, the child is a beautiful young bird to be cared for until it is ready to fly free in the forest. They are fragile, ornamental, even functionless. Yet fly free in the forest they must. We are still an individualist society, however, not a collectivist one. Individuals in American culture must compete with one another for resources and must succeed or fail through their own individual efforts. As adults, we are expected to walk a tightrope with few safety nets around us. Though we may try to protect our children from this stress and may even delay it until they are well into their twenties, they eventually must take their places in a society that prizes autonomy and individual accomplishment above all else.

While our parenting styles in the 1800s and even the early 1900s may have prepared our children for this role, our approaches to parenting in the 1990s do not. Our children, as they mature, are not finding a smooth transition into our competitive society. Over the years, I have seen progressively more teenagers whose disturbed behaviors, while they varied in form, appeared to arise out of a core fear of growing up. They felt in their hearts, at some unspoken level, that they did not have what it took to "make it" and that they were going to fail. Once the fear was out in the open, often the parents felt free to speak about their anxiety, too—that they were afraid for their children to grow up, that they felt their sons or daughters were "not ready."

It is this group of adolescents that today contributes to the rising statistics with regard to alcoholism, runaways, and suicides, and the rising psychiatric hospitalization rates, especially among the middle class and the affluent. These adolescents aren't ready for adulthood: They are what I have come to call *underdeveloped*. In the next chapter, we will take a look at many of the hallmark characteristics of underdeveloped children, from early childhood to young adulthood.

2 Do You Have an Underdeveloped Child or Adolescent?

In selecting this book, you, the parent, must have some concern already about your child's emotional growth and well-being. Perhaps your son is doing poorly in school in spite of the fact that his teachers say he is capable of making A's and B's. Your daughter is moody and irritable and seems to be very discouraged about herself much of the time. Perhaps you have a child who still seems to be whining and having tantrums, though he's in the third grade now. Whatever the immediate and most pressing problem, it appears that he or she is not motivated to explore life, to test skills, to relate well to others. She doesn't seem to want to push herself, to live up to the potential that you know is there. He would rather depend on you to do things for him than take a risk and possibly fail. Your best description of him is, well, immature. This is where the term *underdeveloped* comes from.

Many children of overindulgent parents do not master developmental tasks at an age that is appropriate for them. By developmental tasks we mean those milestones in development that typically occur at a certain point in the child's life. Some are automatic and have a narrow range of time in which they occur. For example, children will learn to walk on their own, provided no one hampers their movement and their natural urge to explore their world. We don't have to encourage them to walk or teach them how to walk. They usually begin to walk between the ages of ten and fourteen months. They're not mature enough to walk before this, and it's unlikely that they will refrain from walking until they're beyond fourteen months.

Other developmental milestones, however, are not so automatic and occur at times that may vary widely from one child to another. For example, children first become comfortable spending the night at a friend's house at about the age of five or six if they're adventuresome, or seven or eight if they're a little shyer. They don't do so automatically, and some may need encouragement and help with arrangements. The child who is reluctant to spend the night with a friend at age nine or ten is developmentally behind her peers. She is likely to be dependent on her parents and afraid to separate from them, because she does not know how to handle the situations that will come up at the friend's house.

With this introduction in mind, we'll now go into a more detailed analysis of underdeveloped children and adolescents. The twelve traits that follow form the core problems for these children, but they also direct the parent and the clinician to those areas that are most problematic for these children and adolescents. This is a good chapter to read twice. As you notice these problems on a daily basis in your child, you can begin right away to formulate some strategies of your own to correct them.

Underdeveloped children have what psychologists call "poor frustration tolerance."

By this we mean that a child's ability to tolerate frustration is very low. Frustration, as we all know, is a part of adult life. From pulling to a standing position to mastering quadratic equations, frustration will be a part of every child's life, as well, in the course of development from infant to adult. By coping with frustration during childhood, we learn to cope with frustration in adulthood. The ability to cope with frustration and maintain emotional control is one of the hallmarks of a well-adjusted individual, child or adult.

Children of overindulgent parents have had many, many frustrating situations removed from their experience, and they often come into adolescence ill equipped for the frustrations of real life. As children they instead master strategies for getting the parent to resolve the frustration for them. They have tantrums or lose control emotionally when a task is experienced as difficult. They withdraw from the activity or give up, in hopes the parent will take over. They denigrate the activity as something "stupid" and "not worth doing," in hopes of substituting one that is easier and more fun.

Underdeveloped children have what psychologists call "poor task persistence."

Here we are referring to the ability to persist toward a goal, to hang in there until the job is done. Though it often comes hand in hand with poor frustration tolerance, it is a little bit different. Some goals are not very difficult or frustrating, but they may be tedious, time-consuming, or boring. They may take a long time and require several steps to complete—like raking leaves, bagging them up, and taking the bags down to the street.

The ability to set a goal and persist with one's efforts until the goal is realized is also a part of adult life. In fact, it is a necessary part of healthy functioning in any adult role. Whether you are at home reorganizing the contents of your kitchen cabinets or at work as a research scientist conducting experiments that take years to complete, you must be able to persist in the face of boredom, obstacles, repetition, interruptions, and lack of immediate results.

Children of permissive parents come into adulthood with a history of giving up easily on tasks, projects, and goals. They begin puzzles but seldom finish them. When asked to clean their rooms, they pick up a few things but then get distracted. They start to rake the yard but wander away without adult supervision. Parents make statements like "He quit softball because it was 'boring.' He quit Scouts because it was 'dumb.'" Or they describe their daughter this way: "She quit piano lessons because it 'wasn't fun.' She quit the needlework project because it 'took too long.'" By the time they are in high school, they have quit studying, too. Biology is "too hard," English is "dumb," and geometry is "pointless." Overindulgent parents are reluctant to use pressure to get their children to persist at long, complex tasks. Most typically, they take over the task and finish it themselves, as they also can't bear to let the child accept the negative consequences of not finishing the job.

Deena: The Problem of Chronic Giving Up

Deena's family called me after reading an article I wrote in our clinic newsletter. Deena's father, Dennis, said, "Boy, your article describes Deena to a 't.' She has just given up on school. Her grades have been dropping steadily for years. She used to be in the gifted program, but now, at seventeen, she is barely passing. She won't join anything, won't go out, won't make new friends. She has always been shy, but now she's downright depressed and we're worried about her."

Deena's family could be described as a family of intellectuals with a very liberal view of childrearing. They believed in giving their children the freedom of individual creative thinking and decisionmaking. They had had problems with their older son's procrastinating but were pleased when he got himself more organized and on track in his sophomore year of college. What they failed to see was that Deena had a far more anxious personality than her brother. She was more at risk, as "giving up" had become a chronic pattern.

When I met with Deena, she said she was really afraid to grow up. Even though she knew she was bright, she just didn't think she could handle college work. When she looked at her homework, it all seemed so difficult; she would just shut the book and watch television or take a nap. She might take a stab at it here and there, if a friend studied with her, or if her best friend chewed her out, but then she would quickly give up.

As she fell further behind, she got progressively more anxious and overwhelmed. She would watch more television and take more naps. Her parents would complain, but she tuned them out. All their nagging turned into power struggles that Deena would ultimately win. By the end of the semester, she was so anxious about failing, she would study just enough for the final to pass with a D. She knew no decent college would take her with only passing grades and felt she had let her family down and that her future looked bleak.

The focus of Deena's treatment centered around her making a plan to organize her assignments and accomplish her work in a step-by-step way. We even looked at what kinds of rewards she could provide for herself to motivate her to study. Working with her parents, however, was much harder.

They could not see that they could step back and support and encourage Deena's plan. They were sure Deena's plan would fail. They wanted instead to pursue what they had done in the past— make the work easier—this time by having her go to school part-time and take as long as she needed (I call it the "We're so patient" approach) or to continue to nag and threaten her or a combination of both.

If school were the only problem, and the adolescent could persist at other difficult tasks, the problem might be limited in scope. But it seldom is. Deena had no driver's license at seventeen, not even a learner's permit. Driving was "too hard" and "made her nervous."

Since she did not drive, she could not get a job. She would not get involved in church youth activities because she "was uncomfortable" with kids she didn't know. She spent her summers sitting at home watching television while her friends got jobs as camp counselors, restaurant workers, or store clerks.

Underdeveloped children have poor problem-solving skills.

As a clinician, I know that children learn to cope with problems successfully by being allowed to solve the problem by themselves— provided they have some backup adult guidance, should they need it, as to what is a good method and what is a not-so-good method. Underdeveloped children have often been prevented from solving problems by overprotective parents who want to remove problems from their lives. What do I do if someone is teasing me on the bus? What do I do if I leave my lunch at home? How do I fix a flat tire on my bicycle?

It is easy for a parent to step in and take care of these problems. It's not too terribly difficult to drive the child to school, drop off his lunch at the school office, and fix the flat tire for him.

In this situation, however, the child loses valuable information about assertiveness with others, coping with adversity, and the mechanics of bicycle repair. The child is that much less equipped to deal with these problems the next time they occur.

In adolescence, the problems are more difficult for the parent to resolve easily. What do I do when my boyfriend seems to like another girl? How do I get a job? How do I arrange transportation once I get a job? What do I do when everyone at a party is drinking? Here, an overprotective parent can still resolve some of the problems for the adolescent. She can arrange a job through some personal contacts and buy her daughter a car. She can try to forbid her daughter from having contact with that boy or that peer group, although that would be difficult at best. But the adolescent has been prevented, once again, from having the opportunity to learn new skills—the skills of asserting herself with others, coping with conflict, filling out job applications, promoting herself, carpooling, and reading bus schedules.

By young adulthood, this person now has a tremendous deficit in the area of problem-solving skills compared to other young adults who have been solving problems since they were preschoolers. If we think of problem-solving experiences as being like a library—each experience being a volume added to the collection —underdeveloped adolescents have libraries that hold just a few slim books. There is no store of life experiences to draw on. Their peers, who have been pressured to face problems and cope with them, on the other hand, have libraries that have been accumulating over time.

Many adolescents and young adults, when faced with problems they don't know how to handle, simply collapse. They are prone to emotional breakdowns or impulsive solutions that are poorly thought out. They experience overwhelming anxiety or suicidal fantasies, or may run away from home. They often say, "I don't want to grow up." The reason they give is a vague and poorly defined sense of being unable to handle adult life.

I always think of them as the fragile young birds Kagan speaks of. Raised in a cage, sheltered from experience, they are suddenly turned out into a not-so-friendly world. I remember one very overprotected young man who was twenty-three when I saw him and experiencing overwhelming anxiety attacks after leaving home. He said he kept feeling as if he were a bird who flew out of a nest on the side of a cliff and was falling, falling through space. He said he felt his wings just weren't strong enough to support him, that he didn't know how to fly.

Underdeveloped children are reluctant to take risks, to go into new situations and learn new skills.

Another marker of successful adult functioning is the willingness to try new activities that will require mastery and with it the risk of failure. Whether it is taking up golf or applying for a promotion or having children, we all are faced with situations that require us to master new skills. Most of us go into these new situations with some worry about whether we'll be able to "do okay," but we nevertheless push on. Why do we push on? Psychological research tells us that we do so because we have some faith in our ability to handle the situation effectively and because we believe that we are likely to have a positive outcome.

Underdeveloped children know that they do not cope with frustration well, that they have trouble persisting in the face of boredom or difficulty or goals where there are no immediate results, and that they are poor at solving problems. Therefore, by young adulthood, they are lacking an internal belief that they are capable and will effect positive outcomes. Their belief system is not faulty: In fact, it is probably rather accurate.

By middle school, parents often complain that their children are "couch potatoes." "All he wants to do is watch TV, and play Nintendo." These parents are often trying to push these youngsters into activities such as athletics or Scouts but meet with great resistance.

The children would like to have more money but will not approach neighbors about doing odd jobs for them. In high school, they take only the easy subjects. They are reluctant to try out for a part in the school play even though it seems interesting. Some are reluctant to take the exam for their driver's license. They think about doing volunteer work at the hospital but can't get up the nerve to call. They've heard other kids get jobs as camp counselors during the summer, but they're not sure they could handle being far from home all summer.

In fact, they don't see how they could go away to college and be so far from their family and friends. Some can't see how they could manage college at all. Even though their college board scores are pretty high, they feel that the most they could handle would be living at home after high school and taking a couple of courses at the local junior college.

Underdeveloped children typically use avoidance as a coping strategy.

As a clinician who works with adults as well as with children, I am always alert to information about an adult's coping mechanisms when I am taking a history on a new client. How an adult copes with problems in his life is probably the single most important piece of information I can learn about him. How he has coped with similar problems in the past is a good predictor of how he will cope with this problem now and ones like it in the future. More than likely, at least some of his coping mechanisms are maladaptive ones and have contributed to the emotional distress he's experiencing right now.

Underdeveloped children are "avoiders." They rely heavily on approaches that help them avoid dealing with the situation. Most people with major emotional problems, such as anxiety and depression, cope with stress poorly by using avoidant strategies. Here are some strategies avoiders use to get out of doing homework.

Blaming: "It's the teacher's fault. She makes it so boring that I don't want to do it." Or, "It's your fault. You were supposed to remind me this morning to bring home my geography book."

Denial: "Homework? What homework? I don't know anything about any homework."

Grand Emotional Displays: "All right, all right! You're always bugging me about my homework. I can't handle it! I'm too upset about a fight I had today at school with Todd and I just can't deal with homework now!"

Escape: Child is gone when you get home from work and stays away until dark.

Feigning Illness: "I think I'm coming down with something. My throat feels scratchy. Would you call the school in the morning and tell them I was too sick to get my algebra homework done?"

Forgetting: "Oh gosh. I forgot to bring home that homework sheet again. I guess I can't get it done."

Lying: "I did my homework on the bus."

Procrastination: "I'm tired. I'll take a nap first, just a short one, then I'll have more energy to do it later." (Later never comes.)

Rationalization: "Algebra is stupid. I'll never need it to get a job anyway."

Underdeveloped children are unusually dependent on their parents and peers.

It follows logically from the above descriptions that if parents continually remove frustrations from their children's lives, finish tasks for them, and solve problems for them, those children will be extremely dependent upon their parents. Many parents do not mind this level of dependency in the home environment because they view it as a gift or a luxury that they are able to give their children. "I want her to be a little girl as long as she wants to and as long as she needs to," many mothers say. "After all, that's partly why I decided to stay home with my children, so that I can let them be children. I hate to see children grow up so fast."

Yet these same parents are often puzzled when the children do not function independently outside the home. The four-year-old who is unable to blow his nose or go to the bathroom by himself, and who waits for someone to pick him up when he falls down, is more than likely the preschooler who is reluctant to separate from Mother at the classroom door.

The nine-year-old whose mother picks out his clothes, packs his lunch for him every morning, helps him with his homework every evening, even to the point of putting the completed homework in his bookbag for him because he tends to forget it if she doesn't, is often the nine-year-old who does not function well in the classroom. He is described as not following instructions, waiting for the teacher to help him get started, dawdling, daydreaming, sometimes crying and complaining the work is too hard, and seldom finishing his work.

By adolescence, these dependent children are faced with the developmental tasks of separation and individuation—detaching from the family and forming a sense of identity as separate persons. This task, which is difficult for anyone, is made much harder because of their history of dependency. These teenagers come into adolescence often verbally abusive and rebellious but subtly just as dependent as ever.

I have found over the years of working with families like these that the most direct way of picking up on this pattern is to ask the adolescent a question. It doesn't have to be a complicated question. It can be as simple as "Can you tell me what kind of difficulty you've been having at school?" or "How would you like things to be different in your family, if you could change things?" or even "Tell me some of the things you've been unhappy about."

Inevitably these preadolescents and adolescents will turn to their mothers and whisper, "Mom, you tell her." They seem unable to grapple with a question that requires them to sort out some information, organize it, and express it. They are unable to suggest a solution to a problem or propose an alternative method. Offering an opinion that is uniquely their own is a novel experience.

They will turn to their parents for solutions but immediately find fault with their parents' ideas. They are quick to complain, but when asked to participate in a family meeting by offering suggestions, they are often silent. They know clearly that they don't like the way their parents are handling conflicts between them, but they have nothing to offer as to what would be a better method of resolving the conflict.

For children who come into the teen years with prolonged

dependency upon a parent, loud complaining, arguing, and negativism with a parent appears to be one solution. By putting themselves in constant conflict with their parents, they achieve a measure of separation by completly rejecting their parents or having their parents reject them.

The other solution seems to be the transferring of dependency from the parent to a peer. Unable to manage a period of independence that would normally occur between childhood and the young adult years, these teenagers become emotionally "married" to someone at fourteen. By "married" I mean that they have at least daily contact, sometimes several times a day; they forsake all others in terms of dating or even close friendships; they are extremely jealous and possessive of each other; their mood rises and falls in accordance with how peaceful or stormy the relationship is with the other teen at that moment in time; and they become convinced that they cannot survive without each other. Parents often see these relationships as unhealthy but are powerless to intervene. The strength of the dependency upon the boyfriend or girlfriend is in direct measure a reflection of the strength of the dependency upon the parent.

While attaching oneself to a boy or girl so intensely and so early may grant the teenager a measure of separation from her parents, this approach certainly has its hazards. By becoming "married" at such a young age, the adolescent misses out on mastering some of the developmental tasks of adolescence that need to be dealt with as well. Some of these are: learning how to be alone and consolidating an identity, learning how to make and keep long-term friendships with a person of the same sex, and learning how to end a relationship when it is hurtful.

They fail to learn what they need to know to answer some important questions:

- "What kind of person is right for me?"
- "What kind of person is wrong for me?"
- "What do people like about me?"
- "How can you tell whom to trust?"
- "How can you tell if a girl [or a guy] really cares about you or is just using you?"

- "How do you patch things up when your best friend hurts you or betrays your trust?"
- "Who am I alone, apart from my boyfriend [or girlfriend]?"
- "How can I be in a relationship with someone else and still be myself?"

Ashley: The Problem of Unhealthy Adolescent Dependency

Ashley was a fourteen-year-old girl who had drifted away from her family and seemed out of control. Her mother had been through three marriages, and her father had been through two. Both were deeply caring parents who felt guilty about all the changes their two daughters had had to go through. Ashley had felt unhappy and neglected during her mother's marital problems and had lived with her dad off and on.

When she turned twelve, peers suddenly became very important. She dropped out of all activities at school and neglected her homework in order to stay on the phone or out with her friends. Her parents were unhappy with the situation, but they were reluctant to intervene. Ashley drifted back and forth from one parent's house to the other's, depending upon where she had the most freedom and the best access to her friends. She began to skip classes to be with her friends, or she would fail to come home on the bus. Then she was in trouble with the authorities at school.

Her parents grew increasingly concerned, but when they set limits, she only went to the other parent's home or stayed away. As she continued to get into trouble, she drifted toward a rougher group of friends. She developed a crush on an older boy who was in trouble himself. She loved him because "he puts up with me. No one else does. Everyone's mad at me." When asked about Todd and how he felt about her, she said, "He loves me because he needs me and because I put up with his drinking and his bad temper." She then became more isolated as she distanced herself from her old friends, her teachers, her parents, her sister, and even the activities she used to enjoy. She felt constantly moody and depressed. She began to wear black and carved his initials in her arm. She didn't feel very good about anything anymore except her total love for Todd.

In working with Ashley's parents, they could see that they had to set some limits for her. They agreed to decide for her where she was to reside for the next year. They decided it would be dad's home, as he was able to cut back his hours at work and supervise her more closely in the afternoon. Mom felt guilty about giving up custody of Ashley again but felt it was in Ashley's best interests to stay with her dad. At her dad's home, a contract was developed that would address her needs as well as her parents' desire for realistic limits. Ashley would be allowed to continue seeing Todd. She could only do so, however, if she also maintained at least one after-school activity at all times. Ashley was allowed to choose her own friends, provided her dad met each and every one of them and she supplied him with their address, phone number, and parents' names. She agreed to divide her time equally between Todd, schoolwork, other friends, and her after-school activity. In this way the parents did not get in a power struggle with her over Todd, yet there were other involvements in her life that would compete with him for her time and attention. By getting a boost to her self-esteem from these other activities, she didn't have as strong a need to depend on Todd for a sense of acceptance.

Mom also agreed that when Ashley called to complain that Dad was too strict, she would listen sympatheticaly but encourage her to work it out with her dad. Mom and Dad agreed to have a family meeting at least once a month with Ashley to review how the contract was working.

Underdeveloped children have low self-esteem.

It is often a mystery to parents how their children could be so loved and yet have such low opinions of themselves. "We have given them all the love we could give. We've told them we love them every day of their lives. Yet here she is unhappy and depressed and always so down on herself." Many mothers have said, "I tell her she looks terrific. She's pretty and smart and can do anything she wants to. But it doesn't seem to stick."

In doing psychological testing with underdeveloped children, I've observed over the years that though these children may score high on anxiety, high on depression, and low on self esteem measures, they consistently say yes to questions about whether they feel loved and whether they feel they are an important person to their families.

Apparently, for many children, knowing they are loved has little correlation with high self-esteem. How can this be? It seems to defy conventional wisdom about self-esteem in children.

The answer seems to be that children may, in fact, be wiser than their parents. Though these children and adolescents know they have unconditional love at home, they know, at some deeper level, that one day they will leave home and go out into the wider world and that there they will have to compete with others and succeed or fail. The larger society, at least in our culture, does not offer them unconditional love and acceptance. They will compete for mates, for jobs, and for resources. Their performance will be compared with and measured against that of others. They are sure they are loved at home. It is "out there" they are not so sure of.

What underdeveloped children seem to lack is a reservoir of past experiences in which they have had to push themselves or prove themselves. From learning to snap her own jacket, to doing her homework on her own, to landing her first job through her own efforts, to buying her first car with the money she earned, a child increases her confidence in her abilities bit by bit, day by day, in small increments. Unconditional love is simply a beginning foundation for good self-esteem. It is an opening deposit, you might say, on a bank account of successes in living. Into the account go problem-solving experiences, successful efforts at independence, goals that were accomplished, fears that were overcome because they weren't avoided. Self-esteem is the subjective feeling about how full or empty that account is.

Referring back to the section on problem solving, recall that we take risks because we have the belief that we are capable of handling whatever arises and the faith that if we push on, we are likely to see a positive outcome. Children with low self-esteem have no belief in their capabilities and no expectation that a positive outcome is more likely than a negative outcome.

By adolescence, underdeveloped teenagers are not keeping up with their more independent, self-confident peers, and they know it. They fear that they are not going to make the transition out of the home and into the world as successful young adults. They feel like losers and see their future as one long string of failures. It is our task as parents to allow problems and obstacles to occur in their lives that they are capable of handling so that they get to experience a feeling of mastery.

And it is up to us to allow them to struggle with stressful experiences so that they are able to develop a history of successes and, to a lesser degree, a handful of failures, as well.

Underdeveloped children are unable to cope with strong negative emotions.

Another aspect of maturity is the ability to experience and to regulate strong emotion. By strong emotion we mean anger, disappointment, grief, loss, fear, betrayal. Psychologists know that suppressing strong emotions altogether is not healthy. The principle to keep in mind is that we all must learn to manage and regulate strong negative emotions.

As young children, our emotions are simple, much like our palate is. When we are infants, we can experience only pleasure, pain, and fear, just as we can taste only sweet, sour, and bitter. Our capacity to control emotion is very poor also. If we feel pleasure, we smile, gurgle, and fall asleep. If we feel pain or fear, we cry. As children grow and mature, they learn to experience and distinguish much finer gradations of emotion, just as they learn to distinguish much subtler tastes and textures. The pain of losing someone you love is different from the pain of a bruise. The pain of losing someone through death is different from the pain of losing someone through rejection.

Healthy children learn to experience these feelings, become aware of them, name them, and talk about them. They also learn to control those feelings sufficiently so that they are not derailed by them. Though a child may strike out for the third time out of three at-bats, he learns not to throw his bat at the pitcher and storm off the field, because his teammates would not accept it. A child learns that even though she didn't get the part in the school play that she wanted, she must keep her feelings in control so that she can go to her classes and listen effectively and take notes. Both children in these situations, an eight-year-old and a sixteen-year-old, know that there are expectations for them at their age level as to the expression of their emotions. They must find ways to postpone the expression of their feelings until they find a time and place and situation where it is appropriate and acceptable.

Whether one feels this is right or wrong is moot. It is simply a fact of life in our society. Adults will be subjected to many situations that evoke strong emotions. If one is constantly unable to manage strong feelings, then one will simply not be able to function effectively as an adult.

Will: Easily Overwhelmed By His Emotions

Will was a twelve-year-old boy who was brought for consultation by his parents, who were concerned about his explosive outbursts. Will had always been a disorganized, forgetful boy who was somewhat immature and relied heavily on his mother to keep him on track. Will had a way of wandering away from chores half-finished, losing his possessions, and forgetting to write down homework assignments.

Will was brilliant and was in the gifted program at school. Yet his mother organized his assignments for him, got him started on his homework every night, bought different colored notebooks to put his homework in, and hounded him over and over about his chores.

When Will fell behind in school, he would panic. Several times, when he realized he had not completed work that was due the next day and he would have to take a zero grade, he became hysterical, screaming at his mother, crying uncontrollably, and making threats to hurt himself. Once he removed the screen from his window in an effort to jump out the window and kill himself.

Will's mother was frightened. "Bob travels a lot, and Will is getting too big for me to handle alone. If he's doing this at twelve, I'm afraid to think what he'll be like as a teenager."

When the next-door neighbor asked if Will could pet-sit for her while she was going to be out of town, his mother objected. "I know what will happen," she said. "Will will forget to go over there, and I'll end up having to feed the dogs. Then I'll be angry at Will, and he will shout back at me."

Will wanted to try, so Will and I worked out a plan for remembering to feed the animals on his own. He reasoned that since he played Nintendo every day, several times a day, that the best place to put a reminder note was on the television screen. His note read, "You don't eat till the dogs eat." Will was able to handle the job, to his mother's surprise, and earned his first income outside the home.

By adolescence, these youngsters view deprivation, disappointment, frustration, loss, and rejection as unusual and as out-of-the-ordinary. These experiences are not supposed to happen to them. They seem to think that such experiences are unfair, that other kids their age are not having to have these feelings. As the stakes get higher in adolescence, the feelings get more intense as well. They come into adolescence with no adequate preparation for the intensity of feelings they will experience. They have developed no coping mechanisms at all.

Many times I have asked, "What have you learned to do when you feel that way, to make yourself feel better?" only to be greeted with blank looks. Healthy, well-adjusted teenagers can come up with, "I read a book to get my mind off of it." "I go outside and shoot some baskets." "I call my best friend and we talk for hours." "I turn on some music and write in my diary for a while."

Underdeveloped adolescents all too often feel strong emotion and look for escape, since they can think of no way to cope with the situation. Many turn to alcohol or getting high, "so I won't have to feel anything." Many are explosive and verbally or physically abusive toward family members. The parents of such teenagers may report that their adolescent son constantly fights with his girlfriend and has pounded a hole in the wall with his fist or smashed the phone down so hard he broke it while arguing with her on the phone. Or they may report that when they confront their daughter about her poor schoolwork, she leaves home for several days. She usually turns up at a friend's house, but when she comes home after these runaway episodes, she has no more plan of what to do about her schoolwork than when she left.

Underdeveloped children are easily overwhelmed by the accumulation of several stressful events.

This problem is a direct result of the problems listed above and does play a major part, I believe, in the high rate of suicide and running away among today's adolescents. Children who are poor at solving problems, who do not believe in the possibility of successful outcomes for their efforts, who have a low opinion of themselves, and who are thrown into turmoil by strong emotion, inevitably are swamped by having to deal with several problems at once. They are like fragile boats out on the open seas when a typhoon strikes. They are literally drowning. They lack the coping mechanisms, the emotional resilience, and the resources to ride out the impact of constant battering.

Some may argue that today's youth are more prone to suicide attempts and to running away because there are more problems to deal with. Drugs are certainly more available, and adolescents are having sex earlier. Today's adolescents are also more affluent, and with this comes pressure to look attractive, dress well, act sophisticated, and own a nice car. Some would assert that sexual abuse is more common today (although some would not). Still others would assert that our society today is more competitive than it was fifty years ago and that there are greater pressures on children to be successful.

If it is true that children today have more problems to cope with and more stresses to withstand, the case can be made that they are less equipped to deal with them than in previous decades. Of families I have seen over the years who call with the initial presenting problem of a teenager who has run away from a middle-clas family or made a suicide attempt, roughly 80 percent are what I call underdeveloped children from overindulgent families. These are middle-class families who have been unusually permissive about allowing the children to retreat from stressful situations and who have intervened over the years to solve problems for them and protect them from the natural consequences of their actions. They are as likely to come from intact families as from divorced families. They have not been physically or sexually abused or subjected to any significant trauma.

They are overwhelmed by the average, ordinary stresses of everyday life. Their family is new to the area and they are having to make a new set of friends. High school work is more difficult than middle school work, and they must study to keep up for the first time. They now have a social life and are having to juggle their time between school, band, and phone time. They have a job for the first time, and their boss expects them to be at work on time and to sweep the floors at closing. His girlfriend wants to be free to see her other friends on the weekend and not just him. It is these stresses that soon become "too much."

Underdeveloped children have a poor sense of concern for and responsibility toward other members of their family and community, a factor that impairs their interpersonal relationships. They often act without considering how their actions will affect others.

A common complaint I hear from many parents is, "They don't offer to help me prepare dinner. They watch TV, waiting for food to be put on the table, then complain that they don't like what I've cooked. It makes me so mad. Sometimes I lose my temper and say things I wish I hadn't."

A father I saw recently was furious at his son. He had just given the seventeen-year-old a new sportscar. The boy was gone from the home constantly. His grades were dropping. When he was asked to take his younger brother to basketball practice, the son refused. He said it was "my car to do with as I please." The fight that erupted between father and son led to the son leaving home for several days.

Maria: The Problem of Lack of Concern for Others

Maria, a seventeen-year-old Hispanic girl, lived with her mother and stepfather, an accountant. She left home after a fight with her mother and stepfather about her failing grades. She was also upset because her stepfather was putting pressure on her to watch a video on study skills. She was gone for two days before she called home to say where she was. She told her younger sister, Jamie, aged eleven, where she was but made her promise not to tell Mom that she had called.

When she decided to come home, I recommended to the family that she not come home until she had listened to everyone in the family as they said how her actions had affected them. Little Pedro, aged six, said the fighting scared him and made him want to cry. Her stepfather said he was hurt that he had gone to such trouble to get the video for her and she had completely rejected his efforts. Mother was hurt and angry that she did not know where Maria was for two days and that Maria did not care enough about her feelings to call home and let her know she was all right. Jamie was confused because Maria had asked her to lie, and she was afraid Mom would punish her for keeping the secret. She had always looked up to her big sister before. Maria was genuinely surprised that her family had been affected in this way.

Maria listened patiently and acknowledged what she had done to each person. I then asked her to make amends to each family member individually. She was unsure just what I meant. We went through the process slowly—offering her apology, making a promise not to do the behavior again, and making restitution, wherever possible, for the hurt feelings. The process of listening, taking responsibility, and making amends was, in fact, new and instructive for the whole family.

Many parents operate under the loving yet misguided idea that if they give unstintingly to their children, and let no need go unmet, the children will be happy, well-adjusted, and generous. After all, our culture promotes the myth that "unmet needs" underlie all emotional problems. Yet these children come into adolescence not as giving and compassionate human beings but as professional consumers. They are seen by their parents as egocentric, very particular about what they want, and with needs that are almost insatiable.

If they have a concern for others, it is expressed in an abstract way, e.g., "We ought to do something about the homeless." They complain, however, that they are put upon when asked to help a younger sibling with homework or to go along on a visit to a sick relative.

Power struggles become much of the focus between parent and child, the child claiming he "doesn't have enough" or "the right one," and the parent feeling exploited. Interestingly enough, some of these children and adolescents experience a kind of depression around their sense of uselessness to anyone. They often feel like "just an appendage." Many times they complain they are a burden to their parents because they really don't do anything important for anyone, and their parents are continually complaining about how much they cost.

Often, in sessions with these families, I find myself using the "hotel" concept. In a hotel, you come and go as you please. You don't have to check in with anyone. You eat when you want to, go to bed when you want to. Your room is always picked up by someone, the bed is made for you, and there are always clean towels in the bathroom. The people of the hotel are there to serve you.

But this is not a hotel. This is a family. There is a difference. In a family, much is given and much is expected of you in return. The work that is done in a family is to be shared, for no one person can or should do it all. The people there give to you of their time, interest, and attention, but you are to give back to them your time, your understanding, and your companionship. The people in a family are not nameless and faceless servants. They have feelings about you, and 90 percent of what you do affects them.

Underdeveloped children have a poor sense of identity.

As these children move into adolescence, one of the tasks before them is to forge a storng sense of their individual identity: to challenge their parents' values and begin to develop some values of their own, to develop a sense of their own strengths and weaknesses, and to find a group to which they feel they belong. Many adolescents can tell you, "I do well in English. I'm in drama club. I'm not very good at math. I sort of fit in with the preppy crowd. I think I'd like to go to college and be a teacher. I've always wanted to do something to help others."

Or they might say, "I'm a jock. I like to work on my car. I'm not very good at English. I like things like math and electronics. I think I'd like to join the navy after high school. I've always wanted to serve my country."

Underdeveloped adolescents have no such clear picture of themselves. They cannot answer such questions as "Tell me what you're good at, what you're not so good at." Many are very negativistic, they are anti-everything. T-shirts that say "Anarchy Reigns" are typical of this sentiment. A certain amount of rebelliousness is healthy, but the question "What do you believe in? What do you stand for?" is revealing. Well-adjusted teens will say, "I'm against abortion," or "I'm a vegetarian," or "I believe in world peace and an end to world hunger." To many, their youthful idealism is refreshing in a world that is all too jaded at times.

Underdeveloped teens, however, answer this question with quizzical looks. Some will answer, "What do you mean?" while others may give a flip answer like "I believe in partying." Some will even turn to a parent and say, "What should I say?"

Even more revealing is a look at their peer group. Most teens can tell you which peer group they belong to. Even those that don't belong to one of the standard groups—the jocks and cheerleaders, the preppies, the "brains," the alternate crowd—are able to say, "I'm not in any group, really. I'm just sort of your average, nice person. I have a lot of different friends and fit in pretty well with most any group."

Underdeveloped adolescents are often very confused about just where they fit in. Sometimes they want to be with the preps, but they're afraid they might not be popular enough. At other times, they might want to be with the "brains," but they're afraid they might not be smart enough. Still others fear rejection so much that they drift toward the group that is the most alienated from the mainstream. This group is variously called the punks, the headbangers, the druggies, or the heavy metal freaks.

One thing I have learned about this group is that this group is the easiest to belong to because it has no standards for admission. You don't have to be smart, good-looking, talented, athletic, or popular to belong. You don't have to endorse any values or believe in any principles. You can be anti-everything.

It is a group for misfits and outcasts. You can be at the bottom of the social order of the high school and yet find companionship and acceptance there. This group accepts its members with no expectations, no criteria, except complete loyalty to each other. It is like a holding place for those with no clear identity as to where they fit in society. Its members support each other emotionally through the confusion of identity formation, until they move out, either to rejoin the mainstream or, to a lesser degree, to become permanent outcasts.

Underdeveloped children have unrealistic goals or no goals.

Goalsetting, in general, is very difficult for this group. We have seen earlier how these children seldom reach goals because of their poor frustration tolerance and poor task persistence. In their failure to reach small goals in childhood, much learning is lost about the nature of working toward goals. By "learning" we mean information that we, as adults, may take for granted.

For example, we know that any long and involved project must be broken down into small increments. We must organize those increments into a sequence and begin with the first step. We must anticipate obstacles and have a plan of how to overcome them. We must assess what resources we will need along the way and have a plan of how to obtain them. We realize that the goal is a long way off and that we will need to try to stay focused on each small increment and obtain some satisfaction from completing each one in turn. We know that we must weigh out the cost-benefit ratio from time to time and conclude that the long-term benefit is worth the cost.

While these statements may seem obvious to us, they are aspects of experience that are missing for children from overindulgent families. These adolescents often answer the question "What would you like to do after high school?" with unrealistic goals such as "Be a famous rock star." A goal like this might not be so unrealistic if the adolescent boy actually had a band and wrote his own music, but it is typically offered by an adolescent who does not play an instrument. Some adolescents will answer, "Go to college and become a lawyer," even though they have failing grades, they say they hate school, and the family has put no money aside for their education. Often the answers are simply very vague, such as "Get a job." A sign of our times, I think, has been the increasing popularity of the answer "Be rich."

When these answers are pursued for more detail, e.g., "What do you need to do to become a famous rock star?" or "What is the exceptional talent or skill that will make you rich?" the answers are revealing. These adolescents usually have no answer. Being a famous rock star or being rich is supposed to "happen" somehow. And it is supposed to happen to them, and not to everyone else, because they are, well, somehow just "special." It becomes very clear that they have no idea of what the individual, incremental steps are that are involved in reaching such a goal. They have no clear sense of the time involved, the talents and skills that will be needed, the financial costs, the personal costs to them in terms of personal sacrifice and emotional strain.

When it becomes clear that this young person has no concept of how to get from point A, where they are now, to point B, where they want to be, then the sad awareness sets in that this individual will most likely never reach his or her goal. They will have many disappointments. They are bound to find adult life much more difficult than they had anticipated. Moreover, they will not understand why they are having such a hard time of it. It had all looked so easy when they were younger. They will be constantly scaling their goals downward to something more reachable and will be learning as adults some of the aspects of human experience that they missed out on as children. More than likely they will eventually understand who they are and set realistic goals for themselves, though it will happen for them at a later age than their peers. This will be arduous and it will be painful, and the personal costs to them will be greater than for their more mature peers.

Lisa Ann: A Boat Without a Rudder

I recently saw nineteen-year-old Lisa Ann, again, at the request of her mother. She had been in and out of treatment with me several times over the past eighteen months, keeping a few appointments for a while, then failing to show up. When I first saw her, she had dropped out of school in the tenth grade. Her mother was asking that I send a letter to her guidance counselor requesting home schooling for her. It seems that Lisa Ann had become depressed over the tragic deaths of two friends and had stayed out of school for several months. Then she was too embarrassed to go back. Before I could refuse, mother was able to get the clearance for the home-based program and had gathered up all the textbooks, assignments, and exams for Lisa Ann.

Over the following months, Lisa Ann made no effort to do any of her academic work at home. She eventually took a minimum wage job and dropped out of treatment after six visits. I heard from her ten months later when she was discharged from a psychiatric hospital. She had gone into the hospital with the diagnosis of major depression, following the breakup of a relationship with a boy-friend. But it was not the loss of that relationship which was most troubling for her. It was her life.

Lisa Ann was living at home with her mother, drifting from one low wage job to another, seldom staying at any of them for more than three months. She had promised to pay her mother $200 per month for her car payment, but hadn't yet made any payments. Mother was on her case for coming in late at night and for spending all her money on gas so that she could ride around visiting friends. When asked what she wanted to do with her life, she would only reply, "I have no idea."

We worked on weekly goals, hopefully making them small enough and providing enough clear directions and assistance with phone calls that she could attain them. She was able to follow through with one car payment, change to a new job, and make one phone call about taking the exam for her general equivalency test, but then cancelled appointments again.

I recontacted her through her mother and she came in again. This time, Lisa Ann was more direct and open about her depression. "I don't want to grow up," she said, "I don't know how. I thought growing up was something that just happened to you. Suddenly you're just all grown up one day and you have a life. I never knew you had to go after one. I don't want to do that. I want you or mom or someone to just give me a life."

A CHECKLIST FOR PARENTS

The following is a list of behavioral examples of underdeveloped children. The examples are grouped by age range, so that you can compare them with your child's behavior and put a checkmark next to the ones that are similar.If you find that half or more of the items are experiences you're familiar with, then your children fit this pattern. You've already made progress in identifying what some of their problems are.

School-Age Children (7–12)

_____ 1. My child has always had a short temper and blows up easily when something is difficult for him. He's broken many models and games in his room.

_____ 2. My nine-year-old girl often wants to quit soccer midway through the season. We have a tough time getting her to hang in there.

_____ 3. My son handles problems so poorly. When he studied hard for a math test and still got a bad grade, he just gave up altogether and decided to fail.

_____ 4. My school-age girl is forever telling us she doesn't have homework or that she did it on the bus. Then we find out later that she just didn't do the homework. This problem of lying as an easy way out is getting to be a habit.

_____ 5. "I forgot" is a common problem at home—"I forgot to bring home my homework." "I forgot to take out the garbage." "I forgot to come in for dinner." "I forgot to brush my teeth," etc.

_____ 6. My eight-year-old boy is so disorganized, he's wearing me out. I have to supervise his getting dressed in the morning and pack his lunch and his bookbag for him. And doing his homework with him is so tedious and time-consuming. The teacher says he can't get started on his work in class without extra prompting from her.

_____ 7. No matter how much I tell my daughter she's pretty, she's smart, she can do anything she wants if she would only try, she just doesn't believe it.

_____ 8. My son becomes so angry and defensive when you point out a mistake he's made or criticize his effort in any way. I think he's very down on himself.

_____ 9. My twelve-year-old has been in trouble in school for blurting out things like "That's no fair! That's too much homework!" or "You pick on me and nobody else!"

_____ 10. I get upset with my son when he refuses to help around the house. He argues with me about doing his chores. He doesn't like anything I cook, yet he won't go grocery shopping with me.

_____ 11. My twelve-year-old daughter is remarkably irresponsible toward her four-year-old brother. She resents having to watch him. In fact, when he gets hurt, she doesn't even act concerned.

_____ 12. My eleven-year-old daughter shocked me when she said "I'm so unhappy I just want to die." I am worried she might be suicidal.

Adolescents (13–18)

_____ 1. My teenager says most of the courses taught in school are "stupid" and the teachers are "boring," though he only says that about subjects that are difficult for him.

_____ 2. My daughter gave up looking for a job after filling out applications at just three places. She wouldn't even call them back.

_____ 3. Sometimes I'm baffled by the poor judgment my daughter shows when handling an everyday problem, like name-calling on the bus, or other girls borrowing her clothes.

_____ 4. My teenage son won't get involved in any activities outside of school. I've suggested he call the hospital about volunteer work, but he just won't make the call.

_____ 5. My fifteen-year-old daughter complains that she wants a car so that she can get motivated to get a driver's license. But she won't even read the driving manual so that she can take the test. Frankly, I wonder if she's afraid to drive.

_____ 6. My teenage son is very rebellious and constantly rejects whatever we say, yet he will stop and ask for my advice before making even a small decision.

_____ 7. My teenage son fights constantly with his girlfriend about her wanting to spend more time with her friends. He gets so upset he can't stay off the phone and he can't think about anything else.

_____ 8. We confronted our teenage son about his heavy drinking on the weekends. He said he "just wanted to blot out everything," that he "couldn't handle it anymore."

_____ 9. Our teenage daughter demands so much from us, more than we can afford. We have endless arguments over her need for nice clothes, concert tickets, and a nice car.

_____ 10. Our teenage son has a car, but he cannot tell you what the finance charges were, what the monthly payments are, and how much the insurance will be for a driver under age twenty-five.

_____ 11. My teenager (sixteen or older) cannot answer the questions "What has been your biggest accomplishment so far? What skills helped you achieve it?"

Young Adults (19–30)

_____ 1. My twenty-one-year-old son has come back home to live with us after running out of money and getting into debt. His goal is to get out of debt, but he continues to run through his money as if there's plenty more coming from somewhere.

_____ 2. Our twenty-two-year-old daughter has come home to live with us. She's dropped out of college twice and is waiting tables. She says her goal is to "go back to school one day," though that's about as specific as she gets.

_____ 3. Our twenty-five-year-old son is drifting through life. He seems depressed and confused.

_____ 4. Our twenty-six-year-old daughter who lives at home only makes enough money to cover her clothes, car payments, and entertainment, yet she's not concerned about it.

____ 5. My twenty-two-year old son, who is only a junior, is on academic probation again. He says he likes to party too much and that maybe he's just not ready to buckle down yet.

____ 6. My twenty-four-year-old daughter will spend the night out and not tell us where she's going or when she'll be back. She says she doesn't have to, she's an adult now.

____ 7. Our daughter moved in with a boy at eighteen, even though she was accepted to college. She said later on that she was afraid she couldn't handle it.

____ 8. Our twenty-six-year-old son spends his weekends with his girlfriend, though he knows his dad has some big jobs to do around the house and could use the help.

____ 9. Our adult daughter who lives with us does not know what our house payment is, how much our utilities bills or our food bills are. She could not tell you what our budget is for running this home.

____ 10. My son, who is twenty-one, does not have his own bank account but has a joint account with us. He does not make phone calls to government agencies or make appointments with important people. I do that for him.

3   Are You a Parent Who Loves Too Much?

By now, you, the reader, may have recognized that your child or adolescent may fit several of the characteristics listed in the previous chapter. You have also begun to get a sense of where some of your ideas about parenting came from and how they may be misguided. In order to help you focus on problems you may have in your parenting style, the following are some characteristics of overindulgent parents, along with detailed case studies of families in trouble.

The overindulgent parent is one who fails to set realistic limits.

In other words, this is the parent who can't say no. All of us, as parents, have been known to give in to children's demands from time to time, especially when overtired, overstressed, and overwhelmed. There are times when we must simply assess the benefits of holding the line versus the costs, in terms of the conflict and disruption that may occur when we continue to say no. We may decide that, for that given occasion, the benefits are simply not worth the cost.

The overindulgent parent, however, is one who has difficulty setting limits on an ongoing basis. "I can't bear the anger and the talking back," these parents complain. "I want my household to be peaceful and happy." Some may have grown up with fighting in their own households. "When my daughter starts arguing with me, I get a knot in my stomach. I literally feel ill."

Other overindulgent parents try to set limits but give in out of a sense of defeat and frustration. "I patiently try to explain my position— why I'm telling him no. My mother always said, 'Because I'm your mother, that's why.' I didn't want to be like that. I felt if you reasoned with your child, they would understand, and they would go along with you. But what seems to happen is that they argue with each one of my reasons until I'm worn out, and I just give in."

Still a third scenario goes something like this:. "Well, when we found out what our thirteen-year-old son had done, we blew up and told him he was grounded for a month, which was probably too long. So there we were, with him confined to the house night and day. He was bored, complaining, and irritable. When he wasn't annoying us, he was just watching television or playing Nintendo. He wasn't doing homework; he wasn't doing chores. It was like a vacation for him. Meanwhile we were suffering from being cooped up with him. We began to wonder, 'Who's being punished here, him or us?' So when he asked if he could go to a friend's house, we said, 'Go ahead.' We were glad to get him out of the house."

From these examples, we can see that the reasons overindulgent parents have difficulty setting limits are varied and complex. These are not parents who fail to set limits because they are neglectful and simply don't care. Some are tired, overstressed, unable to manage confrontations. Some are unsure of themselves and question their own actions. Still others set limits that are inappropriate and ineffective.

A very common pattern occurs when the parent becomes easy prey for the child or adolescent who knows how to make the parent feel guilty or inadequate. I have learned over the years to ask children, usually in front of their parents, "What will you do to get Mom or Dad to give in? What works with Mom? What works with Dad?" It's amazing how many children and adolescents are ready and eager to reveal their secrets. One ten-year-old answered, "I go up to my room and lie on my bed and cry real loud. Gets her every time."

Some adolescents use the threat of running away to test the limits, understanding that the parent may be terrified of the possibility that their living away from home may result in an unwanted pregnancy, promiscuity, or involvement in drugs, alcohol, or crime. In even more dysfunctional homes, adolescents may threaten property damage, physical assault against the parent, or suicide in a bid for control and may actually follow through on their threats.

Kelly's Parents: Afraid to Hold the Line

Kelly was twenty-one and living at home with her parents and her twenty-seven-year-old sister, Jennifer. Her father was a successful auto dealer, and her mother was a homemaker. Both Kelly and Jennifer had difficulty developing an identity as an adult, becoming responsible and independent—in short, growing up. Kelly had tried college, but came home after her first year, having failed most of her classes. She was open with her parents and told them that her heavy use of marijuana interfered with settling into college work. After many months of not doing much of anything, Kelly got a part-time job in a pizza restaurant. At twenty-one, her friends were going back to college for their final year, yet she had no idea who or what she wanted to be in life. She wanted to go back to college but felt, realistically, that she was not mature enough to handle college work. She wanted to travel to exotic places but was afraid to. She would have liked to move out but could not make enough money at minimum-wage jobs to support herself. She spent her time at home alone up in her room avoiding the family. She felt ashamed that she had failed at independence and worried that she might still be there at twenty-seven, like her sister, Jennifer.

Kelly's parents were also unhappy with the situation. Kelly's room was a mess, and she seldom picked up after herself. She spent many nights away from home, staying over at friends' houses, yet seldom told them where she was or when she would be home. They complained that they never knew her whereabouts and were always worried about her safety. They objected to her ongoing relationship with her boyfriend, who drank heavily and became violent from time to time, yet she steadfastly refused to break off her relationship with him. She loaned the family car to him to drive and he wrecked it, yet they still could not get her to stop seeing him. Instead, her father simply got another car from his company and gave that vehicle to her to take the place of the one that had been damaged. When her parents were asked if she and Jennifer were paying them for their room and board and use of the car, they answered that they asked each to pay them one hundred dollars per month, but that they felt ashamed taking it, and, well, actually, neither had ever paid them.

Kelly's parents were intelligent and well educated. They were quick to see that they did not provide limits for Kelly but admitted that they had very clear reasons for doing so. Kelly was immature, naive, and had poor judgment. She was a lamb among wolves. Any time they attempted to place limits on her, she threatened to move out. The thought terrified them. There was no way Kelly could hold down a job that paid enough to support herself. She would be at the mercy of her drinking and pot-smoking friends, who would take her in but lead her back into drug use again. Worse still, she might move in with her boyfriend, who might beat her, or even kill her, one night in a drunken rage.

As unpleasant as it was, they felt forced to endure Kelly's immature and self-centered behavior as long as they could stand it, because in doing so, it literally meant saving Kelly's life. When asked if there was anything Kelly might do that would be the last straw, they responded with blank looks.

Kelly's parents never were able to set limits with her. Clearly, what they needed to do was to help Kelly develop a plan of how to become independent and to gradually ease her out of the home. But their fear of putting any pressure on Kelly kept them stuck and feeling helpless.

Kelly, though, was slowly able to detach from them. When I last saw her, she was making plans to move to Colorado to live with a friend there. This would help her separate from her boyfriend as well as from her family.

The overindulgent parent fails to set clear and realistic guidelines for the child's behavior, followed by clear-cut, predictable consequences.

Over many years of working with families with troubled children, I have learned to ask, "What are the rules in this family about that behavior?" When the parents and children look at me with a sense of puzzlement, I know that these parents are probably overindulgent. Many families do not have a clear idea of what behavior a child at a particular age should be capable of performing. Underestimating the child's capacities, they allow a child to engage in a very immature behavior far past the normal limits expected for that age.

Still other families do not have any particular approach to expectations for the children, but develop their expectations in an after-the-fact approach. That is, they react to misbehavior with punishment after it occurs, but the children report that they did not know what was expected of them and what the consequences would be. As far as they knew, there was no rule outlined for them in advance so that they could make their decisions accordingly. By then, the parent is frustrated, upset, and highly emotional. Often the frustration has been building for a long time. To the child, this parent seems erratic, moody, and unpredictable. The parent seems to strike without warning, zigzagging about like a tornado.

Over-indulgent parents also fail to follow through consistently with appropriate consequences for misbehavior. Many parents will set out clear expectations and will even announce a cogent set of rules for the children's behavior, such as "Complete your homework before dinner," and "Bring your dirty dishes to the kitchen after you've finished eating."

However, when I have asked the children in a family session, "What is the consequence for not doing this, not abiding by this rule?" the children often reply, "We don't know. We're just told to do it." When I persist with, "But tell me what happens when you don't do it," they reply with, "Nothing," or "We get lectured about it."

The parents, listening to this dialogue often counter with, "We try reasoning with them, we repeat the rules, but they simply don't listen." It soon becomes clear that without any meaningful and rational consequences, the rules are pointless and ineffective.

I have found overindulgent parents to be characterized by their profound helplessness when confronted with problem behavior. Often they say, "Well, there's just nothing we can do. We really have no control over him. We are at his mercy." When hearing this, it is easy to assume they are talking about a teenager, but I find that they are just as often talking about a child as young as three or four. When the rules are vague and there are no predictable consequences, then there usually is no control and the parents are naturally going to be feeling helpless. It is easy to determine if this is a problem in a family by simply asking the children, "Who's the boss here?" Children will often say candidly, and in front of their parents, "We are."

The Schultzes: No Rules, No Consequences

The Schultz family was one of the nicest families you might ever meet. Both parents, Frank and Catherine, had come from large, close-knit Catholic families, and that was the ideal they strived toward when building their own family. They felt if they loved their sons a great deal and gave them everything possible, they would grow up to be good citizens. They had five sons, ranging in age from nine to eighteen, and when they came to family therapy sessions, they completely filled my small office. Frank was an engineer, Catherine a kindergarten teacher, and they were active in their church. Yet they were referred to me by child abuse caseworkers. Frank had erupted in a burst of anger at his son Joseph in a bowling alley and hit him in the head several times with a bowling shoe. The manager of the bowling alley, seeing this, called the police.

Frank was waiting to be tried on criminal charges and was terribly ashamed. He was a model citizen and had never been in trouble with the law. Yet in talking to this loving and close-knit family, it was easy to see how tensions had been building. The five sons were noisy and were always quarreling with each other. They created a disturbance in church virtually every Sunday, yet there was no consequence for this misbehavior. In fact, one Sunday the family left the church and proceeded with their plans to spend the rest of the day at an amusement park. When asked, "What is the rule about creating a disturbance in church?" they replied, "There isn't one." In fact, several of the boys said they couldn't believe that Dad had taken them on to the amusement park after being disruptive in church.

At home, the boys seldom carried out their chores, and if they did, they did them after numerous reminders from their mom and dad. They did them sloppily and with grumbling and complaining. When asked, "What is the rule for not doing chores," they replied, "Well, there isn't one. Dad just gets mad at us and yells awhile." Frank responded, "When I don't have the energy for an argument, I just do their chores myself."

The second oldest son, who was generally extremely quiet, piped in after several meetings and disclosed how much he hated the frequent quarreling in the house. The younger boys were constantly arguing and complaining about each other to the parents; the parents would argue with the younger ones about what they had or hadn't done. They couldn't watch a television program without an argument breaking out. He couldn't study up in his room because of the noise downstairs. He didn't like living there anymore.

Frank was especially moved by his son's disclosure. He knew the constant bickering was getting on his and Catherine's nerves, but he had no idea it was bothering the older boys as much as it did, and that it made them not want to live there. He came to see me by myself and said, "I've been blaming them all this time for their behavior. I'm just now beginning to see that I'm the problem."

Over the next few months, he and Catherine worked together to put more of the responsibility for the chores and for conflict resolution on the boys. We worked toward viewing the family as a unit, a "team." If one boy was disruptive in church, the whole family was penalized. If one boy left soda cans in the family room, Mom didn't buy any sodas for the next week. If two boys had a disagreement, they were to go outside and stay outside, no matter what the weather, until they solved it. By using the "team" approach, peer pressure took over and began to work, where parental pressure had been ineffective before. Frank was pleased that this was becoming the close-knit family he had hoped to achieve.

The overindulgent parent fails to put the burden of responsibility on the child for his or her own behavior.

Children from overindulgent homes often behave counter to the norms of their peer group or school, yet they have developed a network of excuses or rationalizations for their misbehavior.

Teaching children to take responsibility for their part in a conflict or disagreement or to own up to making a mistake is one of the more difficult tasks of parenting. Most of us are reluctant to admit to faults or be punished for mistakes, and children are no different. Parents, in their zeal to stand by and support their youngster, often get caught in a power struggle between the child and the school or between the child and the athletic coach, in which they are firmly allied with the child. Overprotective or overindulgent parents mistakenly buy into the child's excuses or the child's placing of blame on the teacher, the coach, etc.

A parent's first commandment is to place a protective barrier between the child and the larger society when it comes to true danger of emotional or physical harm. The overindulgent parent confuses true danger with emotional stress. For example, a child's constant clowning and disruptive behavior in class may have gained the child a reputation as a troublemaker with the class and with the teacher. This often results in the child being singled out for punishment when a group of children is being disruptive, sometimes when the particular child wasn't even involved. The child claims, "It's her fault. Whenever she hears laughing, she automatically looks at me to see what I'm doing." Most parents focus on the child's past behavior that contributed to the problem. Overprotective parents instead focus on the child's emotional distress and view the teacher as harsh and unfair.

Fred: Learning to Make His Son Take Responsibility for His Actions

Jay was eleven when I first saw him with his family. He was a bright boy and a good writer of horror stories, but he was in frequent power struggles with his father, Fred. Fred was a very sociable man, but he was alternately indulgent and explosive with Jay. (We'll come back to Fred in another chapter.) At school, Jay was a constant source of irritation to the teacher, the bus driver, and the cafeteria and hall monitors. One day he would be in trouble for throwing food in the cafeteria; the next day it would be spitting in the water fountain; still the next it would be making noises in the back of the class or teasing a girl on the bus.

No matter what the situation, Jay always had an excuse. "The other kid started it, he threw food at me first." "I had to spit somewhere." "Everyone was doing it. She just singled me out because she doesn't like me." "She deserved to be teased. She's fat and ugly."

Jay never viewed himself as responsible. Instead, he saw himself as a nice guy who liked to have fun and who was victimized by rigid people who got their kicks out of telling kids what to do. Fred wanted to be a thoughtful, understanding parent, and he spent much time trying to sort out just who did start the food fight, and was there no other place to spit, and was there a whole group of kids who were making gross noises together. Jay and Fred would end up in shouting matches over who exactly was to blame and which excuse was acceptable and which was not.

Over a period of time, we worked steadily toward getting Jay to take responsibility for his own misbehavior. Fred made it clear to him that in order for him to listen to Jay's account of what happened, Jay had to do three things: He had to take responsibility for some part of the problem, however small it was; he had to say what he could have done to stay out of the conflict; and he had to state what he was going to do differently to make sure it didn't happen again.

Some of our approaches were creative. When Jay couldn't seem to remember to bring home notes from the teacher about his behavior, and falsified a report card, we had him buy ten postage stamps and put them on envelopes that he addressed to his parents. Then he wrote the following note to his teacher: "I, Jay, have a serious problem with not remembering those things which are unpleasant to me. I also have a problem with truthfulness. Therefore I would like you to send all important communications to my parents in these envelopes until such time as I can remember better to bring things home on my own and can be trusted."

The overindulgent parent protects the child from experiencing the natural negative consequences of his or her own behavior.

Most of us know, as adults, that the most valuable lessons we absorbed were learned by living, not by lecturing. Painful as well as joyful experiences have a freshness and a vividness that stay with us for a long time, even for a lifetime. We all have wonderful stories to tell our children about the meaningful experiences we've had in our lives, and children love to hear them. We all hope that in telling the story, we can help our child not to make the same mistake we did.

Yet overprotective parents often see their role as one of intervening between the child and the larger society to prevent these meaningful experiences from happening, because they might be painful for the child (and for the parent). Yet by not being allowed to experience painful consequences, children are condemned to repeat the same mistakes again and again. When children are young, the painful experience may be as simple as having to go without lunch or borrow money or food for lunch because the child left her lunch at home. But when children are older, and their out-of-control behavior begins to meet up against social norms and laws, the stakes are much higher and the consequences of parental intervention are much graver. A parent who habitually pays the fines for traffic tickets for an adolescent who has been caught speeding is a parent who subtly encourages the child to violate traffic laws. To do so is to push the adolescent toward behavior that may result in injury or death to himself or others.

By intervening between the child and naturally occurring consequences in the child's social environment, the parent is promoting the illusion that the parent will always be there to "bail out" the child. This is unfair to the child because it simply is not true. First of all, every parent has a limit and will sometime, at some point, stop protecting the youngster. Children become quite angry when this happens, and they have a right to feel so because they were misled.

Secondly, there may come a time when the parent simply can't come to the rescue because he or she is out of money, ill, elderly, or experiencing personal problems. Then that adolescent or adult child will feel abandoned and lack the skills to cope.

Thirdly, there may come a time when the parent is powerless to intervene because the adolescent has broken the rules at school or has broken the law and it is out of the parent's hands. At that point, too, the adolescent or young adult is likely to feel shocked and betrayed.

Lastly, by intervening between the child and the consequences that come about in the society in which he or she lives, the parent is also sending a message about the degree of confidence in his or her capacity to handle the situation competently. The parent is saying, in effect, "You can't handle it. It would destroy you," and "You need me to get you through this. Without me to rescue you, you'd be thrown to the lions and eaten up."

Christie's Parents: Facing the Consequences of a Daughter Out of Control

Christie's parents first called when they had just gotten back into town from Texas. Christie, aged fifteen, and her boyfriend, aged seventeen, had taken the family car and left Atlanta, heading west. They had had enough of school and felt they could somehow manage on their own. They got as far as Texas when the car broke down and a policeman stopped to help them. When he discovered they were juveniles, he took them to police headquarters and called Christie's parents. Christie's parents had already flown to Florida and back, believing the two had gone there to stay with the boyfriend's mother. They immediately took the next flight out for Texas, horrified that their daughter might have to spend the night in jail. Between the plane flights and the car repairs, they were out several thousand dollars, but they were relieved to have their daughter home safely.

In fact, they were so relieved, they thought nothing of buying Christie the expensive prom dress she had selected. Christie must have been very unhappy to have taken off like that, they reasoned, and the prom dress might be just the thing to pick up her spirits. Paying them back for their expenses was out of the question, since

Christie didn't have four thousand dollars to give them. Things settled down for a while. Then the police arrested Christie, who, with a group of underage drivers, was found drinking in the back of a parked car. They came to the station as fast as they could and brought her home again. They were concerned about the drinking but were relieved that at least the car was parked and Christie wasn't driving.

They were so happy Christie hadn't been harmed in these escapades that they didn't give a moment's thought to the date for their hearing before the juvenile court judge. Surely it was only a formality. But the judge took very seriously the several charges that Christie had incurred by that time. To her embarrassment, he lectured her about her behavior in front of all the people in the courtroom. He revoked her driver's license for six months and sentenced her to do community service. He imposed a nine o' clock curfew on her. He put her on probation with the warning that she would do time in the detention center if she ran away again. Her parents were shocked. Then he turned to them and gave them a public dressing-down as well about their lax attitude toward Christie's conduct.

I only saw Christie and her family for a few visits after that. Their encounter with juvenile court had shocked them into realizing that they could no longer protect Christie from the consequences of her actions. Christie's fate was now in the hands of the judge and her probation officer. If she made one slip during her probation, she would go to the detention center, and they had no choice but to give her firm limits and close supervision.

The overindulgent parent directly or indirectly encourages dependency in the child.

Overindulgent parents, especially mothers, will state with pride that they minister to their children's needs selflessly and with complete devotion. Yet what they fail to see is that there is a boundary between healthy involvement and the promoting of an unhealthy dependency on them. Children need dependency from time to time, especially during times of acute distress or trauma. When a child has been injured or has suffered a major loss, he or she is likely to regress to a more dependent or immature pattern of behavior, and it is at these times that it is important to let the child do so temporarily, and to provide a level of dependency upon the parent that is usually not needed. When this brief seeking of dependency is gratified, most children quickly regroup and move on toward the task of mastering age-appropriate skills.

Overindulgent parents, however, do not seem to be able to distinguish between this brief need for dependency under unusual situations and the child's far greater need for independence. Most children come into the world primed to seek out new experiences, to take in information, to explore their world and master it. An infant of four months is fascinated with his newfound ability to reach and grasp an object. An infant of five months beams with excitement at discovering she can roll over by herself and propel herself across the floor under her own power. By the age of six months, many a mother begins to feel pangs of sadness at how the infant attempts to get out of her lap and onto the floor so he can physically separate from her and take charge of his world.

Yet the striving for independence, which is so instinctual, often meets with difficulty and frustration as new tasks may be difficult to master. It is here that a parent, hopefully, makes the decision to cheer the child on from the sidelines with an "I know you can do it. I have faith in you."

The parent who loves too much or loves dysfunctionally steps in with "Here, let me do it. That's too hard for you." Even more destructive is the "Oh, here, give it to me. You're taking too long," or "Look what's happened. I gave you a chance to do it yourself, and you've messed it up."

It is out of a healthy and appropriate love for the child that a parent sets the expectations at a level just beyond what the child can handle, then provides the tools and the skills to respond to the task. The healthy loving parent conveys to the child the firm belief that the youngster can handle the new task, then stands back and waits. Such a child is then provided with opportunities for successes that translate into pride, self-confidence, and the incentive to try even more difficult tasks.

It is out of misguided love that a parent steps in and takes over. This act, though meant to convey devotion, communicates to the child, "You can't do it," "I don't believe in you," "You will always need me," "You can't make it without me." The reinforcement of dependency in the child robs the child of the many opportunities she might have otherwise had to feel competent and masterful.

Jimmy's Mother: Afraid to Let Him Grow Up

Jimmy had turned eight when he was referred for family counseling. Jimmy was a very likable and affectionate dark-haired boy who always sat as close as possible to his mother, holding her hand throughout the session if possible. At a time when many boys prefer being with men and are embarrassed to be hugged by their mothers, Jimmy viewed his mother as his best friend. The two had slept together since his dad had been killed in a car accident. Jimmy was described as a sweet but forgetful boy who seemed to get lost when the teacher gave instructions and just wasn't able to follow through with class assignments. While the other students got to work, Jimmy daydreamed and drew pictures, waiting for the teacher to come around to his desk and help him get started.

Everyone was troubled about his behavior except Jimmy. He related to me that he really didn't mind not getting the work done, because he enjoyed the hours Mom spent with him at the dining room table every night helping him with his in-class work and his homework. He loved being with his mother more than anything else in the world. Not only did he need her, to remind him what to do and to help him with his assignments, but he was afraid to be apart from her. Jimmy's mother was devoted to him and needed him as much as he needed her. She enjoyed having him sit as close to her as possible and continually stroked his hair while he held her hand. Not only did Jimmy's dependence on her fill the gap in her life left by the loss of her husband, but she felt that by doing so much for him, she was making up somehow for the loss of his father.

Carol: Letting Her Son Oversleep

Carol was having problems with her son, John, sixteen, who had come to live with her for his last two years of high school. He had grown up with his father after the divorce, and she did not know what to expect from a sixteen-year-old boy. She was doing far more for him than she should have, somehow hoping to make up for the years she was not there. Their power struggles were becoming volatile.

Together we made a contract with John. He was to have an alarm and get himself up in the morning. Mom was to stay out of it but be cordial, have her own breakfast, and go on to work. John was to be responsible for getting himself to the bus stop on time. If he missed the bus, he was to call a cab. John was incredulous. Growing up in the suburbs, he had never ridden a cab. How much would one cost? How would you call one? We had John select a cab company and call ahead for instructions as to how long it took the cab to get there, how much the fare would be, etc. Carol made sure John reserved money for cab fare on his dresser.

Carol was nervous about backing off but could see the necessity for it right away. The first morning she left the house with John still in bed, she fought her urge to go back and get him up. John did get up late, and he did have to call a cab. The cab did get him there on time, however, and the ride was a thrill. His friends cheered when they saw him step out of a cab at the drop-off point. He probably would have done it again except that having to pay the ten-dollar fare out of his own money was a lesson he didn't want to repeat.

The overindulgent parent reacts to the child's growing independence with anxiety, rejection, or sadness.

Not only does the overindulgent parent do for the child many tasks she can actually do for herself, but the parent reacts to the child's own efforts to separate and become more independent in such an emotional way that the child feels compelled to pull back to a more dependent state. Many parents, especially mothers, develop such strong bonds with a child, and derive so much of their identity and sense of purpose from that relationship, that to let the child go and care for herself is quite painful.

This is particularly the case in families where mother stays home with the children and has few outside interests. Her whole identity may derive from being needed by her children, who are extremely dependent on her. If, in addition to these factors, the marriage is an unhappy one, and the father is often absent or uninvolved with the children, the bond with the children becomes even stronger and there are few other demands on the mother as intense. To begin to withdraw from that "enmeshed relationship," mother will have to suffer a major loss and reevaluate her goals and priorities. When she does so, she will be forced to make significant and possibly difficult changes in her own life.

This is also the case with single mothers, who have made their children "my whole life" and who have totally devoted themselves to their children in a misguided effort to compensate for the divorce and the loss of the father. Though these women typically have worked, they, too, will have to experience an empty nest as the children move into adolescence and young adulthood. Rather than view the adolescent's separation and pulling away as normal and healthy, they seek to reestablish the close bond by making the adolescent feel guilty.

The impact of mother's emotional state upon the child when the child becomes more independent is often overlooked and very much underestimated by overindulgent parents. It can be as subtle as her saying to a friend on the child's first day of kindergarten, "It's so sad to see them grow up so fast." Many times I've heard mothers of adolescents say, "She just stays up in her room all the time, talking on the phone with her friends. She never spends any time with us anymore. It is so disappointing and painful to be treated this way, when I have tried so hard to have a close relationship with her. I never believed she would do this to me."

As an example of this problem, let's go back to Kelly and her family.

Cynthia: Ambivalent About Letting Kelly Grow Up

Kelly's mother, Cynthia, had never worked, and her life revolved around her family. In fact, she had no close friends and no outside interests other than going to her exercise classes, usually with one of her daughters. Cynthia confided in Kelly her unhappy feelings about her long and troubled marriage to Kelly's dad. Kelly felt uncomfortable about this, but felt she had no choice but to be her mother's confidante, since she had no one else to talk to. Kelly, in turn, confided in her mother because that made her mother feel needed and loved, though it usually ended in an argument when her mother learned about her risky experimentation with men, sex, alcohol, traveling alone, and so on.

But when Kelly backed away from this "best friend" relationship with her mother, her mother was clearly hurt and lonely. "How can you treat me this way?" she would ask, when Kelly would spend several days away from home at a friend's apartment. "You have completely rejected all of us." Their relationship, like that of many mothers and their adolescent daughters, was emotionally intense and stormy. It swung back and forth between being close and confiding, sharing secrets together, to openly hostile and rejecting.

Kelly wanted to grow up and leave home, yet she was afraid of her mother's reaction. What would her mother do when she was lonely?

Whom would she talk to? Even more so, she worried that if she didn't figure out how to be independent, she might end up like her mother, as she saw her—lacking in self-confidence, afraid to go out into the world and take risks, completely dependent on her husband, lonely, and afraid to see her daughters grow up.

The overindulgent parent attempts to provide immediate gratification of her child's needs.

Many parents, especially mothers who see themselves as totally devoted to their children, feel they must meet all the child's immediate needs. Believing that frustration is stressful, punitive, and downright neglectful, they go about the task of providing a smooth, harmonious, frustration-free daily existence. These mothers often bond intensely with their children, and the child's pain becomes their pain. To relieve the child's pain is to relieve their own pain as well.

To these mothers, love = devotion = immediate gratification. These mothers are often vociferous about breastfeeding past the first year, having small children sleep with them in the parental bed if they should cry at night, and in fact, picking the child up and playing with him whenever he cries and for whatever reason. If the child wants a drink of water, he gets a drink of water, and if the child asks that it be in a special cup, she puts it in the special cup. If then the child asks for ice cubes in his drink, he gets the ice cubes, and if he also wants the special spoon to sip it with, she goes to the dishwasher, pulls out the spoon, washes it, and gives it to him. Her goal is a happy child who feels loved and who appreciates her devotion to him.

"After all," many mothers have said to me, "if I'm going to stay home with my children and be a full-time mother to them, then that's what I'm going to be—100 percent dedicated to them. That's what I'm there for. If I wanted them to eat just any old thing for lunch, then I might as well go to work and put them in day care." This statement does have its own internal logic. These mothers are devoted, but their love and intentions are misplaced.

Linda: Coming to Terms With a Small Child's Demands

Linda once put her three-year-old daughter Kirsten in her wading pool on a summer afternoon. First it was too cold, so Linda added some warm water. Then it was too warm, so she added cold. Kirsten wanted some rubber toys to play with, and Linda got them. Her daughter wanted some boats, then cups, and Linda ran back in the house to fetch those too. Soon the pool was crammed full of toys, and Kirsten wanted to eat a snack in the pool at the same time. The child was becoming increasingly agitated, since there appeared to be no limit to this game, and Linda was becoming increasingly agitated as well. Finally, Kirsten asked for one more thing and Linda began yelling "No!" hysterically.

At lunchtime, this game of demanding one thing after another became so aggravating, Linda had to go to her bedroom in order to avoid screaming. In fact, Kirsten was eating lunch alone every day while Linda "hid" in another room. This was not the warm, close relationship Linda had envisioned for them.

Linda called, seeking professional help after an incident in which her husband, in frustration with the child, threw her into a chair. Linda was afraid he was becoming abusive. Only later did she admit that she was afraid that she, too, might do the same thing.

I saw Linda for approximately two years after that. At times, she discussed her own abuse as a child and how it had affected her. Yet other sessions were focused on Kirsten, on understanding the difference between abuse, appropriate limits, and the lack of limits. She was able to see that Kirsten's ambivalence and frequent changing of demands was her three-year-old way of trying to find out if her world was a predictable place with clear boundaries. Linda's rush to gratify those demands only made Kirsten more confused and anxious.

Linda worked at making rules for Kirsten: She could have only two choices at dinnertime. If she didn't eat, she didn't get dessert or snacks. If she played with pins in the pin cushion, she went to time-out. She could not interrupt people on the phone. She could not get up out of bed or call out more than twice, or her door would be closed.

At five, Kirsten was not as whiny and demanding as she had been at three. She was more enjoyable to be with. Linda had gone back to work and was much happier, too. The world had become more predictable for both of them, and Linda was enjoying Kirsten rather than hiding from her.

It is difficult for these parents to understand why their children are not happy when their needs are immediately gratified. We hear so much in the media and in the professional literature about psychiatric illness in adulthood being linked to the failure to "gratify basic needs" in childhood. John Bradshaw, a popular psychologist and speaker, has amassed a national following with the message that all unhappiness in adulthood comes from our not having our needs met as children.

Unfortunately, it has not been clear just what these needs are. Children, and, in fact, all people, need to feel loved and accepted, to feel that they belong to some group and that they are important. However, they also have basic needs for clear rules, clear limits, clear consequences. They have a basic need for a stable and predictable environment where they can learn to wait, to do without, to cope with frustration, to accept less than what they want sometimes. The desire for immediate gratification is not a basic need that must be met.

The overindulgent parent seeks to protect the child from stressful experiences of all kinds.

I have already touched on some of these — the stress of learning to accept "no," the stress of not having needs gratified immediately, the stress of having to accept the consequences of one's actions. In order to underscore this point, I would like to review how this desire to protect the child from normal stresses is broad-based and permeates these parents' approaches to nearly all situations.

Overindulgent parents view all stress as harmful and seek to protect the child from all painful experiences. They view competition, and with it the possibility of failure, as stressful, and are quick to let the child withdraw from competitive experiences. They view long and arduous projects as stressful and allow children to give up on them. They view rejection by peers as unnecessarily painful and allow children to withdraw from group activities where they might feel as though they don't fit in. They view conflict with others as stressful and allow children to withdraw from situations where they are faced with having to resolve conflict. They view any strong emotion such as loss or grief as stressful and seek to mitigate strong emotion as well. To the overindulgent parent, love = a happy childhood, and a happy childhood = no stress.

As an example, let's go back to the Schultz family.

The Schultzes: Letting Their Son Solve
His Own Problem

Oldest son Brian graduated from high school and, after working during the summer and saving up some money, he began attending a small college in a nearby town. The first few weeks went well, but one weekend he asked his dad to pick him up because he wanted to come home for the weekend. Some boys down the hall played their stereo very loud on the weekend, and he couldn't study.

Frank dutifully drove the two hours there to pick him up that Saturday and bring him home. He made the four-hour round-trip on Sunday to take him back. Thereafter, Brian called dad every weekend to pick him up so that he could come home and study. Frank began spending eight hours every weekend in the car and was getting progressively irritated with his son. When it was suggested that Frank put the burden on Brian to solve his problem, Frank hesitated at first because this approach seemed harsh to him. Also, he was not confident that Brian could solve the problem.

Gradually, Frank saw that his caretaking of Brian was under-cutting his son's efforts to grow up now that he was a young adult out on his own. With difficulty, Frank told Brian he was going to have to handle the problem himself somehow. They discussed several solutions that might work, and he instructed Brian not to come home anymore on the weekends to study. After a few weeks of not hearing from Brian, his dad called and asked him how the studying was going. "Oh, fine," Brian said, "I study with my friend Jack in another dorm on the weekends now."

The overindulgent parent seeks to shield the child from conforming to the demands of the social group and the larger society.

Again out of a misguided sense of love and protectiveness, this parent seeks to make the home a haven of unconditional acceptance and views the outside world as uncaring and cold. The only place where the child's true special attributes are recognized is at home, and the larger social environment is a place where the child will have to "fit in" and "be like everyone else"—an experience that could be painfully deflating to the youngster or adolescent.

An antagonism builds up between the family and the outside world, which becomes as "the enemy." Since society may expect the child or adolescent to undergo painful experiences, and the parent believes he must insulate the child from painful experiences, the parent becomes allied with the child against heartless, uncaring society with its strict rules and expectations.

Wesley's Parents: Understanding the Need to Be Special vs. the Need to Fit In

Wesley was a six-year-old with an IQ of 139, clearly a very gifted child. He was the only child of a very bright but absent-minded father who had never been very successful and a mother who was very bright herself and a teacher. Wesley's parents had been eager to provide him with as much intellectual stimulation as possible from birth and focused on their view of him as a rare and unique gem whose value was underappraised by the school system. No limits were provided to him, in the belief that limits might stifle his intellectual curiosity. Everything possible was done for him in the hope that by removing stress from his life, all his energies could be harnessed toward absorbing knowledge.

By first grade, Wesley could read on a fourth-grade level, but he panicked when he had a runny nose because he did not know how to blow his nose. In the classroom, he got up out of his seat and wandered around the room, browsing the bookshelf for something interesting to read. On the playground, he alienated the other children by trying to take over the game and telling them how to play it. The school counselor kept complaining to his mother, "He just doesn't fit in."

While his mother was concerned, she was secretly happy. It was yet another confirmation of his uniqueness and meant that he was destined for greatness. She was angry at the school for imposing these limits on him and felt the school should make exceptions for Wesley and should build a curriculum around his academic needs and his quirky personality.

Wesley himself was not very happy at all. He was afraid to sleep alone, afraid to ride the bus, afraid to go outside because there might be bees out there. He was ridiculed by the other children and seen as a "geek."

Overindulgent parents are notorious "givers."
They are generous to a fault when it comes to their children—at

least when it comes to material goods. They often say, "I love to give to my child. I don't expect anything back. It just makes me feel good to give to her." Most of these parents are hardworking, responsible people who have persevered to reach a certain level of success—a level where, for the first time, they have expendable income, or at least good credit with which to go deeply into debt. Many will deny themselves in order to provide for the material wants of their children. Some will take second jobs in order to provide personal televisions, designer clothes, and cars for their teenagers. Nothing is "too much" for them.

There is a hidden hook, however. I have found that though these parents say they expect nothing back, in reality, they long for appreciation, admiration, and approval from their children. They feel insecure with themselves and their accomplishments and are often lonely and unhappy in their marriages, so the quest for love from their children consumes much of their energy yet is rarely satisfying.

Fran: The Problem of Giving Too Much

Fran, in her forties, was a very sensible and down-to-earth woman. She had only one child so that she could make sure that her one son had everything. She and her husband worked hard to provide him with every material advantage and saved for his college education. When he decided against college and went to trade school instead, they used the money to put a down payment on a house for their son and his new wife. Fran's husband then took a second job on weekends to make extra money to furnish the young couple's house.

When Fran selected a washer and dryer she could afford for them, her daughter-in-law said it was "not nice enough" for her. Fran was heartbroken. But when the couple was expecting a baby the following year, Fran and her husband increased their workload to furnish a nursery for them. Fran was heartbroken again when her son and daughter-in-law gave her a small and inexpensive Christmas gift that year. She then began to develop problems with her health. All her medical tests were negative, and her doctor said it was stress. When the baby came and they rarely called Fran to come over to see it, her stress deepened to depression.

It took Fran several months to realize that her chronic giving was making her stressed out and angry, and that it was not ultimately helping her son and daughter-in-law pull their lives together. She used her illness to justify to them (and herself) a lighter workload and her inability to give as much. She gave when she could, yet said no when it became stressful for her. The illness actually helped her focus on her health, exercise more, and practice her relaxation and meditation exercises. In fact, as she began to do less for her son, she began to see that she did not need to do her mother's banking either, or to take work home from the office. To her surprise, her relationship with her son and grandson continued to be a positive one.

Overindulgent parents take over the role of problem solving for their children.
This is an easy mistake to make. It seems only natural, when our child comes to us with a problem, that we should step in and solve the problem. When our children were infants, we solved virtually all problems. In fact, it was our quick and effective response to the baby's "problem" that made him feel that he could rely on and trust the adults around him.

Yet by the time the infant is a few months old, he begins to encounter obstacles that he is equipped to overcome by himself. It may be as simple a task as reaching an object that is just out of reach. It is by continually using his skills to solve problems that he develops a sense of mastery over his world and a belief in himself as a capable person.

Sue: Learning to Back Off

Let's go back to eleven-year-old Jay. His mother, Sue, was furious with him for getting thrown off the bus. Now she would "have to" drive him to school herself, which was just rewarding him for bad behavior. When it was pointed out that she didn't "have to" drive him, that he could walk or ride his bicycle, she protested. It was too far to walk, and it would be embarrassing for him to ride his bike. It took some persuading to let her let Jay solve the problem. Even Jay pleaded with her to leave it up to him to get himself up in the morning and off to school. Two weeks later, not only was Jay getting up early, but he was making the long walk to school and not complaining. He had made a new friend who walked with him in the mornings. They had blazed a new trail through some areas they had never been in before and thought it was quite an adventure.

By the teen years, the problems become much more complex and the consequences more painful and far-reaching. A teenager must grapple with the problem of how to end a phone conversation and get back to studying, how to get a job, how to cope with malicious gossip that a former friend may be spreading about her around school. Out of concern for her emotional pain and frustration, overindulgent parents inevitably step in and offer advice. The advice is almost always excellent, yet, in my experience, it is seldom followed. These advice-giving sessions usually end up in intensely emotional arguments, the teenager tired of being talked down to, the parent tired of her advice being solicited and then rejected. Many hours must be spent in retraining the parent to step back, let her daughter grapple with the problem, examine her options, weigh the consequences, and make a final choice.

The following is a dialogue between Lauren, aged seventeen, and her mother, Peggy, which went something like this:

LAUREN: I've got to have some money! I'm tired of wearing these same old clothes all the time. And I need a car, too; I can't go anywhere without a car.

PEGGY: Why don't you get a job?

LAUREN: Where?

PEGGY: How about that pizza place near our house?

LAUREN: Ugh! I hate fast-food places! I can't stand all that grease.

PEGGY: How about one of those shops up at the mall?

LAUREN: But if you work in a store, you have to work on Saturdays, and I couldn't stand that. I want to be able to be with my friends on Saturday. And besides, how could I get up there without a car?

PEGGY: You could walk or you could ride a bicycle. It's only a mile.

LAUREN: You have got to be kidding! If anybody saw me walking or riding a bike, I would die of embarrasment. I can't believe you would even suggest such a ridiculous thing!

PEGGY: You could find out when the other girls go to work up there and arrange rides with them.

LAUREN: I can't do that. I would feel so stupid doing that. I just have to have my own car. Can't you buy me a car and I'll pay you back once I get a job?

PEGGY: I can't afford to buy you a car, and, besides, you haven't paid me back the money you borrowed for the prom dress. Why don't you talk to your uncle? You know he offered to buy you a car if you pulled up your grades. He's waiting for you to call him and talk it over.

LAUREN: But he wants me to make ridiculously high grades, like all A's and B's. I can't do that. I would have to be studying for several hours a day, and I wouldn't have any time for my friends or for a job. And I can't talk to him! He's old and grumpy and weird! You talk to him for me!

PEGGY: I have talked to him, but he says he's waiting for you to call him. That's part of the deal he's set, that you have to call him.

LAUREN: God! You are making everything so hard for me! Why won't you just buy me a car?

PEGGY: You know I'm a single parent and we have to make do on my income alone. You can call your dad and ask him if he'll help you out.

LAUREN: You know he won't. All his money goes to his new wife and kid. He just dumped us and he doesn't care about us anymore. If you and Dad hadn't divorced, I wouldn't be in this fix. There would be more money to go around, and he'd buy me a car. This is so unfair to me that you and Dad got divorced and now I have to suffer!

PEGGY: Okay! Okay! I'll do what I can.

Overindulgent parents are often verbally abusive and try to make their children feel guilty.

This last point is perhaps the dark side of being an overindulgent parent, and the one that is the most difficult for parents to admit. Overindulgent parents, as I have said, are extremely loving parents, though their love is often misguided. They will fail to set limits or invoke consequences until the child is completely out of control. Then they will explode in an emotional tirade and a volley of overly harsh punishments. They will give and give, seemingly with no limits, until the child finally asks for one too many things. They react with a barrage of insults, calling the child greedy and self-centered. After doing tasks for the child that he should be able to handle himself and solving his problems for him, they will complain that he is a burden and a loser. They will intervene for him in his conflicts with others, bail him out of his mistakes and disasters, then collapse out of exhaustion with angry recriminations about how it is the child's fault that they are exhausted and broke.

Peggy: A Loving Parent Loses Control

Peggy, mentioned a few pages ago, was overly indulgent with Lauren and could set no limits. She wanted to protect her from making serious mistakes, yet Lauren, at seventeen, was out of control and getting into serious trouble—failing her courses, abusing alcohol, hanging out with kids who "used" her, and becoming sexually promiscuous.

This mother and daughter had always been "best friends," but now they were at war. Peggy would solicit information from Lauren about what was going on between her and her boyfriend, what she did at a party, how much homework she had each night. Yet when Lauren gave her detailed, personal information about her life, Peggy would explode in anger. Peggy, who was a sensitive individual, was shocked at what she had heard herself say to Lauren, not once but during many fights. "You're a loser! You're a tramp! You'll never amount to anything! I can't stand you anymore! I'm through with you! Just pack your things and get out!"

Like Frank Schultz, who hit his son with a shoe, she couldn't believe she had said those things to the daughter she loved so much.

Peggy and Lauren reached a crisis one night during one of those stormy encounters when Peggy let loose a tirade of insults. To her surprise, Lauren moved out. Peggy called on a Saturday morning in a panic. I instructed her to allow Lauren to stay where she was for at least a week for a cooling off. When Lauren was ready to come home, we worked out a contract. Lauren would abide by her mom's rules and would not confide her secrets in her mom. Peggy, in turn, would not be verbally abusive. I saw them for only a few sessions after that. Six months later, Peggy sent a note saying that she and Lauren were continuing to work toward mutual respect and that though they had their ups and downs, they were doing well all in all.

A CHECKLIST FOR PARENTS

Put a checkmark next to the items that are true for you.

_____ 1. Sometimes I blow up after a problem has gone on too long and give out a punishment that's too harsh. Then I let my children off restriction before their time is up.

_____ 2. I try to reason with my children when I give out consequences, but they use that as an opportunity for endless arguing—and they often win.

_____ 3. I have a hard time setting limits with my adolescent due to the threats he or she has made to leave home, drop out of school, run away, etc.

_____ 4. My children cannot readily answer this question: "What are the rules in this house about clothes left on the floor?"

_____ 5. My children cannot readily answer this question: "What are the consequences in this house for not doing homework?"

_____ 6. I often feel completely powerless with my child, whether he's four, fourteen, or twenty-four.

_____ 7. If asked, "Who's the boss around here?" my children are likely to answer, "We are."

_____ 8. I often let my child make excuses or blame others for her misbehavior. I want to be fair and to listen to her point of view. I'm not sure where to cut it off.

_____ 9. I have to admit I can't bear to see my child unhappy because he's been deprived of something. After all, that's why I earn the money.

_____ 10. When I have to follow through with a punishment and my child is really unhappy and crying, I feel so guilty that I just can't do it.

_____ 11. When my child is unhappy because of how she's being treated by someone else, I feel I must come to her aid and protect her.

_____ 12. My children don't have a lot of responsibilities around the house. We want their childhood to be carefree and enjoyable.

_____ 13. I know I do a little too much for my son, but he really needs me, and I don't mind doing things for him. I know he'll grow out of it one day.

_____ 14. I have to admit, the day she started school was a sad day for me, and I'm not looking forward to her graduation.

_____ 15. My children are my whole life. I guess they always will be.

_____ 16. The children come to me for everything—for help, advice, emotional support, money, direction, love.

_____ 17. I am so angry at my fourteen-year-old son. We used to be so close after his dad and I divorced. Now he just stays up in his room, listening to music, and won't have a thing to do with me.

_____ 18. I am totally devoted to my child. I try to gratify her every need. I don't want her to grow up thinking her mother (father) didn't love her.

_____ 19. I have been pretty liberal with my son about letting him back out of things that were stressful—giving a talk in front of the class, confronting a bully on the bus. I don't feel you should make kids do things they can't handle.

_____ 20. I have been known to take a stand with my child against the school or pay for an attorney to help him out with minor brushes with the law. I believe when you're a parent, you love your child and you stand by him no matter what he's done.

_____ 21. In many ways, I take pride in the fact that my child doesn't fit in. I want her to be her own person, to stand apart from the crowd. Schools nowadays are too conforming.

_____ 22. If I can solve a problem for my son, I certainly will. That's what I'm there for.

_____ 23. On occasion, I have really lost it and said some angry things to my thirteen-year-old daughter. Once I told her if she didn't like it here, she could find somemewhere else to live.

_____ 24. I am hurt, angry, and frustrated about how my young adult daughter is turning out. I have tried so hard to be a good parent. I just don't know what went wrong.

If you've checked more than eight items, read on.

4   Parenting Styles, Problem Solving, and Coping Skills in Children

Though the field of child psychology is relatively new, researchers have learned a great deal over the last thirty years about children growing up in different types of families. One area of research has been focused on what we call parenting styles—how parents approach everyday situations with their children. Psychologists have observed parents interacting with their children and rated them along several dimensions of behavior. Then they have asked teachers and fellow students to rate the children in these families on scales that measure such qualities as leadership, self-confidence, and popularity with peers.

The categories or dimensions of behavior researchers have chosen are the same ones used to describe friendships or marriages. One dimension is that of warmth versus hostility. Warm parents are described by people who observe them as nurturant, affectionate, positive, accepting, and child-centered. Warm parents are more likely to use reasoning and explanations when children misbehave. Hostile parents are described as angry, punitive, harsh, rejecting, and critical. Though all parents are angry at their children some of the time, hostile parents are characterized by negative interactions with their children much of the time.

Another dimension is restrictive versus permissive parenting. Restrictive parents are viewed as highly controlling, demanding complete obedience from their children and having very strict rules with regard to modesty, table manners, neatness, noise, fighting with each other, etc. Permissive parents are very lax about setting rules and grant their children a wide berth as to obeying the rules. They are also characterized by less consistency in how they enforce the rules.

A third dimension is that of anxious emotional involvement versus calm detachment. Parents who exhibit high involvement are very sensitive to everything that happens to their children, confide in their children, have their children confide in them, and are very sensitive to their child's feelings toward them. Parents who are less involved are much more detached. They are more likely to see their children as separate people from themselves and set clearer limits around what adult issues and feelings the children are exposed to.

If we plot these dimensions on a circle, we get something like Figure 1, taken from a diagram developed in 1964 by Wesley Becker of the University of Illinois. The more restrictive parenting styles are on

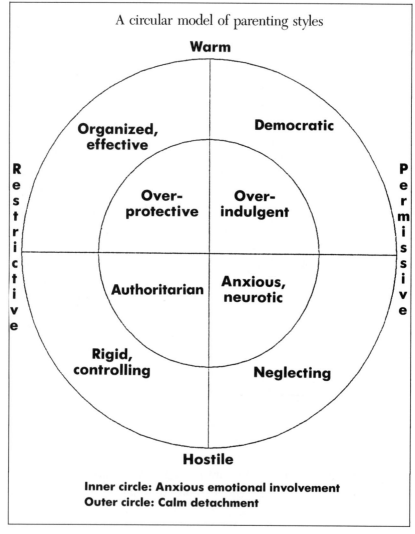

Figure 1

the left. There we find rigid, controlling parents who are more hostile with their children and more distant. There, also, we locate the authoritarian parent is hostile and controlling but more emotionally involved. The overprotective parent, while a warmer parent, is also a very emotionally involved parent. The organized, effective parent is more on the controlling side but also warm and appropriately detached.

On the right are the more permissive parenting styles. Parents who are permissive yet hostile and detached are described as neglecting. Anxious and neurotic parents combine permissiveness with hostility and anxious emotional involvement. The overindulgent parenting style, which is the focus of this book, combines permissiveness with warmth and anxious emotional involvement. Permissive attitudes combined with warmth and more detachment make up the democratic style.

Though not all researchers have used these exact dimensions, much of the research on parenting styles can be described by looking at the diagram in Figure 1. For example, most studies of juvenile delinquents suggest that they come from homes described as neglecting. Parents in these homes seem very lax about rules and are very emotionally detached from their children. Yet when the children get into trouble, the parents are very harsh and punitive. Particularly common in the homes of those who later engaged in criminal behavior was the combination of a very permissive mother, and a very hostile father, and a great deal of inconsistency.

When we look at adults who grew up as children in anxious, neurotic homes, we find that they are more likely to have many psychiatric problems: alcoholism, anxiety, depression, low self-esteem, and a higher tendency to suicide. These children, it seems, by being so close to their parents, tended to internalize their parents' hostile attitudes toward them.

If we move upward, to the overindulgent section, we are likely to find children who are out of control. They are likely to be seen by classroom teachers as more disobedient, irresponsible, and disorderly in the classroom. They often cannot pay attention and have poor work habits. At home, they are likely to be described by their parents as rebellious, aggressive, disrespectful, and disobedient. They are characterized by moderately low self-esteem. Interestingly, the older children view their parents as not very interested in them or attentive to them.

They often lack a sense social responsibility toward others and are less independent than some other groups. As adults, they are likely to be low achievers. Boys from these families seem to do more poorly than girls. They are described as hostile, uncooperative, domineering, and unable to get along well with their peers.

Just next to them on the circle are children from democratic homes. These children are allowed a great deal of autonomy and parents use reasoning instead of punishment. Like children from the overindulgent homes, they have a tendency to be out of control some of the time, but they are more often bold, assertive, outgoing, and self-confident. They tend to be a bit domineering toward their peers but are well liked. As adults, they tend to be high achievers.

If we look at the children on the left side of the circle, we are more likely to see children who are overly controlled and inhibited in general. Children of overprotective mothers have been found to be more submissive, dependent, and timid than their peers. They also have a tendency to be neat, obedient, and polite. While these behaviors may be desirable to parents and teachers, such children are not often viewed as leaders among their peers. They tend to be more anxious and afraid of failure. This parenting style seems to be particularly harmful for girls who are already a bit more passive and anxious.

Many studies suggest that children from the authoritarian and rigid, controlling families don't fare so well either. They tend to be unhappy, withdrawn, and have difficulty trusting others. They have the lowest levels of self-esteem.

Children from the organized, effective homes seem not clearly distinguishable from those from democratic homes. While they may be a bit more controlled in their behavior, they are still likely to be seen as competent among their peers, independent, outgoing, and well liked. They are optimistic and cheerful. They have high self-esteem. Studies of high achievers in adulthood indicate that they most likely come from this kind of home.

One researcher, Diana Baumrind of the University of California, did a series of studies in the late 1960s and early 1970s comparing three different parenting styles. One style, which she calls "authoritarian," is very much like the authoritarian and the rigid, controlling styles described by Becker. The "permissive" style corresponds to the overindulgent style on the diagram. The style which she called "authoritative" seems to correspond to a blend of the democratic and the organized, effective styles. Her research pointed out very specific sets of traits in these parents.

Authoritarian parents attempt to shape, control, and judge the child's behavior and attitudes in accordance with a set standard of conduct. This standard is usually absolute, inflexible, and something not to be challenged. It often comes from a rigid moral or religious belief system. They value obedience to authority as a virtue and believe in using punitive measures to "break the child's will" if the child challenges their authority. They believe in keeping the child in her place, which is a very inferior place to that of the parents. They believe in restricting the child's freedom to come and go or make decisions for herself. They assign household responsibilities in order to instill a strong respect for work. They value order and traditional structure as an end in itself. They do not encourage verbal give-and-take, believing the child should accept what they say without question.

Baumrind described permissive parents as those who try to behave in a nonpunitive, accepting, and affirming manner toward the child's impulses, desires, and actions. They consult with the child about decisions and give explanations for family rules. They make few demands for household responsibility. They present themselves as a resource for the child to use as he needs. They allow the child to do as he pleases as much as possible, avoid exerting control over him, and do not force him to conform to outside standards or expectations. They try to use reason and persuasion but not outright power to get the child to do what they want.

When she observed the permissive parents, Baumrind found that they were very passive in the face of disobedience. They scored low on measures of firm enforcement of rules. They also scored low on measures of encouraging independence. They did not discourage dependency and even tolerated a great deal of babyish behavior from the child. They were more likely to be angry over their lack of control in the home. In terms of discipline, they refused to use force to gain control, they were unclear about their role as parents, and they could be coerced or manipulated by the child. They did not make strong demands on the child to pay attention. They avoided open confrontation with the child, ignored the child's defiance, and tried to remain "sweet and patient" when the child disobeyed. The permissive parents seemed to have few clear positive goals for their children and strove for non-interference with their children's natural development.

Authoritative parents were described as those who attempt to direct but not control their child's activities in a rational and reasonable way. They will give explanations for why they want the child to do something, encourage verbal give-and-take, and listen to the child's objections when she refuses to obey. But, if need be, they will have the final say and exert firm control when it is necessary and when it is in the child's best interests to do so. They value independence in the child and take pride in their child's ability to be self-sufficient and make her own decisions. Yet they also value the child's self-discipline and capacity to conform to society's norms when necessary. They manage to assert firm control over the child without compromising the child's individual interests, autonomy, and self-esteem. They are warm parents who affirm the child's importance and uniqueness. They are not loyal to an outside higher authority but to what seems best for the child's emotional growth.

When Baumrind studied these parents in more detail she found that the children were encouraged to assert themselves, express their opinions, even argue with their parents in an attempt to get the parent to change the rule. In some cases, if the child made an exceptionally good argument, the parent would bend the rule. These parents used reason and explanation as far as they could, resorting to force and punishment only as a last resort and when necessary to safeguard the child's well-being. These children accepted their parents' firm limits because they seemed well intentioned, fair, reasonable, and in their own best interests. They also respected their parents because they saw them as caring, concerned, and predictable. These families also set firm rules about the rights of others and set high standards for the children around their responsibility toward other family members and toward their peers. And finally, these families stressed independence at an early age. They gave their children a great deal of freedom within their firm boundaries and rewarded them for self-sufficiency. Dependency on the parents and babyish behavior were actively discouraged. These children also viewed this push toward independence as loving and as child-centered.

As expected, children of authoritative parents were rated by their peers and by other adults as more nonconforming, independent, imaginative, and confident than children of the other types of parents. They were also rated as more adaptive, likable, well-socialized, friendly, and dependable. Interestingly, Baumrind found that firm control was especially important for boys, as the boys from permissive families fared particularly badly. Girls, however, seemed to do best in authoritative families who were a little less controlling yet a bit harsher in the demands they made on them. Baumrind found what other researchers had found: that too much warmth, acceptance, and nurturance appeared to be maladaptive for girls, as they had trouble breaking their dependency on others. Too much control was also more destructive for girls than for boys in that it was found to make girls excessively compliant.

In summarizing a large body of research, we can say that those children who are most successful and competent at life tend to come from homes whose style of parenting is described by nine factors.

The first factor is that of *warmth*. Warmth is shown by competent parents through expressions of love and affection, naturally, and affirmations of the child's self-worth. It is also expressed, however, by a deep and abiding interest in the child's life, his friends and activities and schoolwork, and an attentiveness to him when he talks about himself. It is expressed through a moderate level of acceptance, patience, and understanding. The warm parent also is one who gives frequent positive feedback to the child about how well he's doing and praise where appropriate.

Parents of successful children also score high on measures of *firm control* in the home. The parents make clear rules about those issues which are most important—typically those matters that have a bearing on the child's safety and well-being and those that pertain to respect for the rights of others. They let the little stuff go but hold firmly to the rules about these big issues. The children understand the rules, can state them, and know what the consequences are. The parents do not hesitate to punish their children for misbehavior. They begin with discussion and reasoning. If these are not effective, they progress to isolation, denial of privileges, and restriction of freedom. They rarely use physical punishment, threats, coercion, or withdrawal of love. They report that their punishments are effective. Their children view them as fair and feel their punishments are deserved.

The third factor is the *lack of anxious, emotional involvement or enmeshment*. The most healthy parents in all the studies are those who have a healthy level of emotional detachment from their children and also do not see the children as extensions of themselves. They respect their children's right to be separate people with their own thoughts and feelings. They do not share adult concerns with the child. They do not demand to know their children's secrets or all their private feelings. They do not view their children as friends but maintain clear-cut boundaries between themselves and their children. They are not swayed by their children's angry outbursts, verbal attacks, or efforts to make them feel guilty when they discipline their children.

The fourth factor is that of *consistency*. Parents of successful children have been found, in study after study, extending as far back as the 1920s, to be consistent about what they do. Though they may be a bit permissive or a bit controlling or a bit harsh, they are consistently so. Their rules are enforced in a consistent way across time; their discipline is carried out in a consistent manner. In these homes, there is a reasonable amount of consistency from one parent to another. There is likewise a consistency between what the parent tells the child to do and what the parent himself does. This consistency, combined with firm control, gives the child a stable and predictable home base from which to operate.

Another factor we see turning up in study after study of successful parenting styles is *democratic decision making*. Competent parents do not turn over decisions to children, but they do invite children to have their say. They actively solicit their children's opinions on appropriate matters, such as what foods they like to eat, what videos they want to watch, and where they would like to go on the family vacation. They stimulate their children to think about their choices carefully, to weigh out the pros and cons, and to look at the issue from several angles. By doing so, they promote their children's ability to think for themselves and make good choices.

In fact, these families seem to promote *independence* in all areas. They stress the importance of doing a task "on your own, without any help from me." They hold back and resist the urge to help, even when the child may become frustrated. They seem to know when a task is too difficult and the child really needs help, and when it can be mastered by the child with just a little push from Mom or Dad. When these parents are asked, At what age should a child be able to dress herself? put herself to bed? cross the street? stay home alone for a while? etc., the ages they give are younger than the ages given by other parents.

This factor of independence overlaps with a factor that some researchers call *maturity demands*. We find that in homes of successful children, immature and babyish behavior is discouraged. Parents emphasize, "You're too big for that now," and "You're a big kid now. I think you're capable of taking better care of your things," etc. They give their children household responsibilities appropriate to their age. They have expectations for their children about keeping their rooms in order and taking care of their clothes and toys. They reward their children for being responsible, self-sufficient, organized, and helpful.

They also make demands on their children to become *socialized*— to take in society's rules about how we are to act with one another. All the various groups of competent parents insist that their children, starting from an early age, incorporate these social rules. They make demands on their children to control their aggressivess toward each other and to control their impulses. Children in these families are not allowed to verbally or physically abuse each other. They are praised for controlling their tempers. They are required to be respectful to adults and often to care for younger children or elderly people. Politeness and good manners are highly valued in these homes.

Lastly, many of these homes where we find healthy parents and healthy kids are homes where *nonconformity* is encouraged. It seems that the parents' emphasis on independence, self-sufficiency, and democratic decision making in the home also contributes in some way to helping these children march to the rhythm of their own drum. They are a bit rebellious away from home and often challenge authority figures. While teachers may be uncomfortable with this at times, children from these homes seem more imaginative and more capable of formulating original ideas. They are not as strongly swayed by peer pressure, but instead are guided by inner values and principles.

How do well-adjusted children solve problems?

Another area of focus for researchers who study healthy parents and healthy children has been the area of problem-solving skills. Myrna Shure and George Spivack, two researchers at the Hahnemann

Medical College in Philadelphia, launched an area of research in the 1960s that is still continuing today. Spivack first noticed when working with troubled adolescents in a residential treatment center that they seemed to show exceptionally poor judgment when solving everyday problems. He and Shure then set about to determine just what it is that constitutes good judgment and good problem-solving skills in children, how these skills change with the age of the child, and whether parents can teach children to have these skills. Other researchers who came after them have looked at what kinds of families these good and poor problem solvers come from.

They found that children as young as four years of age are solving problems with their peers and that some are doing better at it than others. In fact, those who are doing well are well liked by adults and children, and those who are doing poorly are already identified as behavior disordered. Shure and Spivack posed this problem to preschoolers:

> Here's a problem. Jimmy wants a chance to play with the truck, but Johnny keeps on playing with it. What can Jimmy do so he can have a chance to play with it? Tell me as many things as you can think of.

By far the most important factor that separated the well-adjusted from the behavior-disordered preschoolers was that the former group could think of *more alternative solutions* to the problem. The more poorly adjusted children could think of only one solution, and it was usually aggressive. The more competent children also thought of aggressive solutions, but they could add to this a stock of nonaggressive solutions as well. Somehow, by being able to generate several solutions to a problem, they could more easily choose from these and pick a good one.

Shure and Spivack found that in their research on older children of elementary school age, this ability to generate alternative solutions continued to be a strong factor associated with children's doing well in school and getting along with their peers. Other problem-solving skills, however, begin to emerge as well. Children from six to twelve years of age begin to be able to formulate a goal and determine which steps are necessary to accomplish the goal. They can anticipate obstacles and plan for them. They can formulate alternative plans if the first one fails. They have a better ability to see what caused a particular situation. They have a better sense of the consequences of their actions. They can see that A leads to B, and B leads to C. They also seem to acquire a sense of timing—when is a good time to do something, and when is a not-so-good time. These skills separated the well-adjusted children from the behavior-disordered children across several studies and were found to be unrelated to race, social class, or intelligence.

By the time children are in their teens, two new skills are added to this repertoire. One is the ability to manage strong, negative emotions such as anger, fear, jealousy, and rejection. The other problem-solving skill is the ability to see a situation through the eyes of another person. The researchers called this skill "role-taking ability," but we could just as easily call it compassion or empathy. Though all these skills described so far were important, it was this factor, more than any of the others, that separated successful teenagers from less successful ones.

Other researchers have found good problem-solving skills to be of tremendous importance to understanding how people cope and adapt to life successfully. Poor problem-solving skills are characteristic of a wide variety of psychiatric patients in hospitals, of teenagers who don't use contraceptives, of teenagers with unwanted pregnancies, of juvenile delinquents, of abusing and neglectful mothers, and even substance abusers. Teenagers who cannot generate alternative solutions to problems have been found to be more depressed and suicidal. Some studies suggest that these poor problem-solvers come from more permissive homes characterized by inconsistency, poor controls, and frequent conflict.

It comes as no surprise perhaps that good problem-solvers come from homes most similar to the authoritative style of parenting, where there is good control, rules are clear and consistent, and consequences are explained. There is democratic decision making in the homes of good problem-solvers, demands are made for maturity and independence, and respect for others' feelings is important. Some have suggested that it is this push toward independence that is the important ingredient. Children who are pushed to mature early and to be self-sufficient are also being encouraged to solve problems by themselves. Each and every problem the child solves becomes an opportunity for the child to learn new information about what the consequences of some of her actions are, about good plans and bad plans, and about how her actions affect other people.

The exciting part about this research is that Shure and Spivack found that parents can teach children to be good problem-solvers. Simply put, parents can be trained to stop solving their children's problems and, instead, to put the burden of problem solving on their child, through a question-and-answer format. Parents are taught to ask these types of questions:

- What is your plan?
- What else can you think of?
- What do you need to do first?
- What if you run into a problem?
- What will happen if you do that?
- Can you tell me the pros and cons of each plan?
- How do you think she will feel if you do that?

I call this the Socratic method. Socrates was noted for his teaching style of not lecturing but asking his students questions, and by doing so creatively, leading them to formulate new and interesting solutions to philosophical problems. Parents who are taught to do this with their children see a reduction in their children's behavior problems. This approach is now widely used in classrooms by teachers. The misbehaving student is sent to the "opportunity room" to think and to write a "plan" for what he could have done differently. Teachers review the plan with the child and ask him if he thinks his plan will work. Parents can use this approach with their own children, starting with the first few questions with younger children and progressing to the last questions with adolescents. Some examples of using this approach will be offered in later chapters.

How do competent children cope with stress?

From early infancy, we are confronted with a barrage of stressful situations. In encountering stress, we must find some way to cope with that stress, whether we cope internally (such as changing how we feel or think about the situation) or externally (such as doing something about the situation). In the early years of this century, Freud and his followers made the simple assumption that the nature of the stress the individual encountered (such as harsh toilet training or parental death) had an enormous impact on shaping the child to become a particular kind of individual. Clinicians have long observed, however, that how the individual copes with the stress makes all the difference in the world. Those who seem to cope well with stresses seem to do well in life, in spite of having encountered enormous problems growing up. Those who cope poorly, responding to stresses in ways that seem clearly inappropriate or poorly thought out, seem to compound their problems. In fact, a whole new area of research called "resiliency studies" has come out of these case studies of people who overcame enormous odds as children and grew up to be productive and happy individuals. These studies do not ask the question, "Why isn't this person unhappy in light of the trauma she suffered as a child?" which has never been answered adequately, but instead ask the more interesting question, "What are the attributes or coping skills of this person that have enabled her to build a good life for herself in spite of childhood trauma?"

In the early 1980's, Susan Folkman and Richard Lazarus, at the University of California, Berkeley, began to study adult coping skills in a systematic way. They found that how people coped with problems depended on what they felt they had at stake, on whether they felt they could do anything about it, and on what they then chose to do. They developed a list of eight types of coping patterns that people used when confronted with a stressful situation. Briefly, they found that people's coping patterns varied with the type of stressful event they were faced with. For example, seeking the emotional support of your friends worked well for coping with a death in the family, but developing a plan of action was a better bet for coping with the loss of a job.

While there is no one best coping style for every situation, some broad generalizations can be made about coping patterns, based on a large body of research. We know that distancing oneself from the problem ("I didn't let it get to me") and self-control ("I sat quietly and thought about it for a long time") are almost always good approaches. So are accepting responsibility ("I apologized") and developing a plan ("I knew what had to be done, so I doubled my efforts to make things work"). Positive reappraisal, or making lemonade out of the lemons life hands you, is always constructive also. Seeking social support is sometimes a good idea and sometimes not. It depends on the confidant's reaction. Confrontational coping, or expressing one's anger, has also been found to be sometimes a good idea and sometimes not.

Most dramatically, researchers have found that escape-avoidance is almost always a disastrous choice of coping style, no matter what the situation. Forgetting about the problem, engaging in wishful thinking, binging on food or alcohol, running away from the person or situation, sleeping excessively, etc., have extremely negative outcomes for the individual. Not only does the person not solve the problem, but this pattern intensifies the person's belief that she is incapable of solving similar problems in the future. Studies have linked this coping style to the development of a wide variety of psychiatric and substance abuse problems.

We now know that children and adolescents approach stressful situations with coping patterns that are very similar to those of adults. They are different, however, in that the stability and the support of the family are always an important factor for them. Unlike an adult, who acts as a free agent, they always live in the context of a family that may offer a lot or a little in the way of resources to the child. Also, the child's age and level of development is always a factor in how he copes with a problem. As children develop, they broaden their range of approaches to coping with stresses in their lives. They become more "inward" in the sense that they develop more ways to manage their thoughts and feelings as well as ways to solve the problem.

Studies show that well-adjusted adolescents use the same positive coping patterns described above. When faced with rejection or failure, they might confide in a friend, turn on the radio and dance, write in a diary, read inspirational works, develop a plan, talk to their guidance counselor, work out with weights, make a joke out of it, or relax and watch a little television. The most destructive coping styles among teenagers, across all studies, are ventilation of feelings in an angry way and avoidance. Losing control of their temper, being verbally abusive, and making threats they later regret are examples of the former, while using drugs or alcohol, smoking, binging on food, sleeping, avoiding the people whom they feel uncomfortable with, and avoiding talking about uncomfortable subjects are examples of the latter. Often, wishful thinking also turned up among the coping styles of teenagers in trouble, along with other types of avoidance. These adolescents would "hope it all worked out somehow" or "wait for someone to solve the problem for me."

We now know that adolescents who cope with stress in these ineffective ways are more prone to acting out behaviors, to eating disorders, drug abuse, and running away from home when they can't face peer and family problems. We also know from research that inconsistency is a hallmark in the homes of these teens who cope poorly with stress. Studies show that their parents are more likely to restrict the children from coping adaptively, and that they often fail to provide adequate models of coping themselves.

It is this issue which is of particular relevance to overindulgent families and underdeveloped children. As we saw in chapter 2, underdeveloped children and adolescents rely heavily on avoidance and escape to cope with problems. By middle childhood, they are less likely to try new things because they fear failure and are poor problem-solvers. By adolescence, they are unable to manage strong negative emotions and are easily overwhelmed by the accumulation of everyday problems. Many begin to rely on angry outbursts and avoidance to handle their problems. These problems compound themselves by late adolescence and contribute to higher suicide rates, heavier alcohol use, more social isolation, and an increased tendency to drop out of school and run away from home.

In summary, research psychologists in the area of child development have known for several years what many of the childhood antecedents of adult behavior are. We know that overindulgent and permissive families are families in trouble. This parental style may be warm and loving, but it is characterized by poor or no limits, and inconsistency. Parents in these families are overly close with their children and tolerate a great deal of dependency from them. Their goals with their children seem to center around making the children happy and content and not interfering with their lives. Children from these families tend to appear most often in that group that are seen as disruptive, out of control, unhappy, and low in self-esteem. Because they are not pushed to solve problems independently, they are poor problem-solvers by the time they are in elementary school. They often cannot work independently in the classroom but need much external structure and direction. They continue to have poor problem-solving skills well into adolescence. They can generate few good solutions to problems and cannot develop an effective plan of action. As teens, they are more likely to act out, to be impulsive, and to engage in reckless and dangerous behaviors.

We know that overindulgent families score low on measures of demands for independence and maturity and demands that the child be socialized, i.e., be polite and exercise self-control. These parents seldom require their children to be conscientious about the rights and feelings of others. At a time when these youngsters should be developing the capacity to see life from another person's point of view, they are still quite immature and self-centered. Their capacity for close and enduring relationships in adolescence does not develop smoothly.

By high school and early adulthood, they make up a large portion of the group we call underachievers. Many are depressed at their lack of success in so many areas of living—work, school, social life, and family. They have poor coping skills when it comes to stress and are more likely to resort to hostile outbursts and avoidance when upset. These behaviors make them at high risk for a range of psychiatric problems and substance abuse. They are also more likely to be in trouble for juvenile offenses such as truancy, running away, driving without a licence, and so on.

On the other hand, there are those children who are consistently self-confident, sociable, outgoing, poised, and high in self-esteem. They are well thought of by peers and teachers alike. The parents in these families use an authoritative parenting style—they are warm but firmly in control. They emphasize independence and self-reliance from an early age. They insist their children be respectful of the feelings and rights of other people, both children and adults. They use reasoning in disciplining children and give children a wide range of participation in making family decisions. These children have high self-esteem, and they are good problem-solvers. They can generate many solutions to a problem. They can develop a step-by-step plan in working toward a goal, overcome obstacles, persevere toward their goals, and accept frustration. They are compassionate toward others and have a sense of responsibility for the consequences of their actions. Through all this, they also seem to develop adaptive ways of coping with stress. They can size up a situation and decide whether to approach the problem by confronting it directly and making changes, or by seeking help and advice from others, or by changing their outlook and controlling their emotions. They almost never handle problems by hostile outbursts, impulsiveness, escape, avoidance, and wishful thinking.

The field of education has reaped a harvest from this research. Teachers and counselors are now employing it to teach children how to solve problems and to cope with stress. It is time now to share it with the concerned parent who wants to give her child the best chance at a good life.

5   How Did We Get to Be Overindulgent Parents?

Over the years, I have come to know many parents who have difficulty setting limits with their children and who know that they give too much to them. They are aware of the problem and are concerned about it. They have been told by friends and family alike, even teachers, "You need to follow through more consistently," or, "Your children take advantage of you." They have insight into the problem and can say, "I know I let him get away with too much."

The problem that brings the parent to a clinic for help may be marital difficulties, depression, or a child who is underachieving at school or even in trouble with juvenile court, but the parents all make similar statements: The parent sees the problem but feels helpless to do anything about it. She is enmeshed in a destructive relationship with the child or adolescent but cannot break out of the pattern until she has addressed the problems in her own life or in her past. These emotional difficulties in the parent's life contribute to a set of faulty beliefs about his role as a parent and to maladaptive ways of interacting with his child. Let's look now at some recognizable patterns.

Perhaps the most common cause of overindulgence is *parental guilt over divorce, work, or remarriage.* With the advent of the women's movement and the increased expectations most Americans have had for a higher standard of living, a steadily growing number of women have chosen to return to careers after having children. Current figures show that about 60 percent of all mothers with preschool-age children now work outside the home. With the destigmatization of divorce and the increased possibilities for women to support themselves economically through work, the last twenty years have noticed a dramatic upsurge in the divorce rate as well. Currently, about half of all marriages end in divorce.

Often these two trends—of more working mothers and higher divorce rates—are linked together. For example, a woman who is increasingly unhappy in her marriage may go back to work in order to prepare to support herself and her children. A woman who finds herself suddenly divorced may be forced to go back to work to support herself and her children. A woman who is divorced and remarried may continue to work, even though she is remarried, because she never wants to be totally economically dependent on a husband again. While these changes have brought women in our society a sense of enhanced freedom and control over their lives, these gains have been purchased with a high price of guilt.

Most American women have a romanticized picture of mother-hood, one that includes marriage to a man who makes enough money to support the family on his income alone, a nice home, and the opportunity to stay home with children during their tender years, and certainly does not include divorce. While this may have been the predominant model in the fifties and sixties, it is a reality for only a small percentage of families in the seventies, eighties, and nineties. In over half of American families, the mother goes back to work when the children are still small in order to provide the basic necessities for the family. These children will be cared for by someone or some group of people outside the home. Half of the marriages will end in divorce. The mother may remain single for many years, or she may remarry fairly quickly. She is likely to marry a man who is also divorced and probably has children from a previous marriage. Over 60 percent of second marriages end in divorce, the most common reason being conflicts over "your" children and "mine."

These changes are difficult for children, and their lives are often marked by a sense of loss. In the initial divorce, they lose the compan-ionship of the parent, usually the father, who moves out of the home. They usually lose the standard of living they were accustomed to, due to the worsening of their mother's financial circumstances. They lose the stay-at-home mother when she goes back to work, and they are often alone in the house in the afternoons. If their mother cannot keep up payments on the house, they are forced to move, losing the house, the backyard, the neighborhood, and the friends that went with that home.

If their father is irregular about visitation, they lose the sense of being valued and loved by him. If their father soon has a new girlfriend, they feel completely displaced by her. If the new girlfriend or wife has children of her own, they feel cheated by the fact that those children get to spend more time with their father than they do.

Naturally, many children are unhappy following a divorce, and they see their lives as irreparably broken. They feel deprived of security, love, attention, and a comfortable lifestyle. Most of all, they feel they have lost the sense of a "family"—a solid and secure container that forms a nurturing and protective net around them. One nine-year-old boy said, "Divorce is like a limb of your family tree broke off and went away and it will never come back again." A ten-year-old girl said, "It's like when we were a family, we were like a flower. Then the divorce came. All the petals and leaves fell off and nothing is left but the stem."

Faced with such sad children, it is easy to see why mothers feel guilty. How can one possibly compensate for this sense of loss? Mothers in this situation are often desperate to do anything to overcome this feeling of deprivation in the children's lives. Unhappy children are often irritable and uncooperative. When pushed to complete household tasks, to compete in athletic events, or to do homework, they are more likely to give up easily or burst into tears.

Any mother faced with a child whose father just called and canceled a visitation for the third weekend in a row would be hard-pressed to be firm and in control and continue their daily routine as if nothing had happened. Many well-adjusted adults would be inclined to take the child out and have some fun as a diversion, or to take the child shopping and buy him something to lift his spirits.

Peggy: Allowing Her Guilt to Undermine Her Authority

In chapter 3 we met Peggy and her teenaged daughter, Lauren. Peggy had a habit of trying to solve Lauren's problems for her. It was one of many ways in which Peggy was overindulgent. She also spent more money than she could afford on her and set too few limits. Peggy related the history that she and her first husband, Greg, had married right out of college and soon had two children, Lauren and her older brother, David. When the children were still young, Greg had a "divine revelation" that he was living a sinful life in the suburbs, and he left them. He went back to theology school and became a street minister, founding a shelter and soup kitchen for the homeless.

The children took it hard. Not only had their dad left their mom, but he had renounced them and their lifestyle as well. Greg went on to meet a woman who believed in his vision, and they married and renovated the shelter together. They took vows of poverty and lived in two small rooms in the back of the shelter.

Because her ex-husband was indigent, there was virtually no child support for Peggy and the children. She had a good job, but it was barely enough to make the house payments and raise two children. The children suffered, too, because their father took little interest in them. He denounced David and Lauren as "materialistic" when they asked for money. He would agree to visitation only on condition that they come to the shelter and work in the soup kitchen. They wouldn't go. They both felt he was more interested in saving street people than he was in them.

Both David and Lauren felt painfully rejected, and Peggy felt acutely guilty. She tried to buy them what she could to assuage their feelings, even if it meant going into debt on credit cards. She made a hasty and ill-timed second marriage to a man who seemed sensitive and caring and had a good income. Several years into the marriage, however, she realized he was an alcoholic and deeply in debt. When that marriage ended, she inherited the debt that he had incurred jointly with her. Pat now felt even more guilty— guilty for the children that their father had abandoned them, guilty that she had put the children through a second failed marriage, and now guilty that she was so deeply in debt and had no money to buy them what they wanted, much less needed.

When she tried to set limits with Lauren, Lauren played on this guilt, and Peggy usually gave in. Lauren, at seventeen, had seen all of her mother's mistakes and knew how to use them against her. Lauren had felt and continued to feel deeply rejected. This feeling was genuine, yet over the years, she had learned to capitalize on her sadness and mother's guilt to sabotage her mother's authority.

It often surprises people to know that women initiate the majority of divorces nowadays. In doing so, they often suffer the burden of guilt for the divorce and the changes that accompany it. Even so, fathers are not immune to the effects of divorce guilt either. The most common source of guilt is simply guilt over not being there. Divorce in our culture most often relegates fathers to marginal roles in a child's life.

Mothers get custody of children in 90 percent of divorcing families. For those fathers who are noncustodial parents, the typical visitation is two weekends a month, and a few hours one night each week. This amounts to about 17 percent of the child's time. They are not there in the home to oversee homework, take the child to piano lessons or Girl Scout meetings, or oversee household responsibilities. They are not there when the child is upset, or has a problem, or needs help. Often they are not notified about a child's performance in a school play, or a soccer game, or a church function. They may not be allowed to meet with the child's teacher or see the child's test scores.

Many fathers, faced with the aching loss of a sense of importance in the child's life, attempt to make up for their absence by making their time with the child as fun packed as possible. Guilty fathers take the child to amusement parks and video arcades, on fishing, camping, and hunting trips, to movies and to restaurants. I've seen many fathers buy expensive luxury items for the child, such as computers, mopeds, all-terrain vehicles, and a color TV and telephone for the child's room—all to ease their guilt as well as entice the child into keeping up the visits, if the child is beginning to balk at being away from his friends on the weekend. As these children grow into adolescence and become more focused on their peer group, these fathers hold out cars as the enticement to keep up visits or even live with them. They hope that perhaps the car will make up for the lost years or establish some kind of bond between them.

Still other divorced fathers feel guilty about the circumstances of the divorce. The father may have hit the mother, may have abused alcohol, or may have left the mother for another woman. The father may feel ashamed of what he has done to his wife and his children, and that his actions led her to file for divorce. The children's mother may be deeply hurt and bitterly angry. He may feel guilty that the children are now primarily cared for by one parent who is sullen, depressed, withdrawn, and leaning on the children for emotional support.

Many men divorce wives who are disorganized, unmotivated, or emotionally unstable. They leave the marriage with grave concerns about whether the children will be well cared for, but have been told by their attorneys that there is no way they can get custody unless the mother is clearly neglectful or abusive. These men agonize over the poor care that their children receive, yet feel completely helpless to do anything about it. They are afraid that if they make demands on the mother, she will retaliate by making negative comments to the children about him or revoking his visitation. They tolerate the situation knowing there is nothing they can do to compensate for the mother's poor care of the children other than what they can do on their visitations.

Men typically remarry sooner than women, and most are remarried within two to three years. The father may then feel guilty that the children feel displaced by his new wife and her children, for now their father has become a primary parent for someone else's children, while only a marginal parent for them. If the father kept the house, his new wife and her children may move into the very bedrooms his natural children used to occupy.

For the 10 percent of fathers who do get custody of their children, it is usually in the cases in which the mother abandons the children or is severely emotionally disturbed. These fathers know the heartache the children experience when the mother leaves them to pursue a new love possibility or simply disappears. In our culture, in which the love of a mother is regarded as a sine qua non for emotional health, abandonment by the mother is a stigma only a few children experience. It marks the children as "different" in a way that divorce used to. Many fathers in this situation feel the children are overwhelmed with rejection and must be handled with great care. Many would do almost anything to make up for the hurt that the children feel. Custodial fathers who finally ended a marriage because the mother was alcholic or mentally ill must face the children's pain when that mother is inconsistent with visits or is "out of it" when the child goes to her home. Many of these fathers delayed custody at the time of the divorce and only pursued it years later when the mother had finally deteriorated to such a point that they stood a chance in court. By that time, however, the child had lived with years of neglect and possibly abuse. These fathers feel they have to make up for all the child didn't get over the years. They hope to make the child's last few years at home with him so happy and carefree that they wipe out the memory of the disturbed and neglectful mother.

Matthew: Struggling With a Divorced Father's Guilt

Matthew was a thirty-year-old rising young executive with a

software firm when he came in with his second wife, Lanie, for marriage counseling. While there were many conflicts between them, none was more emotional than the conflict over his relationship with his first child, Michael. Michael was the product of his failed marriage to Faith. It was a marriage that he realized was a mistake from the beginning. Matthew married Faith in his senior year of college, thinking that they had similar interests and goals in life. He was going to school, working full-time, and interviewing for management positions. Somehow he failed to take into consideration that Faith had quit fashion school after one year, had no career goals, and would not work. Matthew continued to be successful in his career as Faith continued to flounder and to lack direction. Matthew became overbearing and dictatorial, giving her orders on how to take care of the home and how to pay the bills. He gradually took over all decisions in the marriage. When Michael was born, he felt compelled to take over there as well and tell her how to care for him. When Michael was eight months old, Faith sued for divorce, charging that Matthew was too overbearing and that he was suffocating her.

Matthew remarried after a few years and had a second child, but continued to feel guilty. He felt guilty that he had made such a poor choice in his first marriage and that he had been so overbearing and had caused the marriage to fail. He felt guilty that he had brought Michael into the world under these circumstances and that he lived so far away that he saw him only one weekend a month. He felt guilty that Michael felt jealous of Katy, his second child. Michael's mother neglected his hygiene, did not discipline him, and did not give him educational opportunities, and Matthew felt partly to blame for these too. He felt bad that Michael lived with a stepfather who cared little about him. This was his only son, and this life was not at all what he had wanted for him.

Matthew's solution was, first, to make no demands on Faith whatsoever for fear that she would further restrict access to Michael. Of course, legally she couldn't deprive him of his visitation rights. But she could choose not to put his phone calls through to Michael, not to give him gifts that Matthew sent, to say negative things about him, or to move even farther away.

Therefore, when Faith neglected Michael's oral hygiene so badly that his teeth became decayed, his father said nothing but paid to have Michael's teeth recapped. When Michael came for visits, Matthew expected Lanie and Katy to rearrange their weekend to accommodate Michael. Michael was aggressive—he had bitten Katy—yet Matthew was reluctant to intervene firmly. He had "talks" with Michael. He could not bear to spend the rare weekends with his son putting him in time-out or spanking him. Michael's table manners were poor and his language was peppered with obscenities, yet Matthew felt that he and Lanie had to bear with it. Matthew bought Michael almost anything he wanted. He knew that Faith misused the child support money and that it didn't go to Michael.

The end result was that Matthew, in the name of love, was contributing to a worsening situation. Lanie could not bond with Michael because his language, behavior, and hygiene were so objectionable. She was resentful that she and Katy took second place to Michael. She resented all the money that went out toward Michael. She resented having to be the one to do the discipline. She began to dread the weekends with Michael and was cool and distant toward him. Because Lanie was so aloof with him, Matthew felt even more guilty and redoubled his efforts to be more indulgent with Michael to make up for it.

By the time I saw Matthew and Lanie, their marriage was in serious trouble. It took several months to begin to work together toward making reasonable expectations for Michael and setting realistic limits for him. Matthew was able to see in time that his overindulgence with Michael was not only hurting his family but that it was not helpful to Michael either. Matthew was advised to work through his attorney to assert his legal rights and to join a support group that advocated for the rights of fathers. These would be more effective means of addressing his concerns and his guilt than the overindulgent pattern he had taken on.

Perhaps the second most common reason parents are overindulgent has to do with the parent's own childhood. Often, overindulgent parents have a *childhood history of divorce, neglect, poverty, parental alcoholism, or abuse*. People are often surprised to see the figures on childhood stress. About one in four girls is a victim of sexual abuse; for boys, the figure is estimated at about one in seven. About one in four children grows up in a family marred by alcoholism. There are no good figures on physical and verbal abuse, since the definitions vary from one study to another, but the figures for these kinds of abuse are likely even higher. Though they are not nearly so much so today, in the 1950s and 1960s, poverty, divorce, and illegitimacy were serious social stigmas, and adults today remember the pain of being the only child in the classroom to have parents who were divorced or to wear ragged hand-me-downs to school.

Adults who come into parenthood with this background often have one advantage but two strikes against them. In terms of an advantage, they are often independent people who virtually raised themselves. They are gritty, determined survivors. They learned to cope with what they didn't get at home by hard work and by getting what they needed outside the home. They learned to make do with what they had, even if it was substantially less than what they wanted, or to do without altogether. They learned to bond to their siblings and peers at an early age. They learned to make their own fun, to create their own amusements. They were often thrust into positions of adult responsibility at a very early age. They had to care for younger children, to put a drunk father back in the hospital, or to call the police when their parents were fighting.

These survivors have come into adulthood toughened and hardened by pain and deprivation, but with deep emotional scars that no one can see. They are emotionally hungry but are trying to keep that emotional neediness in check. They are determined to give their child what they didn't have so that their child will never be as unhappy as they were. They have a list of "nevers": Their child will never have to do without; their child will never be spanked or talked to harshly; there will never be loud arguing in the house; their child will never feel that his or her life is hard or difficult.

These parents operate on the assumption that by filling up the child's life to the brim, somehow their own inner emptiness will be filled as well. For these parents, any sound of conflict in the home brings back memories of their own parents' drunken and abusive fights. Any complaint of deprivation on the child's part brings back memories of their sense of inferiority and humiliation. The child's angry retort, "You're so mean to me," recalls their own painful experiences with physical or verbal abuse.

Many of these parents came from stable, middle-class homes where a parent was simply cold, critical, or uninvolved. Their hope is to overcome their neediness by being a loving, warm friend to their children. For them, almost any form of limit setting that makes their child unhappy evokes painful memories from their own childhood. They perceive it as a failure on their part to be the kind of parent they had hoped to be.

The second handicap is that they have no model of how to accomplish what it is they're trying to accomplish as parents. Not only do they have an unrealistic ideal that they're striving for, but they have no road map of how to get there. "What is a reasonable punishment for a child and what is unreasonable, abusive?" They do not know where to draw the line. "When do I try to be a warm, friendly companion to my child and when do I try to be the stern parent?"

Not knowing how to strike a balance, these parents are seen by their children as unsure of themselves, swinging wildly from one pole to the other. "What do I do when reasoning with the child in a warm and friendly way simply does not work?" These parents, having never observed another approach other than physical abuse, are staunchly opposed to using some form of abuse to coerce their children into compliance, and rightly so. Yet when the "companion" approach does not work, they often explode in a tirade of verbal abuse or even hit the child.

"I want my child to be allowed to have a say in what's going on. I certainly never was. Yet I end up being talked to disrespectfully, and she ends up getting her way." These parents were overcontrolled, undervalued, not listened to. They have good ideas about wanting something better for their child, but they have no models for drawing the line between freedom of expression, participatory democracy, and outright defiance.

"Isn't it bad to have arguments in front of the children? Won't it hurt them to expose them to our fights?" These parents know that parental conflict can strike fear in children's hearts, yet they do not know what a normal amount of conflict is, or how average, well-adjusted parents deal with differences of opinion, especially as they relate to the children. One parent may override her misgivings about being too permissive and capitulating too readily to the children, and give in to them out of fear of exposing them to too much conflict.

"How much responsibility should I give them? I don't want their lives to be as hard as mine was." These parents, again, are at a loss when it comes to knowing what a reasonable amount of responsibility is for children, since they have never known it or observed it. They only know that their own lives were very hard and that they gave up childhood very early. They swing to the other end of the spectrum, assuming that no responsibility is the best alternative. Yet they fail to see that it was their own early assumption of responsibility, painful though it was, that made them the very capable people that they are.

Fred: Influenced By His Own Painful Past

Recall that we met eleven-year-old Jay in chapter 3. Jay was frequently involved in mischievous escapades at school and in power struggles with his father, Fred. His most clear-cut problem was his refusal to take any responsibility for his behavior and to see that the negative consequences he experienced followed rather predictably from his behavior. Jay's father, Fred, was a large and gregarious man who had moved south from New Jersey to start his own business. His mother, Sue, was a nurse.

Though Fred was most often warm and friendly, he was also moody and unpredictable. His angry and explosive outbursts at Jay set the tone for the whole family much of the time. Sue explained that Fred had come from a home in which he was neglected and mistreated as a child. He had been kicked out of the house at sixteen and forced to make his own life. He still maintained ties with his family, even though he had never been able to count on them for anything and they, in fact, had tried to exploit him financially. Though he said he hated them, he could not stop seeking their approval.

Sue said they had had a rocky marriage and had sought marriage counseling more than once. Fred could be dominating and controlling, yet also needy and attention seeking. He would go all out for you, but he also expected and demanded that you give a lot back. If he didn't get the response he wanted, he would get panicked about being rejected and abandoned, and explode. Then, realizing that by exploding he was pushing away the very people he needed most, he would be remorseful and beg for forgiveness.

Fred had gotten into a pattern of acting out this pattern with Jay. He would overlook Jay's misbehavior, saying that he, too, had pulled a lot of pranks in school. If the principal called about Jay,

Fred would rush to his defense. He didn't want Jay to suffer as he
had. He wanted Jay to know that he cared about him. He would do
Jay's chores for him if he forgot, and do them cheerfully. If Jay
needed something, no problem, he would get it for him.

Fred operated with Jay on the belief that by giving Jay what he
wanted, he would get back from Jay the devotion and approval that
he craved, and the deprived child still within him would feel loved.
But, as many parents know, that doesn't happen. Jay tended to take
Fred's devotion to him as a given, and even took advantage of him.
He didn't seem to value or esteem his dad much one way or the
other.

When the pranks, the failing grades, and the chores not done
escalated to a breaking point, Fred would unleash a torrent of anger
and frustration at Jay. He was known to kick over garbage cans, to
shove Jay against a wall and call him a bum. Later, feeling regretful,
he would come up to Jay's room and apologize. Jay took in all this
with an attitude of indifference. He saw his dad as completely
unpredictable. He felt the main problem was that his dad just didn't
like him but was stuck with him.

A third pattern we see with overindulgent parents is the *mother's
codependency*. "Codependency" is a term popularized in the late
eighties and early nineties which has come to mean almost anything
and everything. In its purest form, as used by experts on alcoholism, it
referred to the kind of woman often found married to an alcoholic
man—she was a caretaker to him, she was often hurt by him and his
disease, and she viewed herself as a victim and a martyr yet was
dependent on the relationship and seemed to need to play those roles.
She seemed to have no other sense of identity than this one. She
complained endlessly about his disease, his dependency on her, his
inability to function productively in society, yet she stayed with him.
She was seen as being, in some respects, just as dysfunctional as he was.
Because he was dependent on her, and because she was dependent on
that dependency, she was called "codependent."

Codependency—the dependency on being needed by someone
who is himself or herself a dependent or dysfunctional individual—is a
term that aptly describes many overindulgent mothers. They are
dependent on having their children be dependent on them. They
derive their sense of identity, their sense of importance, and their sense

of self-worth through this codependent relationship with their children.

The codependent mother is a woman who, through a failure in the developmental process or through a lack of good coping skills, has turned to the children to meet needs that are best met elsewhere. Let's look at a few examples. One is the woman who failed to master the adolescent stage of development—separation and individuation. During the years of roughly fifteen to twenty-five, when other teenagers were challenging parental values, experimenting with different peer groups, learning to live apart from the family, and resolving the questions of values and career identity, this type of woman married young or became pregnant at a very young age and that became her identity. She skipped over all those difficult tasks of growing up that are best accomplished before marriage and parenthood. She comes to view herself as an extension of her husband and children. When asked to describe who she is apart from her husband and children, she draws a blank.

The young woman who is more independent and insightful is able to look ahead to the future and anticipate that her job as full-time mother will come to an end. She grows in confidence during the years of mothering and learns much about her values, her strengths and weaknesses, and her skills as an individual. She begins to form a sense of herself as a person while the children are young and begins to explore new interests outside the home when the children are school age. This is usually an unconscious process. She begins to pull back from her complete involvement with her identity as a mother as her children begin to pull away from her. It is a smooth process with only a few bumps along the way. By the time the children are eighteen and ready to leave home, she lets them know that she is ready for them to go, because she has many goals of her own that she would like to accomplish.

For the woman who is not so well adjusted and not so insightful, the children become a refuge from the outside world. She does not view them as a temporary job, she views them as a permanent position. By unconsciously encouraging their dependency on her, she guarantees job security for herself for life. These women react to their children's dependency with a sense of bemusement. "He's my baby and I dote on him. You know how that is." They normalize their behavior with comments like "I'm just like all mothers, I guess. He'll always be my precious baby."

They react without concern to situations that would concern most families. "Yes, he's twenty-six and he's come back home again, but that's all right. He's always welcome here, and he could stay with us forever if that's what he wants." These mothers react to the teenager's efforts to individuate as if they were personal acts of betrayal. "You love them when they're babies, then, when they're teenagers, they break your heart."

They lack an objectivity about the process of growing up and why the child or adolescent does what she does. Even when the young adult has left home and married, these mothers exert a strong tidal pull on the young son or daughter—away from other commitments and toward home, even over large geographical distances.

A second type of codependent mother is the woman who is unhappy in her marriage and unhappy with herself and has turned to the children for love and a sense of self-esteem. Recall that, in chapter 2, a noted anthropologist concluded that in modern, industrialized nations, people have children for purely sentimental reasons. We have children in order to be loved and admired. When we are feeling beaten down by life, nothing can make us feel more loved than a small child rushing to us with open arms. When we are feeling inadequate or feeling like a failure, nothing can make us feel more like a hero than a small child who sees us as omnipotent because we know how to read or to write or to fix a broken toy. It is an exhilarating feeling, and all parents fall victim to it.

The insightful parent, however, knows that this "love" and hero-worship is temporary, too. As the child increasingly grows in skillfulness, he will see our skills as less and less extraordinary. As he comes in contact with other adults outside the home, he compares them with us and may even conclude that we are less heroic than others whom he admires. The sense of being loved for being all-knowing and all-powerful is a fleeting one. It passes quickly during the school-age years. By early adolescence, the child loves his peers more than us, and by late adolescence, he loves a girl more than he loves us. Soon he will have a wife and children of his own to love, and we will be but a distant figure in the background of his life.

For the mother who is in a very unhappy marriage, who is depressed, and who has few outside interests, the love and admiration of the children are vital to her survival. They are all-consuming. Since romanticized notions of motherhood in our culture have created almost a cult of motherhood, she feels no compunction in saying, "My children are my whole life." Since maternal love in our culture is viewed as a soothing balm that cures all ills, it does not seem inappropriate to her to say, "I love them completely and it is important for them to love me. I don't want to do anything to lose their love." Somehow this web of mother-child love and adoration is thought to provide a cocoon of safety against the stresses of the outside world.

In reality, what clinicians see in their offices are women who are unable to find gratification outside the home in work, hobbies, volunteering, travel, friends, a new marriage, and so on. Slowly, over time, these women are able to see that they are anxious about seeking some source of gratification outside the home. "What if I make a mistake? What if I fail? What if no one feels I have anything to offer? What if I offer to volunteer and they tell me they don't need me? It's been so long since I did anything outside the home, I just don't know if I'm capable. I left all that behind when I had children. I feel safe, comfortable, in charge at home with my children. I don't know if I want to go back to all that stress."

What these clinicians also see increasingly are children, adolescents, and even adults who feel that they serve as props for their mother, keeping her from collapsing. They feel bound and obligated to her, to keep her happy, to compensate for their dad's neglect of her. They view every separation from her as a betrayal and fear that if they pursue their own goals, she will fall apart. Some even fear that if they grow up, move away, or break contact with her, she will actually die. It is as if an emotional umbilical cord still connects them. "No one will love me, no matter what I do, like my mother will." "No one will love my son, no matter what he does, like I can."

Annette: Locked in a Codependent Relationship With Her Teenaged Daughter

Annette was a woman who came in requesting help in managing her daughter, yet stayed in treatment for two years. Annette was an intensive-care-unit nurse, and her husband, Doug, worked for a shipping company. Both had come from large Catholic families in the industrial Northeast and had similar ideas about what kind of family they wanted. They had four children and managed to put them all through Catholic schools on their modest incomes.

In addition to working full-time, Annette did "everything" for the kids, in Doug's words. She had also taken on all the disciplining and the limit-setting, as Doug was a rather passive, "easygoing" person who believed in letting the children do pretty much what they wanted.

When Annette came in for help, she had reached a breaking point. She wondered if she was having a nervous breakdown. She found herself screaming at the children a great deal. She had become "obsessed" with her daughter Lynn, who had just turned eighteen, and her relationship with her boyfriend, Mark. Her approach to parenting had always been "Do everything for your children and they, in turn, will love you and appreciate you."

She and Lynn, her oldest, had always been very close, almost like friends. Lynn had always been very dependent on her: She came to her mother for approval on what to wear, how to style her hair, for help in what to do about a problem with a friend.

This relationship was what Annette had always wanted. Annette had come from a family in which she was close to neither parent. Her father was harsh and punitive. She felt she could never do anything to please him. He wouldn't send her to nursing school, believing she wasn't smart enough to make it, so she had had to put herself through school. Even now, though she was in her forties, his rejection of her could devastate her. Recently, he had stopped in the city on his way to Florida and had looked up her sister but not her. Annette's bitterness toward her sister as well as her father was deep. She couldn't sleep at night for thinking about it, yet she couldn't ask him about it or confront him with it either. She still wanted his approval and couldn't risk losing it.

Annette's codependent relationship with her daughter Lynn came to a crashing halt in Lynn's senior year when she became involved with Mark. Suddenly, she turned away from her mother and became just as dependent on Mark. There were no more long talks, no more coming to Mother for advice. She wanted to be with Mark every minute. Whatever Annette had to say was rejected by Lynn. Annette was reacting like a spurned lover. As Annette said, "She has broken my heart."

Annette would go for days not speaking to Lynn, in an effort to punish her, then lose control in a hostile outburst in which she said things meant to hurt her. Lynn reacted by distancing herself more than ever from her mother, not speaking to her, lying to her about where she was going, and staying out all night.

Annette could not set any appropriate limits with her, however, because she was afraid Lynn might move out. "Then I'll lose her. She might move in with Mark, and he'll have her." Lynn did eventually move out and move in with Annette's sister. This deepened her hurt and bitterness, as now, as Annette viewed it, her sister had both her father's and her daughter's love and approval.

Annette worked hard in treatment to distance herself from these intense love-hate feelings toward Lynn. She was helped a great deal by Doug. Doug was able to see how distressed Annette was and to step in and take over more of the discipline with the children as well as set standards for them to be more independent. Doug was able to say that he had felt neglected over the years by Annette's intense involvement with the children. By helping Annette pull away, they were able to have a closer marriage. They began to set aside time for themselves for the first time.

When Annette entered the women's group, she was adjusting to Lynn's being out of the home and on her own. By then, her second child, Chris, was turning seventeen and beginning to make plans to leave home. The group helped her to see his increasing independence from her as a positive step and to prepare herself for that transition.

As Annette talked only about her children from week to week, the group began to confront her with the request, "Enough about your children. What about you? What's happening with you?" It was a question that Annette could not answer at first. "Me? What do you mean by me? I don't know that there is a me apart from my children." Over the course of a year, Annette began to formulate some goals about going back to nursing school to get her R.N. and was looking forward to the day when all her children were grown. She and Doug were doing well and making plans for things they wanted to do when the children were older.

Still another underlying factor in the overindulgent parent syndrome is *overcompensation for the other parent's neglect, lack of interest, or harshness.* Divorced and working mothers are not the only ones who approach parenting weighted down by a mantle of guilt. Often stay-at-home moms of intact families are ruled by guilt as well. This time it is guilt due to the father's actions. In fact, this problem occurs especially often in intact families, for frequently the father, who is the sole breadwinner, is viewed as the ruler of the family. His career, which is the sole financial base of the family, is viewed as paramount. If Dad works evenings and Saturdays, so be it. Mom will take the children to their soccer practices and their baseball games. If Dad comes home exhausted after a seven-day road trip and all he wants to do is to rest or play tennis or be left alone, then we have to comply, because he is the boss and he works so hard for us.

Children in such families are naturally blocked in their efforts to have a close relationship with their father. It is the mother who is left with the job of soothing hurt feelings when Dad fails to show for a basketball game when he said he would or keeps promising to take the kids fishing but never does. When Dad wants the house quiet so he can rest, even though he has hardly seen the children in a week and they want to crawl all over him, it is Mom who is faced with the hurt looks on their faces. It is easy to see how a mother in this situation might want to let the children forego their responsibilities, give in to their tantrums, seek some new amusement for them, or take them shopping, in the hope that by buying them something they really want, they won't feel so hurt.

Fathers in these intact families, when they do have time for their children, often approach parenting out of guilt as well. They know they work long hours, travel, work weekends, and so on. Faced with needy children, they drop roles as teachers of skills and givers of information about the outside world and focus instead on being good playmates to the children.

Sometimes the neglect is simply a matter of a father who is distant, aloof, and unexpressive. Often men in our culture are not comfortable with expressing affection. They are anxious and awkward with highly emotional situations such as confrontations with children and with discipline. They rarely express praise or emotions of any kind to the children. Typically, they do not come to the family therapy appointments. At home, Mom and the kids are together, but Dad is down in the basement wood shop working on a project. Or he is tinkering with the car. Or he is jogging. Or, increasingly more common nowadays, he is at the computer. These are men who are at ease with things, with numbers, and with technical information. They are not "people" people. Faced with fathers like these, mothers often feel compelled to provide twice the love, nurturance, praise, interest, and involvement that they ordinarily might have, had they married a different kind of man. The children of the distant father feel pushed away, unimportant. Their self-esteem suffers. They often feel sad and lonely. It is out of love and concern for the child that the mother tries to compensate in some way.

Vy: A Mother Trying to Compensate for a Detached Father

I saw Vy and Joe, a couple in their late forties, when they came in for help with their arguments over Paul. Paul, at twenty-six, was still living at home and had no plans to leave. He hadn't been able to save any money, since all his paycheck went into his car, his clothes, and equipment for his band.

They were concerned, but not too concerned. Paul had come a long way in the last five years. Through his teens and twenties, he had had problems with failing grades in school and drug use that culminated in two arrests for possession of marijuana. At least he was gainfully employed now, after finishing two years at the technical school and earning a certificate in electronics. And, after all, as Vy said, "He's always been my baby."

Vy and Joe began married life when Joe returned from Vietnam. Joe had never been a very talkative man. He preferred to work with his hands and had done well as a maintenance supervisor at the auto plant. But after the war, he "went into a shell," as he put it. The atrocities he had seen gave him nightmares. He was nervous and irritable. He withdrew from Vy and the children. "I kept to myself," Joe said. "I couldn't deal with nothing." He turned over the childrearing completely to Vy and stayed busy with hands-on jobs around the house. When asked how long he had been in a shell, he replied, "About twenty years."

Vy and Joe had three girls, and then came Paul. Somehow the girls didn't mind having such a distant father, but it was hard on Paul. Vy saw Paul reach out to Joe and be rebuffed by him. Joe would isolate himself in his shop in the basement and Paul would respond with hurt and anger. Vy was overly permissive with Paul, and she knew it, but she couldn't help it. Paul was special. He was her only boy, her youngest, and her last. And he took his father's aloofness so painfully.

She excused his failing grades and forgave him for his arrests. If he wrecked his car, she got him a new one. She felt it was all she could do for him. Vy was angry at Joe for not being more of a father. Joe was angry at Paul for doing things that embarrassed the family. He was angry at Vy for being a mother hen and being overprotective. Here he was at twenty-six and she still washed his clothes and picked up his room. When he accused her of doing too much, she countered with "At least I'm doing something. You never did anything. I've had to be mother and father to him all these years to make up for what you wouldn't be."

The most common problem with overcompensation has to do, in a sense, with the differences in parenting styles between mothers and fathers. Fathers are more likely to be firm, no-nonsense disciplinarians. They are the "hawks." They give one warning, and that's it. They step in and take over. They are less tolerant of the child's excuses for misbehavior. They are more clear and concise than mothers as a group, but they are more likely to be blunt, even inflexible.

Mothers, as a group, are more likely to use reasoning and persuasion, to give numerous warnings, to follow through only when all else fails. They are the "doves." They are more focused on peacekeeping. They are, as a group, less clear and less firm, but more able to tune in to the child's feelings, to look at situational factors, to be flexible in their thinking and in their approach. They also are more likely to be highly emotional in confrontations with the children.

This hawk-dove dichotomy may be present in as many as half of all marriages with children. It is one that many couples negotiate and come to terms with over the span of the childrearing years. When couples reconcile this dichotomy, the children benefit by getting the best of both worlds—they get the benefits of Dad's firmness and Mom's flexibility. Mother is able to see some of the positives in Dad's style, reevaluate her own weaknesses, and move closer to his style. Father is able to do the same. Their styles merge together over time into a smooth blending of the two while still retaining a slight difference. Or they may yoke their two styles together over time and specialize. In situations that call for the utmost firmness, they turn it over to Dad, and Mother supports him. In areas where the highest emotional sensitivity and flexibilty are needed, they turn it over to Mom, and Dad follows her lead.

In couples where communication is poor and each person stubbornly maintains his or her own position as the best, a process of polarity begins to evolve. They are like magnetic poles that repel each other. Father steps in with his blunt approach, the child cries and goes to Mother for soothing. Mother comforts him. Father is angry. Mother does something indulgent for the child in hopes it will compensate somehow. Over time, Father is growing increasingly impatient at how she "babies" the son. He feels he will have to be harder on him or he will grow up to be a mama's boy.

And so the next time there is misbehavior, the father is even more harsh. The child is more upset and goes to Mother for more comfort and soothing. Mother undoes Dad's punishment when he is not around. The two evolve as coconspirators against Dad. When Dad is around, they may abide by his rules, but when Dad's gone, Mom does things her own way, implying that his way is all wrong. Dad grows increasingly angry that he has been described to the son by the mother in derogatory terms and that she always undercuts him and sabotages what he is trying to accomplish with the son. He resents the bond they have formed and how they seem to conspire against him. She has no respect for him. The son has no respect for him. He becomes verbally abusive to the son. The mother grows increasingly angry about his verbal abuse of the son. She tries to compensate by buying him a new car, paying off his traffic tickets, giving him money on the side. By this point, the adolescent boy is completely out of control. He respects neither parent. The parents by now are engaged in frequent fights over him and are verbally abusive to each other. They are considering divorce.

In still another variant on the overcompensation problem, often it is the stepfather who is perceived to be harsh and unsympathetic. Mother feels she not only has to undo her guilt about the divorce and all the hurt that has caused the children, but overcompensate for the stepfather's harshness as well. As Mother indulges the children in the name of love, the stepfather increasingly steps in as the heavy to restore some order in the house. These two become increasingly polarized over time as well.

Mary and Jack: Conflict Between Hawk and Dove

Sixteen-year-old Amber was first seen after she was discharged from a psychiatric hospital and a youth detention center. Amber had been failing her school subjects, experimenting with drugs and alcohol, and sneaking out of the house at night, and she was sexually promiscuous with boys. The conflict between her and her mother and stepfather had escalated to the point that one night she made a threat to kill her mother and herself.

Amber's mother, Mary, gave this story as background. Mary had grown up in Nebraska with cold and critical parents. "Whatever I did, Mother always found the one thing that was wrong." She wanted to be a friend to her children and to give them a warm, loving family. When she was very young, she married a man who turned out to be immature and to have a drinking problem. When the marriage ended, she had three small children. He provided no child support and showed no interest in them. This had always hurt the children, especially Amber, who was particularly sensitive.

Mary tried to make up for it by doing everything she could for them. She worked two jobs, when she had the time, in order to buy them nice things. She knew she was poor at setting limits with them but hoped that would improve when she married Jack. Jack was a very stern man who had raised children of his own and had rather rigid ideas about raising teenagers.

When Jack was out of town on business, the house was chaotic. The girls ate what they wanted to eat, went to bed when they wanted to, and talked on the phone as much as they liked. The girls argued and fought among each other and used obscenities. Mary felt she needed to give them a break after several weeks with Jack, who was so strict. When Jack returned, he was outraged. Clothes were lying on the floor, soda cans sat on the furniture, and chores were not done. He stepped into the role of dictator, establishing rules and order in the household once again, and threatening to spank them for bad language. Jack and Mary had become completely polarized. Even the girls said, "We live in two different worlds."

By the time Jack left town again, all the girls were angry at him, as all of them were on restriction. After they complained to Mom, she usually let them off restriction because she felt Jack's punishments were excessive. The girls learned not to respect Jack, because he was too harsh and because their mother undercut his efforts. They did not respect Mary either, because she gave in to them and to Jack, and because even Jack saw her as "weak." Amber admitted that her defiance was an attempt to get Jack out of the home, and she felt she was winning.

When the situation is reversed, and it is the father who is overindulgent in an attempt to compensate for what the other parent is not providing, it is more typically a scenario involving a natural father and a stepmother. The stepmother, especially if she has children of her own, is not going to be as attached to his children as he is. She may even see the children as competition for his time, attention, and affection. They may pose a threat to her primacy in his life. She married him because she loved him, not because she loved his children. She may approach his children in a businesslike, matter-of-fact way. She may quickly move into a role of coparent, setting bedtimes, curfews, and rules for clothes left on the floor. The children may resent this and view her as harsh and demanding. The father, who may already feel guilty about the divorce and remarriage, may move into a role of coconspirator with the children, undoing her punishments when she is not around, sabotaging her rules and guidelines. The more he indulges them, the more she feels the need to take even a stronger, more punitive stance with them.

Earlier in this chapter, we looked at a problem that seems peculiar to mothers, and that was mother's codependency. There is another type of problem with permissive parenting that seems more characteristic of fathers, and that is the *father's need to avoid conflict*. Again, there are broad individual differences among men and among women, and men and women are far more alike emotionally than they are different. However, there are also some broad group differences that clinicians often see. One is the observation that women are more likely to engage children in emotionally intense and volatile verbal arguments, which may resolve a problem or may simply escalate into an out-of-control situation. Fathers, as a group, tend to step in and quickly resolve conflict in a less emotional way, and children respond well to these fathers.

There are many men who, however, for reasons of personality style, feel very threatened by emotional displays, arguing, or conflict of any kind and simply leave the situation or placate the child in an effort to quickly smooth over the situation. In our society, women have come to be more comfortable with and adept at handling highly emotional situations. They cry at weddings and funerals. They seem to know what to say when visiting someone in the hospital. They are more at ease discussing their personal feelings, resolving a dispute between the children, reassuring a child who is fearful.

Many or even most men, as was discussed previously, take instrumental roles in our society. They take charge, impart information, and solve problems. Many men feel emotional situations are messy, uncomfortable, out of control. They are simply out of their element. Their motto is "peace in the household, at any cost."

Sam and Wanda: Parents Who Avoid Conflict at Any Cost

I first met Wanda and Sam when their fourteen-year-old daughter, Sarah, was discharged from the hospital. Wanda was an administrative assistant at city hall and Sam had taken early retirement from the navy. For some inexplicable reason, Sarah, at thirteen, had begun refusing to do homework, refusing to go to school, refusing to do chores around the house, refusing to practice her violin, even refusing to bathe. She had begun to sleep all the time. The experts at the hospital had considered many exotic explanations—head injury, schizophrenia, possible molestation—and all had been ruled out. Sarah wouldn't cooperate with any treatment in the hospital, in fact, wouldn't talk. She just slept. They discharged her as "untreatable."

When I talked with Sarah, she was fairly clear in stating, "I just don't want to grow up. I want to be a little girl forever." At home, Sarah mostly ate, watched TV, talked on the telephone, and slept. She was failing all school subjects in spite of being described as "gifted" and "a talented violinist."

The parents were at a complete loss as to what course of action to take. After all, she had defeated the finest minds at the hospital. Wanda wanted to set some limits on her phone time, TV watching, and time spent seeing see friends, but she couldn't handle Sarah's angry responses. Sarah would become hostile and argumentative. Wanda had grown up in a household with conflict and made up her mind to be a "friend" to her daughter. There would not be loud arguing and conflict in her home.

Wanda would set a limit—no TV time until the homework was done—but quickly give in. Often she would turn it over to Sam in the hopes that he would follow through.

Sam was a very small, quiet, soft-spoken man who, for the last three years, had been the homemaker in the family. He had retired after twenty years in the navy and did not want to work at all. Working was too stressful, and he wanted to "hide from the world awhile." He said he felt a kinship with Sarah in that "sometimes I don't want to grow up either."

Sam would try to set limits with Sarah when Wanda became depressed and gave up on her. He was not as afraid of Sarah's angry retorts. He was concerned about Wanda, however, because when he did argue with Sarah, Wanda began to get anxious and have stomach spasms. Sarah would sense this and argue even louder. Wanda would continue to hyperventilate and become nauseated. The whole thing would spiral out of control until Sam gave in to Sarah's demands, in the hope that this would calm Wanda down. Sam simply couldn't bear to see Wanda upset.

As complex as this family's problems were, they began to improve six months into treatment, when Wanda got to know a friend with a mountain cabin. Wanda would go away for the weekend for rest and relaxation. Sam would take over the task of making Sarah clean her room, do her chores, and catch up on her homework. He could carry through on this as long as Wanda wasn't there to get upset.

As Sarah began to see some progress in her grades and in her room, she began to practice the violin again. As her mother gained some distance from the problem, rested sufficiently, and saw Sarah's progress, her mood improved. After ten months in treatment, Wanda was beginning to use completed homework as a ticket for all privileges. Sarah was considering studying for her driver's license.

The last type of parent I would like to describe is *the sophisticated, high-achieving parent*. This situation is perhaps the least common and occurs in the healthiest families overall, but it is worth mentioning. Over the years, I have seen as clients and known as friends many parents who were highly educated and determined to be superparents and raise high-achieving, perfectly well-adjusted children. They took a psychology class or two in college, attended Lamaze classes when pregnant, and subscribed to at least one parenting magazine. The mother breastfed as long as she possibly could to "foster a strong mother-infant bond," though combining this with a career proved very difficult. They put pictures of black and white shapes in their newborn's crib in order to stimulate her visual development. They refused to buy guns for their sons because they "didn't want to encourage the use of violence" and agonized over whether a doll for their daughter might be sexist.

These are knowledgeable parents who use psychological terminology very comfortably. When their young child cries at night, they take him into their bed so he doesn't experience an excessive amount of "separation anxiety." Mother is worn out from breastfeeding around the clock but is reluctant to give it up because it might "frustrate his oral needs." The three-year-old who is still sucking a pacifier is a source of frustration, but the parents are reluctant to put pressure on the child to give it up because it would be "repressive" and may result in "low self-esteem." They do everything possible for the child because they are convinced that making their child feel loved and giving him a happy childhood will make him grow up happy, secure, and well-adjusted, with "good self-esteem."

In fact, "self-esteem" seems to be the new buzzword with educated parents, slowly replacing the old Freudian terms like "repressive" and "oral needs." These parents will say, "I don't want to correct him in a public place because it will give him low self-esteem." Often they call my office for an appointment saying, "We want to see you first to talk about Jeremy's behavior problem so that we can discuss it privately. We wouldn't want to discuss Jeremy's problem in front of him, as it might give him low self-esteem." Sadly enough, Jeremy most likely already has low self-esteem because he is frequently in trouble at school and is rejected by his peers. These children, who are quite bright, are often held back in a remedial class because they are too immature to start first grade with their peers.

These parents have a need for others to see them as sophisticated, knowledgeable, and loving parents with happy, well-adjusted, and well-cared-for children. Where they get into trouble is in their attempt to live up to a fantasy of what it means to be the perfect parent. Their parent-child model is one where there is no messiness, no conflict, and no negative consequences. They are quick to follow trends, without questioning whether the current trend is reasonable, workable, and based on common sense. For example, explaining to a two-year-old why he should not hit Mommy in the face, and encouraging him to find peaceful solutions to conflict, is not likely to be a successful approach. Two-year-olds are simply not linguistically and cognitively sophisticated enough to take in this kind of information.

Some of these parents tend to become invested in projecting an image to others that everything is going well in their households. In their zeal to bring about this idealistic picture, they are reluctant to invoke any natural or logical consequences that might portray to others anything less than this seamless, harmonious situation. They would not let their six-year-old go to school in mismatched clothes (though the child was proud she had picked them out herself), because others might think the parent didn't care about the child. They would not let their nine-year-old go to school without his homework done and receive a zero, because the teacher might think the mother didn't care enough to stand over the child and help him with the homework until it got done. Allowing the child to go to school without a jacket, in order to find out that it is cold and that mother was right, is unthinkable. They could not see themselves as good mothers if the child were under-dressed—they would be too concerned about what other people thought of them.

With these parents, I find that an intervention in their parenting style must focus on the giving up of the trendy, idealistic picture of parenting and instead zero in on what is working. If their current parenting style is not working, and the evidence is clear from the type and degree of behavior problems they're seeing in their child, then it is time to give it up. These parents need to focus on the child and what the child is telling them through his or her behavior. They succeed when they adjust their approach to the child's developmental level, when they let go of their concern for public opinion, and when they use realistic approaches that have a solid foundation.

6 Undoing the Overindulgent Parent Syndrome

Now you are ready. You have recognized more clearly the problems your youngster is having and why. You have identified what it is about your approach that's not working. In the last chapter, you were able to understand some of the very human and forgivable reasons why you act the way you do. Now it is time to do some of the mental preparation that is necessary for you to make good use of the techniques that will be presented in later chapters.

The first step is to *correct your faulty and irrational beliefs*. Parents are human beings, and human beings do have hurts, fears of disapproval and abandonment, and overwhelming guilt at times. Parents regret past actions and decisions, need to be loved and valued by others, and fear being alone and unloved. We adults may have unmet needs from past abuse or neglect and may have few or no role models to go by.

All these issues contribute to what many in the field call faulty, irrational beliefs about roles. These beliefs are distorted and out of line with what research, common sense, and even our own experience tell us children need. We are often unaware of these beliefs, but they still have a guiding influence over our actions.

For example, the overindulgent parent views love this way—"I love my child; therefore, there is nothing I wouldn't do for her"—without regard to the appropriateness of what she is about to "do for" her child. Parental love is viewed as a state of total sacrifice. A healthier parental attitude might be, "I love my child; therefore, there is nothing I wouldn't do for her, provided it is within reasonable limits, and as long as it's in the best interests of my child." The key here is the term "best interests." Total sacrifice and devotion may not be in the best interests of the child. It may even be destructive.

Secondly, the overindulgent parent views his or her role as a parent this way: "It is my job to see to it that my child has a happy, carefree childhood, free of stress, disappointment, rejection, and so on. A parent with this irrational view needs to replace it with this view: "My job as a parent is to raise my child to not need me, to be strong, capable, and self-assured, and to get along with and care for others."

I have found myself saying to many parents that emotional stress is like a vaccination to children and adolescents. When your child gets a vaccination, he is given a mild form of the disease so that his body can build up antibodies to it. He receives only as much as he can handle, a watered-down version of the full disease; but in doing so repeatedly, with successively higher concentrations, the child is finally immunized against the disease in its full strength should he be exposed to it when he is older.

Exposing your child to emotional stress operates the same way. By experiencing frustration, disappointment, rejection, failure, punishment, grief, and loss when she is young, and by finding successful coping mechanisms, she will be immunized against stressful experiences when she is an adolescent or young adult. The key here is to "dose" your child with only as much stress as she can adequately handle and as is normal and appropriate for her age level. Removing stress from her life because it may make her unhappy makes as much sense as depriving her of inoculations because she doesn't like to get shots.

Thirdly, the overindulgent parent measures her self-esteem this way: "My child needs me; therefore, I am an important person to him and to myself." The word that troubles me here is *need*. Does your child need you for your guidance, your wisdom, and your understanding in a way that is appropriate for his age? Or does he need you in ways that other children or adolescents (or even young adults) seem to have outgrown?

A healthier sense of self-esteem about parenting is seen in this statement: "My child is adaptable, relates well to people, and is assertive and independent. Therefore, I must be doing a good job as a parent."

A parent who is heavily invested in having her child need her in an overly dependent way must ask herself some very hard questions: "Do I want my child to need me for his sake or for mine? Do I want this dependency because it is good for him or because it fills an empty place in my own life? Am I unhappy with my career, my marriage, or myself? Am I hanging on to this dependency because I'm afraid to move on with my life in other ways?"

A fourth irrational idea is this: "It's easier to give in and avoid a struggle with her." Certainly it is easier in the short run to bend the rules, let the consequences of misbehavior slide, say "Yes, I guess so" instead of "No," instead of holding the line and risking an all-out pitched battle. This is particularly so if the parent has been at work all day, hasn't been home all week, or hasn't seen the children since the last visitation.

The key here is the term *short run*. Life offers us many problems for which there are easy solutions in the short run, but those easy solutions carry devastating long-range consequences. Letting children slide looks easy in the short run, but in the long run, we create problems for ourselves in the future. The child is being trained to push the limits as far as possible with the certain expectation that you will give in. The cycle of saying no, listening to loud, angry demands, and finally giving in, is being solidified into a recurring, entrenched pattern that is even harder to break. The children are losing respect for the parent, who seems ambivalent and unsure of himself, and are perhaps losing respect for other authority figures as well. The adolescent who learns that "no" really means only "maybe" is put at risk of breaking the law in the future, expecting that society's "no's" are only "maybe's."

A healthier parental attitude is this: "It looks easier in the short run to give in to avoid conflict, but it only makes for more problems in the long run. We're both better off if we resolve the conflict now."

A fifth irrational idea is this: "I must compensate for my child's loss [of the father who is not interested in her, of the mother who was always at home] by giving her twice the love and making her life as easy as possible."

Many more children today have to cope with divorce and mother's working than did children in the past. Stress and loss, however, are not new to children. In years past, children had to cope with parental death more often, with crippling childhood diseases, and with fathers going off to war. They coped with being sent away while mother nursed a sick baby, being the fifth of nine children, or the absence of a father at sea for six months. Children, researchers find, are more adaptable than we think they are. If given good coping skills, they come through these crises. In fact, studies show that children who come through a tragic loss or crisis cope more successfully with stress or loss as adults than those adults who never experienced any major crises as children.

The key here is "successfully." Not all children are taught to cope successfully by their parents. By "cope," we mean, for example, make the best use of the parent's limited time when he or she is available, find something to do when the parent is not available, figure out how to make herself feel better when she is feeling sad or lonely or angry. We actually prevent the child from developing good coping mechanisms when we attempt to gloss over the loss and pretend it isn't there.

A healthier parental attitude is this: "There really is no way to compensate for a loss. It just is. I can only help my child make the best of a tough situation, and find the silver lining in this cloudy picture. I can do this by helping him to be more self-sufficient and more independent, or by helping him get from others what he doesn't get at home. I can help him to talk about his feelings, recognize and name them, and learn ways to manage these powerful emotions he has about this situation."

Lastly, let's take up this irrational idea: "I can't stand back and let her fail [make a mistake, be embarrassed, get a bad grade, etc.]. It's too painful."

Here, a parent must challenge himself with the question, "Too painful for whom? For me or for my child?" Sometimes we confuse our own guilt or worry with our child's experiences. But our children are not extensions of ourselves. They have their own feelings. We may be unable to separate our childhood pain from our child's experience. I remember confiding to my Ob-Gyn how guilty I felt when I left my six-week-old-infant with a family member when I returned to work. I agonized over how abandoned my baby must have felt. She replied, "It's hurting you a lot more than it's hurting him." It seemed callous at the time, but after a few years, it seemed a piece of wisdom, as my son thrived with his aunt and cousins.

Many times, I have seen parents anguish over letting a child experience something that was "too painful" only to find that the child didn't find it so painful at all. One mother of a ten-year-old son decided to stick to a plan to have her son remain in his room and not eat dinner until his homework was done. She had been totally opposed initially, feeling that being deprived of eating with the family was "too painful." The first night of the plan, the family sat down to dinner and he was still in his room. The family ate, put away the food, cleaned the kitchen, and he was still dawdling in his room. He finally came out of his room at nine-thirty with homework in hand. He said, all in all, he was hungry but it was "not so bad." The second night, when he smelled pizza cooking, he finished in record time. He agreed that it was a pretty good plan, as it was making him get the work done.

A healthier parental attitude would go something like this: "What may be painful for me may not necessarily be painful for my child. What is, in fact, painful for my child may be only mildly painful and only last for a short while. Furthermore, this mildly painful experience may be one that my child may derive a tremendous benefit from. It may prevent her from experiencing something more seriously painful down the road, and I love her enough to do what I can to prevent that from happening."

The second step to making changes is to *change what you say to yourself in a proactive way*. You can select some positive statements that help you and guide you when the going gets tough. The following is a list of affirmations for parents who do too much for their children in the name of love. There is one for each day of the month. Tear this page out and put it in a place where you'll see it often.

1. If you love your child, then give her limits. *Love = Limits*.

2. My job as a parent is to raise my child *not* to need me.

3. My child is adaptable, relates well to people, and is assertive and independent. Therefore, I must be doing a good job as a parent.

4. Moderate amounts of stress are good for him. They are strengthening his psychological immune system.

5. I am giving my child problems to cope with, vaccinations against the tough problems she'll have to face later on.

6. My job as a parent is not to remove the lemons from his life. My job is to teach him to be an effective maker of lemonade when life hands him lemons.

7. I am raising my child to be a rugged individualist, to be self-sufficient and self-determined.

8. Each time I make her persist toward her goal and not give up, we both get to delight in the outcome.

9. Each problem he handles on his own successfully, completely on

his own, makes him stronger and stronger.

10. It's a tough world out there, but every day she's getting better prepared for it.

11. I don't take over for my child when he gets frustrated. I have too much confidence in him. I wouldn't hurt his self-esteem like that.

12. I remember what it was like to wait for something, to want something badly, to long for it—and to finally get it. It was so exciting. I want my child to have that excitement too.

13. I remember what it was like to earn the money for something, to work and save for and buy my first _____. I was so proud when I got it. I want my child to have that feeling of pride, too.

14. I remember how proud I was the first time I _____, completely on my own, with no help from my parents. What a sense of accomplishment I felt that day! I felt that if I could do that, I could do anything. I want my child to have that feeling, too.

15. I know that by giving my child responsibilities and obligations toward the family, I am giving her a sense of importance, of belonging, of being valued by the family.

16. I require my child to give to others in the community. I want him to know that people value what he has to offer, that what he does matters to someone.

17. I want my children to feel secure. They don't have to worry. The captains of this ship are firmly in control and have charted a clear course for them.

18. I want to be for my children what I want them to be: self-assured, calm, clear-thinking, respectful of others, self-confident, and responsible.

19. I don't need my children's affection and approval to know I'm doing a good job. I just look at the end result—who they are as people—and I know I'm doing a good job.

20. There is no better teacher than experience. This is as true for them as it was for me, for my parents, and for my grandparents.

21. Raising a child is like holding a bird in your hand. Clench it too tightly and it will peck your hand to get free, or it will suffocate. Teach it to fly and let it go, and it will come back to you.

22. A rare tropical bird, raised in a cage and hand-fed, cannot

survive when set free in the rainforest.

23. I don't need my children's love. In not needing their love, I set them free to love someone else.

24. I'm not concerned about what others think (about her homework not being turned in, or how she was dressed, or about the fact that she got upset when she was frustrated). I know I'm doing the right thing.

25. Remember the saying "Give a man fish, and he'll soon be hungry again. Teach him to fish, and he can supply himself with food for a lifetime." I must apply that idea to my children.

26. When I don't want them to experience something painful, whose pain am I worried about, theirs or mine?

27. I can't compensate for what they've lost. I can only teach them to make the best of a bad situation.

28. I'm looking forward to the day my children are grown and are out on their own. I've got many other things I'd like to do with my life. It's important for me to let my children know this so that they are free to grow up.

29. A "no" must be a no and not a "maybe" (except in unusual circumstances). To teach my child that a "no" is a "maybe" is to teach him to violate the rights of others.

30. Face the conflict now. Get it over with. This will make things better in the future for all of us.

31. I must remember that I cannot make my children happy. I can only teach them to be independent, capable, and caring people. If I do my job well, their happiness will be a natural outcome.

7 Your Preschooler and Young Child: What to Expect in the Way of Maturity and Responsibility

Many overindulgent parents unknowingly make the mistake of viewing the young child as helpless, dependent, unskilled—in short, extremely vulnerable and in need of constant protection, caretaking, and reassurances of their constant devotion in order to feel happy and secure. To view a young child in this way is to see her as the sum of her deficits and to view the parent as all-knowing, all-powerful, and all-giving. Naturally, this may make the parent feel quite important, but it does a disservice to the child. To change this parenting style requires no less than a complete change in the parent's view of childhood. By learning what a child is capable of at different stages of development, parents can help provide opportunities for growth.

Ages Eighteen Months to Four Years

Language undergoes explosive growth in the second and third years. By eighteen months, most children can say about 50 words (though they may be understandable only to family members). Developmental psychologists, however, estimate that young children understand about five times as many words as they can say. Therefore, by the time a child is two, she may be saying 100 words, but comprehending 500! Most two-year-olds, in fact, understand almost all simple conversation about daily household activities and routines and can express most of their wants to adults. They are usually speaking in two- and three-word combinations and using language to meet their basic needs and to get what they want. Two-year-olds understand "yes" and "no" as well as "who," "what," and "where" questions, and can answer them appropriately.

Three-year-olds usually have between 1,000 and 1,200 words in their vocabularies. They can give a simple account of something that

123

has happened to them, speaking in full sentences and with a sense of beginning and end, cause and effect. They will sit still for stories and ask questions about the characters. The three-year-old can answer questions such as "What runs?" and "What cries?" They will, at times, listen to a parent's explanation of a rule and may comply with the rule because they understand the reason for it.

Socially, two-year-olds begin to move away from their mothers and enjoy the company of other children. Their skills at relating to other children, however, are rudimentary at best. They enjoy watching other children and playing alongside them in what is called "parallel play." Toys and possessions are not given up willingly, and "mine" is a word heard often when two-year-olds are together. Children grab, command, refuse, and hit at this age, in a desperate attempt to hang on to what is theirs. Most two-year-olds still only speak to adults and not to each other. When they do speak to each other, their conversation is likely to consist of "No," "Don't touch," and "Give me that." Efforts to teach them social skills are not very successful, and they are likely to respond best to simply being redirected toward a new and interesting activity and away from the conflict at hand.

At the age of three, friends become much more important, and it is at this age that the first and most primitive bonds of friendship form. Cooperative play begins to replace parallel play. Children may not only share toys from time to time but develop simple methods to solve conflict. They begin to develop simple social skills such as asking permission and taking turns.

Children at this age not only play together with clay and paint, wagons, and tricycles but engage in imaginative play. They are beginning to enjoy doll play. They feed, dress, and burp baby and put her to bed. They play house, school, and have tea parties. They like to dress up and take on a role, such as firefighter, policeman, doctor, or Ninja turtle. In a room full of three-year-olds, children will be playing in groups and actually talking more to each other than to the teacher or parent.

The four-year-old is characterized by his enormous energy and enthusiasm for life. Four-year-olds are much more independent than three-year-olds and more adventuresome. They feel much more secure and in control of their bodies and are eager to seek out new experiences. Children this age usually have no problems with separation and thoroughly enjoy preschool and play dates with friends and usually have no trouble being left with a sitter in the evening.

Socially, four-year-olds now prefer children over adults and are capable of cooperative play that is rather complex. Cooperation, sharing, and taking turns are rules that can be recited easily by them and are accepted by them more readily. Friendships begin to form and come to be highly valued by the four-year-old. Four-year-olds still frequently get into areas of conflict with other children, but when asked to problem-solve, they can generate alternative solutions. In other words, when told, "You keep getting into trouble on the playground when you and Sean and Matthew pick up sticks and fight with them," and asked, "What could you do differently?" they are capable of generating two to three ideas of what else they might do.

Emotionally, two-year-olds are known for clinging to "sameness." They have learned the routines and daily activities well and find security in knowing where things are and what happens next. Many children at this age set up elaborate and exasperating rituals, demanding that everyone in the household adhere to these rituals as well. They want things to stay where they belong and for people to do what they always have done in the ways they have always done it. Deviations from this routine are likely to result in angry, emotional outbursts. In fact, poor emotional control is highly characteristic of the two-year-old and not a great cause for concern.

Two-year-olds are also very ambivalent and have a hard time making choices. Choices may seem bewildering and the child may vacillate back and forth, even when the choice is seemingly simple, such as which of two shirts to wear or which of two desserts to eat. Full-blown tantrums appear usually for the first time at this age. It is frustrating to be a two-year-old. The very young child's comprehension of language far outstrips her capacity to express herself, and her desire to run, climb, and explore far exceeds his ability to do so with a sense of caution.

For many children, the frustration, ambivalence, and tantrums of the twos carry over into the threes as well. In fact, the "terrible twos" is more typically a long stretch of development from age eighteen months to four years. Most parents report that getting children to adhere to the rules of daily living gets smoother at about age four. It is at this age that children become much more aware and accepting of rules and regulations. They see that social behavior is governed by rules that everyone can agree on and that activities can proceed more smoothly with rules. They often like to quote the rules. They may say, "We always clean up after snack, before we can go out to play."

Preschool-age children also grow enormously in their self-help skills and can surprise a parent with their self-sufficiency. The independent two-year-old can feed himself with a spoon and fork. He can hold a cup in one hand, drink from it, and set it down skillfully. She most likely knows where many foods are in the refrigerator and can get them out herself. She can also climb down from her highchair and bring her plate to the kitchen.

Most three-year-olds sit at the family table for meals in a booster chair, though the food refusals, dawdling, and messiness may make mealtimes stressful. Most four-year-olds can feed themselves capably at the family dinner table, with the exception of cutting with a knife. Most drink their milk without spilling, and can pour juice from a pitcher into a glass with only minor spilling. They typically still dawdle and are messy eaters. The development of table manners is still a long way off for most four-year-olds.

As for dressing, the two-year-old has usually mastered undressing more than dressing. She can take off her socks, shoes, and pants. She may be able to put on loose shirts, though they may be backward. Many two-year-olds enjoy the struggle of putting on socks and pants, though both legs may end up in one pants leg, and the heels of socks may be over the insteps. If the parent has the time to wait patiently, the child is often able to persist until she gets it right.

Most three-year-olds undress well and rapidly. They are now able to unzip zippers and undo large buttons. They are usually able to put on shirts, pants, dresses, socks, and shoes, though they still confuse front and back, right and left. Again, dressing may be slow and tedious and fraught with frustration, but the three-year-old who dresses himself completely (except for buttons) is thrilled with his accomplishment.

Most four-year-olds are capable of dressing themselves completely, with the exception of tying shoelaces and buttoning small or hard-to-reach buttons. They generally know front from back and left from right with occasional mistakes.

In the bathroom, most two-year-olds can wash their hands with supervision and dry them independently. They can get themselves a drink by turning on a faucet and filling a cup with water. The independent two-year-old can get undressed and get in the tub by herself and make some strokes across her body with a washcloth. She can put on her pajamas with assistance, pick out a book to read, and cover herself with a blanket. Hopefully, if the parent has established a consistent bedtime routine, she will go to sleep with minimal requests for water, snacks, extra hugs, and so on.

Between the age of two and three, most children become potty-trained during the daytime. The age at potty training varies widely, as it is shaped by several factors—primarily maturation, sphincter control, language development, the presence of older siblings, and temperament. Young children can participate in this process by emptying the potty themselves and flushing the contents. Even those still in diapers can get fresh diapers by themselves and take the dirty one to the diaper pail.

In the bathroom, most threes are able to wash their hands acceptably and dry them by themselves. They are usually toilet-trained by day, though they may still wet at night. At the toilet, they may need some help with buttons and snaps and wiping themselves. In the bathtub, most threes delight in more imaginative play and also like to wash themselves, though they need help to do a good job. They can brush their teeth with assistance, put pajamas on, and get in their beds. With skillful handling, most will call out only once or twice after the parent has left the room. The four-year-old is capable of washing his face and hands and drying them without supervision. He can go to the toilet, wipe himself, and flush the toilet, unfastening and refastening his clothes with the exception of small or hard-to-reach buttons. He can bathe himself after a fashion, while the parent usually must wash his hair. Most four-year-olds, however, are capable of clearing out the tub of toys, letting out the water, drying off, and getting dressed. They are capable of brushing their teeth independently, with some supervision.

Lastly, preschoolers are capable of occupying themselves for a period of time. This is important, as children need to begin early in life to find ways to fill their time creatively and productively. Even a two-year-old is capable of playing alone in her room for fifteen to thirty minutes while the parent tends to some other activity. It is helpful to get her started with some activities on the floor and to look in on her every five to ten minutes. Most three-year-olds should be able to play alone in their room for thirty minutes if Mother or Dad has something important to do. Because of their longer attention span and ability to engage in imaginative play, this should not be a difficult task.

Many have given up naps by three and a half, but even so, it may be helpful to schedule in a one-hour "rest time" or "play nap." By darkening the room, and getting out some interesting books, many threes will play briefly and nap briefly, allowing Mother or Dad an hour's respite. It also provides the child with a sense of mastery that he was able to be alone for that length of time or get himself to sleep.

Preschoolers love to follow Mom or Dad around the house and "help out." This is a good age to begin youngsters on a regular routine of household responsibilities, as this natural tendency is likely to wane at later ages. The two-year-old can put silverware in the dishwasher and clean up small messes on the floor with a paper towel. Many enjoy putting wet clothes in the dryer and taking the dry clothes out. Many parents shudder to think of allowing a two-year-old in the kitchen when cooking, but the parent who is encouraging independence will find some part of the cooking process suitable for children of all ages. Even two-year-olds can dump the sugar and flour into a mixing bowl and swirl a large spoon around in the bowl.

Three-year-olds still like to help around the house. They are capable of helping to set the table and bringing dirty dishes to the kitchen. Most can perform simple jobs such as setting the dog's food dish on the floor, cleaning up spills, and putting items in the trash. Threes are capable of putting away their folded clothes in their drawers and putting away toys with supervision. They have some sense of the value of money and enjoy "earning" money for their chores by having shiny pennies put in a clear plastic bank. They do not understand the value of money per se but enjoy experiencing the sense of being rewarded for their work.

Four-year-olds can fill up watering cans and water houseplants. They can empty trash cans. They can gather up dirty clothes and take them to the laundry room. Because they know colors, and concepts such as big and little, they can even sort them. They can put away their clean clothes in the proper drawers. They can help select food items at the grocery store and carry a few lightweight items into the house. Most fours can carry silverware, napkins, and plates to the table. They can clear the table also and bring items to the kitchen. They can refill a pet's water dish and dry food dish.

Four-year-olds love to work in the yard with a parent and can do small jobs, though one should expect an attention span of ten to fifteen minutes. They love to earn money for their jobs—pennies, nickels, or dimes, depending on the size of the job. They understand enough about money to take their bank to the store occasionally to buy something they want.

We know that even two-year-olds are capable of experiencing compassion for others. They will express concern for another child who is crying and ask about a child who is absent from school. Three-year-olds may attempt to soothe a crying child with hugs and pats. They will ask, "Are you better now?" They are capable of feeling sorry for another child who is crying and of feeling remorseful if they have caused harm to that child.

Four-year-olds are ready to participate in a more ongoing way in demonstrating social responsibility and compassion for others. They can bag up their old clothes and old toys and go with a parent to a charitable secondhand store for donation. They love to put the parent's donation in the basket at church. They can bring change with them to put in the basket in Sunday school. My own four-year-old collected money for UNICEF while trick-or-treating at Halloween when he was four years old. Not only did it give him a sense of independence to ring the doorbell and ask for a donation, but he was very proud to bring the eleven dollars in change to his Sunday school teacher. Fours can understand to some degree a parent's explanations about how some people have more than others and some have little at all.

Age Five

By the age of five, most children have become well-socialized creatures. Fives make that big leap from preschool, which typically took up three hours per day, to kindergarten, which is usually six and one half hours per day of sustained attention. They are able to separate easily, move into a group of peers, follow the rules that are set for them there, and develop a bond with someone other than Mother or Dad.

Social skills become very important, as the child is now a social person with clear friendships. She has a sense of who in school is well liked and who isn't, who is invited to birthday parties and who is not. Children between five and six have some notion of what it is that makes some children more popular than others with both the teacher and their peer group.

Five is a time of such independence that the parent can breathe a sigh of relief and feel "we have turned the corner." All the baby equipment is gone, and the child is simply another member of the household, with the exception of a stool at the bathroom and kitchen sinks. Along with the five-year-olds boundless energy is a sense of caution and danger. Fives know not to dash into the street, handle sharp knives, or light matches without supervision.

During the sixth year, most children's appetites improve, and they may actually eat a meal well without much dawdling or playing in the food. However, they are still messy eaters and may spill. Most should be quite competent with a fork and spoon and can use a knife for spreading. Fives are fully capable of helping to set the table and clear the dirty dishes, and this can be a required part of their participation in the evening meal.

Because they can use a knife for spreading, this is a good age for children to begin preparing their own peanut-butter-and-jelly sandwiches. Most can slice fruits and vegetables with a knife that is not very sharp. Most can get their own milk or juice drink from the refrigerator if the container is not too unwieldy.

Children of all ages love to help cook in the kitchen, and the five-year-old can be a pretty good partner. He can count out cups of flour, pats of butter, and tablespoons of oil. (Most fives can count reliably up to ten.) Many, if not most, parents would say, "My five-year-old would just play in the water and make a mess," and this is probably true, but with direction, a five-year-old can actually clean pots and pans and will feel enormously proud of her accomplishment.

In the bathroom, the five-year-old is fully capable of washing his face and hands without supervision. He is capable of brushing his teeth, though he may not do the thorough job the parent would like. Rather than brush his teeth for him, Mother or Dad might want to stand by and give directions and praise. He is also capable of bathing himself, though sloppily, and the parent might want to give some directions and praise here, too.

The five-year-old should need no assistance in toileting—unfastening her clothes, wiping herself, refastening her clothes. This is a common age for children to wet themselves accidentally because they were so absorbed in playing that they didn't realize they needed to go to the bathroom. The five-year-old may need a little reminding and prompting to interrupt her play and go to the bathroom.

The five-year-old dresses himself completely. He can handle most all buttons, snaps, and zippers. He can put his shoes on and fasten them. He can tie a knot, but not very many five-year-olds can tie a bow yet. In fact, a five-year-old can assist a parent in picking out clothes for himself. He can do a large part of the packing for a short trip to Grandmother's house, with a little direction from Mom or Dad. Ask him questions, such as "What will you want to play with in the car on the way there?" and "What will you need to have with you the first night at Grandmother's?" This will begin to establish a foundation for him of framing a problem out loud and thinking through a solution.

Fives are capable of making a small but genuine contribution to the running of the household. They are capable of making their bed, folding and putting away their clothes, hanging up hats and coats. They are capable of emptying their trash basket, cleaning dirty fingerprints off the furniture, and sweeping with a small broom. They love to work outside and can help plant, weed, and fertilize a garden.

They can assist in a small building project by handing the tools to the one doing the repairing, but the parent shouldn't expect much more than about thirty minutes of sustained attention. They can assist in grocery shopping by locating their favorite cereal, cookies, crackers, soup, etc. They can bring in lightweight bags of groceries and put a few things away.

Age five is a time when the parent can offer the child a whole host of opportunities for independence, if the parent is alert to the possibilities. The five-year-old can place the order at the fast-food counter and carry the tray of food. She can place her own order when the waitress at the restaurant comes to the table. She can ask the waitress for "more ketchup, please" or "a glass of water, please." She can ask the store clerk where the bathroom is, with Mom or Dad standing nearby. She can go to the bathroom in the store or restaurant by herself, again with a little supervision. She can lick the stamps and put them on the letters. She can get the mail from the mail carrier, or drop the mail in the mail chute. She can walk the dog on forays to the park. Most parents instinctively do these things themselves, but the child who does them grows in her sense of competence and in her confidence that she can "get around" on her own.

Age five is a good time to emphasize social responsibility and concern for others. The five-year-old is able to do brief care for a younger sibling, such as play with a toddler sibling for fifteen minutes while Mom or Dad is on the phone. He can locate the diapers for mother, encourage the younger child to eat, find the baby's bottle, and so on. For this he needs much praise and encouragement for "how grown-up and caring" he is.

The five-year-old can walk with Dad throughout the neighborhood distributing a leaflet about a community meeting or distribute a neighborhood newsletter. Five-year-olds ask many "why" questions. "Why do we vote?" "Why doesn't everybody go to the same church?" "Is God real?" "Why do we recycle all this stuff?" The five-year-old understands most concepts when they are explained in simple and brief terms. He will enjoy these discussions on trips with Dad to the voting booth or to drop off the recyclables. The five-year-old can continue to take old clothes and toys to a charity and place the donation in the basket at church.

Five-year-olds begin to be capable of "means-end thinking," and this, too, represents a great leap forward. In other words, they are capable of setting a goal, reviewing the steps it would take to complete that goal, and moving along incrementally through those steps. A good example would be the handling of money. Fives are usually able to distinguish pennies, nickels, dimes, and quarters. Though they may not know how much each is worth, they know that paper money is worth the most, quarters are the biggest and best coin money, and pennies are worth the least amount. They are capable of picking out a toy they want to get, doing small jobs to earn the money for it, and slowly saving enough.

Lastly, the five-year-old is capable of demonstrating responsibility toward her possessions. She is able to understand that if she abuses or misuses her toys, they will be taken away for a while. If they are taken away several times, then they must not be important to her, and it is better to give them to a child who has none. She is able to understand that if she leaves a toy outside in the rain and it is ruined, it will not be replaced right away. If she uses another child's toy and breaks it, she must offer to replace it with one of her own. She must make restitution. If she takes one of the parent's possessions without asking and misuses or breaks it, she must face the consequences. She must make restitution for the "theft," and for the misuse. She might offer to do chores for the parent to work off the debt, offer the parent one of her possessions (the parent is then free to give it away), or do chores to earn the money to replace it. These consequences may seem harsh to overindulgent parents, but they come across as sensible and fair to children, and they are as close to "real life" as we can make them at the age of five.

Age Six

By the age of six to seven, children have learned an enormous amount of information about the world around them. Most American children at this age have vocabularies of between 8,000 and 14,000 words. They can read at an elemental level, and this ability to read simple signs and short words gives them a greater range of access to information about the world around them. They want to know the names of the streets around them, where places are on the map, what's on the restaurant menu, etc. They enjoy writing a short thank-you note to Grandma, writing down someone's phone number and address, adding their favorite items to the grocery list.

Children at this age have developed good abilities in handling quantitative concepts as well, and this, too, increases their capabilities. Between six and seven, most children have learned to count to one hundred fairly accurately and to count to one hundred by tens. They understand how much a penny, nickel, dime, and quarter are worth. They can usually add and subtract numbers under ten pretty well. Because of this newfound ease with numbers, most sixes are capable of using the phone to call other children to ask a question or make a play date. (Mom or Dad might want to stand by to offer supervision and to see that this privilege is not misused.)

Because sixes can handle numbers fairly well, this is a good age to start children on an allowance. Many parents are ambivalent about giving allowances to children, feeling children should naturally do what they are told around the house and not have to be paid for it. The parent may want to differentiate for the child, however, between everyday tasks we all must do (i.e., putting one's things away after using them, taking one's dishes to the kitchen, putting one's dirty clothes in the hamper, etc.), and those tasks that are more difficult and are a way of demonstrating one's maturity (feeding the dog, emptying the trash baskets, having one's room picked up by bedtime without being told).

The simplest method is a fee-for-service approach. The parent may want to make up a chart with days of the week across the top and work items in a column on the left, with a monetary value attached to each. The allowance that is given is simply the sum of the jobs that got done that week.

Many overindulgent parents have difficulty with the allowance concept, complaining that the children don't do the work, or only do it after an argument, because they don't care about the money. It is often these same parents, however, who buy the child what he asks for if he has "been good that day." In order for the allowance to be meaningful, it is necessary to put the child on an "earn-your-way" program for toys, and six is a good time to begin.

The parent might approach it in this manner: "Now that you are six, we feel you are old enough to buy all your own toys, with the exception of holidays and birthdays, of course. It might be hard at times. You might see something you want and you can't get it because you just spent all your money on something else, but we think you can handle it. Sometimes we may not like what you choose to buy, but we're willing to let you handle it yourself, provided you don't get something that's dangerous for you."

And then the parent must carry through—no work, no money. And no money must be given or toys bought outside the allowance plan. Certainly, if the child wants something special, she could be offered the opportunity to earn it by doing extra, more difficult jobs. But in six months to a year, the plan will pay off. Your youngster will be working on ways to earn money for what she wants, and the power struggles will be over.

Children enjoy ordering items from catalogues, as it entails several steps in sequence. Also, receiving a package in the mail is quite a thrill for a young child. The child can complete the order form, purchase a money order, mail them from the post office, and look forward to finding the big package on the doorstep when he arrives home from school. Toys that are earned in this manner carry much more value to the child than those that are given upon immediate request.

In terms of self-help skills, six-year-olds are almost fully self-reliant. They can bathe themselves, with the exception of a little assistance with drawing the bath and washing their hair. They should be able to do the rest of the bedtime routine independently. They can dress themselves with the exception of details such as tucking in a shirt adequately or getting a belt through all the belt loops. They can care for themselves at the table, using a knife to cut easy items such as a pancake or a potato, but may need help with cutting meat.

Many six-year-olds can be trusted to go a short distance from home on their own, but this varies greatly with the type of neighborhood. In a safe neighborhood in a small town, a six-year-old might walk a mile to school with an older sibling. The six-year-old who lives on a busy street in an urban area might be trusted only to walk to a friend's home three doors down or to wait at the bus stop in front of the house. Most six-year-olds can cross most streets adequately, as they have learned the rules of when to go ahead and when to wait.

Getting around independently is a great source of self-esteem for children, and even at this age, children can learn new skills. A parent might say, "It's always important to pay attention to where you are, what you're doing, and where you put things. If you can remember where we parked the car in the parking deck and get us back to the car without me helping you, I'll give you a dime. And, if you can find where we are on the directory in the mall and get us to the bookstore, I'll give you another dime." Six-year-olds, by having some ability to read, by knowing left and right, and by understanding small numbers, can do these tasks and do them with great pride.

Six-year-olds are capable of doing all the household chores mentioned at ages four and five plus a little more. They can feed a pet. They can water houseplants. They can vacuum out the car. They can wipe off the dining room table. Tasks that involve social responsibility certainly can be continued also. Six-year-olds can accompany Dad to the grocery store to pick out canned goods and paper products to take to the shelter for the homeless. They can be asked from time to time to contribute some of their (hopefully) saved-up allowance to a charitable cause. They can take along a trash bag to the public beach or along a hiking trail and help Mom pick up trash, not for private gain but because it is the civic-minded thing to do.

The six-year-old is ready to become involved in projects that involve planning, step-by-step thinking, problem-solving, and finishing up at the end. As stated before, the capability for means-end thinking begins at this age, and children learn best by doing. One project could be grocery shopping. Six-year-olds can check around the house for what is needed at the store, pick out and clip coupons, write down the snacks and drinks, for example, help buy them, carry them inside, and put them away.

A small repair is another example. A six-year-old can look over a broken item with a parent, determine what is needed, write it down, decide where to go, help purchase the item, bring it home, get out the necessary tools, clear or prepare a work place, persist at the task until it is done, and finally, put the tools away in their proper places.

The overindulgent parent tends to do these things herself out of fear of unnecessarily burdening the child, but the parent who is preparing a child for self-reliance draws the child into the process as a full participant. She asks questions: "What is the first thing we need to do?" "What is our goal?" "What will we need to take with us?" "Do we need to measure first?" "Should we call ahead first or just go there?" "What will happen if we just go there and they don't have it? What should we do next?"

One of the joys of parenting is delighting in some of the novel and creative solutions that children offer to these questions. Even very young children can form problem-solving strategies that are not only workable but will add to that growing library of life's little instruction manuals.

8 Your Preschooler and Young Child: New Approaches to Common Problems

As a clinician, I have been presented with many of the same behavior problems in children over a span of many years. Working with families of children of various ages gives a clinician the opportunity to see behavior problems as they develop in early childhood and what some of the outcomes are likely to be in adolescence and even in early adulthood. The following is a list of the ten most common problems that overindulgent parents bring to my office. They are problems faced by all parents of young children at one time or another, but they seem particularly difficult to cope with for the parent who has difficulty setting limits and promoting independence.

Problem Area 1: Bedtime

"We're frustrated. We can't get our four-year-old out of our bed at night. It began when she was twelve months old. She had an ear infection and cried at night and couldn't sleep. We would pick her up when she cried and rock her back to sleep. Then she would wake up again and again. Finally, the only thing that would calm her, and allow us to get some sleep, was letting her sleep with us. Now she's so dependent on having us with her when she sleeps, that we even stay with her in our room till she falls asleep. Sometimes this takes up to an hour. Sometimes we just let her stay up with us till she falls asleep out of exhaustion. The pediatrician said to put her in her bed and let her cry it out, but we tried that and it lasted for hours. We just couldn't stand it."

While this scenario is fictional, the elements of this story are typical of a large number of families of young children. In fact, a pediatrician I once visited said that if I had any material on how to get children to sleep, he would put it in his waiting room, because it was the number one question asked of him by parents of young children. While this problem may not seem so serious, it can be quite burdensome as children mature. In the past, I have worked with a ten-year-old girl and even a twelve-year-old boy who were so dependent on sleeping with their mothers, they were terrified of sleeping alone. The ten-year-old girl had become phobic of even playing in her room alone. The twelve-year-old boy would not spend the night at his father's home or go on a sleepover, because he could not sleep without his mother.

The best answer is to start early, in infancy, formulate a plan to help your child learn to sleep alone, and stick to it consistently. Dr. Richard Ferber, a pediatrician and perhaps the prevailing authority on the subject, asserts that learning to fall asleep is one of the first "problem-solving" tasks of childhood. It is also one of the first experiences with separation that children need to master. Infants do learn to get themselves to sleep. Some cry a while, then wiggle into a ball; others might suck on the corner of a blanket; still others may wedge themselves into the corner of the crib in a special position. My son developed a strategy of stroking his eyelashes as a "self-soothing" method of getting himself off to sleep. My daughter stroked the fringe of her baby blanket as her technique. It is fascinating and amazing to me that babies can be so creative and ingenious in their approaches to this problem.

Ferber also points out that the way in which we allow this natural process to take place is to put the baby in his bed while still awake. This flies in the face of many parents' natural tendency to rock the baby to sleep, then lay him down. After all, this seems to be the obvious thing to do when one wants to be nurturant and soothing. When we put the baby down while asleep, however, he is likely to wake briefly in an hour or two, as is natural with babies' sleep cycles. He will realize he is awake and then cry out, summoning the parent, who comes back and rocks and soothes him to sleep again. The cycle continues in this way, until the baby has become conditioned to need the parent to get him to sleep. The overindulgent parent, in her urge to be nurturant and protective, has in effect removed the possibility of a "success" experience from the child's life.

Ferber recommends that if you have gotten off on the wrong track by giving your baby props such as bottles to get to sleep or letting her become dependent on Mom or Dad to lull her to sleep, it is time to make a plan to break this dependency. If she is in the baby phase of development, rock, sing, pat, soothe, put her down in a drowsy state, and let her complete the process herself. If she cries, understand that the crying is out of frustration—not terror or feelings of abandonment.

Ferber recommends that if the baby or young child wakes up at night, pat her, reassure her you're not far away, tuck her in, say good night, and leave. No singing, no rocking, no long talks, no playing, no extra feedings once she's old enough to get through the night without a feeding. Keep your contact to the bare minimum. Check back on her every ten minutes or so at first. She will cry herself to sleep.

Reassure yourself that her crying is out of frustration at learning this new task, just as she would be frustrated with any new task. Gradually, over time, lengthen the periods of time between checks to fifteen or twenty minutes. She, in turn, will gradually lengthen the time between wakings. In fact, you will begin to hear her waken, mumble, stir, or cry out briefly, then go right back to sleep.

What if you have a three-, four-, or five-year-old who will sleep through the night once he gets to sleep, but it's the getting to sleep that's the battle? Here, too, you must develop a soothing and consistent bedtime routine, provide incentives for not getting out of bed, provide penalties for bedtime refusal, getting up, calling out, and so on.

Here, again, children can be creative and ingenious in developing their bedtime routine. They may like reading books, singing songs, reciting prayers, arranging the stuffed animals in a special way, a glass of water by the bed, a silly good-night rhyme, telling stories in the dark, whatever. The important factor is that young children thrive on sameness, on routine, on structure. It makes their world safe and predictable.

Positive incentives are easy to develop. Breakfasttime the next morning is a good time to put stars on a chart for good bedtime behavior the night before. One star for getting up only once. Two stars for calling out only a few times. Three stars for not getting up and for calling out only once. The stars can be traded in for special treats and privileges. This seems simplistic, yet I have seen parents reverse a chronic pattern of bedtime refusals in a young child in a matter of a few weeks, using only positive incentives.

Negative consequences are also helpful, when combined with positive incentives, yet may require more delicate handling. The difficulty is that negative consequences may create more emotional turmoil, which is incompatible with sleep. If positive incentives alone are not working, the parent may want to put five chips in a jar when putting the child to bed, with the warning that each time he gets up, she removes a chip from the jar. Removing chips will mean lost privileges the next day. Certainly, each time he gets up, she should quietly and matter-of-factly return him to the bed and take away a chip.

And what if all the chips are gone and the child is still getting up? This happens all too often if the bedtime refusal problem has become entrenched over a period of years. Many parents, whether they like to admit it or not, eventually lose control and spank the child. While a spanking may not injure the child, it, too, may not work, as some children become more agitated, angry, and noncompliant with spankings. I have found the closing-the-door consequence more effective. The parent states, "Having your door open and the hall light on for you is a privilege. It is a privilege you earn by staying in your bed. If you continue to get out of bed, I will turn off the hall light. If you continue to get out of bed after that, I will then close your door and keep it closed for five minutes. The next time will be ten minutes. If you still continue to abuse this privilege, I will then close the door and keep it closed till you go to sleep." I have yet to see a young child who wanted his door closed at night, even with a night-light on.

Problem Area 2: Clinging and Demanding

"My little girl is very demanding. She's always wanting me to play with her. If I leave the room, she has to follow me. She can't stand for me to lock the bathroom door and will just walk right in when I'm in the shower or using the toilet. She walks in our bedroom without knocking, and my husband is angry about this. She has a fit if I try to leave her with a sitter. I can't get on the phone without her coming to me with some problem that demands my immediate attention. If someone comes over, I can't even talk to them without her interrupting constantly. I don't know why she needs so much attention. Could it be that I'm not giving her enough attention?"

In a scenario such as this, "not enough attention" is very seldom the problem. There are children who are truly neglected, but neglectful parents are not attentive enough to notice this behavior, be concerned about it, and seek a therapist's advice about it. More often, it is the overly attentive parent who is likely to describe this problem, especially if the problem is not related to any recent crisis but has been chronic and ongoing for some time.

There are some children, more typically girls, who seem, by virtue of their temperament, to be more clinging and demanding from a very early age. If this is the case, the parent needs to be more intensive about fostering and encouraging independence in these children rather than giving them more attention. The little girl in this situation needs to know that she is capable of playing alone for a half hour to an hour, even as young as three or four years of age. She needs constant praise for occupying herself competently during her "big girl play period" each day. Stickers, stars on charts, and poker chips in a jar are favorites with preschoolers.

Situations such as the telephone, the sitter, and the visitor can be handled well by "previewing." To preview is to prepare the child in advance for what is about to happen. Just before the sitter or the visitor arrives, have a talk and rehearse what behavior you would like to see. For example, "My friend will be coming over in a few minutes and she'll be bringing her little girl with her. This will be a chance for you to show me what a big girl you can be. I'd like you to play with us together for a little while, then take her little girl to your room and play by yourselves a little while. I'll be watching to see how well you two play by yourselves and give us some grown-up time. If you two play alone for _____ minutes [whatever is reasonable for your child], then I'll be very proud of you, and after they leave, you and I will do _____ [one of your favorite activities together].

If the phone rings, the parent can pause briefly to preview what she would like to see happen while she is on the phone, the positive consequences for not interrupting, and the negative consequences for demanding attention. In this situation, since the parent's attention is such a powerful reinforcer, giving the child special attention afterward for demonstrating independence is a logical positive incentive. Likewise, the removal of the parent's attention, such as a ten- to fifteen-minute time-out, is a logical negative consequence for demanding and interrupting.

Young children, too, thrive on clear rules and boundaries. The preschool years are a good time to establish clear household rules about one's personal space. Examples are, "In our house, when someone is using the bathroom, they shut the door. No one goes in there. They knock and speak through the door if they have to say something. This goes for kids and grown-ups."

Another good rule is, "In our house, when someone is changing clothes, they close the door if they want to, or if they're over six. No one goes in there. They knock and speak through the door if they have to." Still another is, "If the grown-ups' door is shut, their room is off-limits. We knock and speak through the door." Children do not see these rules as harsh and rejecting. On the contrary, setting clear boundaries such as these decreases the likelihood of the child crossing a boundary that has the negative result of making the parent angry at the child. They also give the child a sense of clear boundaries that enables that child to recognize and thus avoid abuse by adults outside the home.

Problem Area 3: Dawdling

"My five-year-old is a chronic dawdler. He just can't seem to get going in the morning. I end up dressing him in front of the television to wake him up. Our next struggle is over eating. He sits and stares at the food on his plate, and I end up yelling at him to eat. Then he can't find his shoes, or if he can find them, he can't tie them. Finally, I have to collect his lunch, bookbag, and coat for him to get him out the door."

Dawdling is a chronic problem with many young children—in the morning, at dinnertime, at bedtime, or at any time the family has to get somewhere on time. As parents rush to pack more and more into the family's day, the power of dawdling to completely wreck the schedule becomes ever greater. Many families respond to this by becoming more coercive and threatening, becoming entrenched in a power struggle they cannot win. The child becomes more sleepy, passive, disorganized, immature, and so on. The parent becomes angrier and simultaneously more caretaking, assuming ever more control as the child becomes increasingly dependent on her.

Creative bids for power, such as dawdling, require creative problem solving on the parents' part. Power struggles need to be avoided, sidestepped. With young children, "environmental change" should always be considered first. By "environmental change" we mean making those adaptations in the child's environment, lifestyle, household routine, etc., that prevent the problem from occurring altogether.

The parent needs to put forth these environmental changes in a completely unemotional, matter-of-fact way. Examples: "I see you're having trouble with buttons in the morning. Let's just put all those button shirts away and go for T-shirts and pullovers." "I see you're having trouble with tie shoes in the morning. Let's just go back to Velcro shoes for a while until you're ready." "I see you're still having such a hard time getting dressed in the morning. Let's just put your clothes on at bedtime and you can sleep in them. Then you'll be dressed when you wake up." (Sounds crazy but it works.) "I see that you're just too sleepy to get up quickly in the morning. You must not be getting enough sleep. I think we'll just have to move your bedtime up by a half hour till we find just the right amount of sleep that you need."

Some power struggles can be avoided through simply letting some unimportant things go. One example is that of letting the child sleep in his clothes for the next day. Does it really matter what he wears to bed? Does the bed really have to be made in the morning? Can it be made after school instead? Does the child really have to eat a standard American breakfast in the morning? Some children find food repugnant in the morning. Would simply a granola bar be an acceptable substitute? An apple? A glass of milk? Some raisins?

Children love praise and positive incentives, and these can work well, too, once you've accomplished all you can through environmental changes and eliminating nonessentials. Examples: "If you get up and get dressed quickly, we'll have some time together to read the cartoons or read a chapter each morning in that book we've been wanting to read." "If you get up and get going successfully all week, then Friday will be our special morning. We'll get up early and go to McDonald's and have breakfast there before school, just you and me."

For some children, a form of external monitoring may do the trick. Kitchen timers are excellent for this. They provide a bridge for the child to move from monitoring by the parent to self-monitoring. The parent and child discuss how long each phase of the morning routine should take: fifteen minutes to dress, fifteen minutes to eat, ten minutes to brush teeth and get organized, etc. The parent sets the timer. The child tries to "beat the clock" by completing her task before the bell rings. If she succeeds and gets through her morning routine in under the suggested time limit, she can earn stickers, stars, chips, some time to watch cartoons on television, and so on.

Your last resort is some form of negative but logical consequences. Example: "We've made all these changes in how we do things, yet you're still having trouble getting going in the morning. I'm just not willing to fuss at you to eat anymore. If you don't want to eat, then we'll just skip breakfast and see how that works for a while. And I just cannot dress you anymore. You're too big for that. I'll set the timer for you and give you one warning, about ten minutes before it's about to go off. Then, if you're not dressed, you'll just have to go as you are. I'll bring your clothes with you so that you can change from your pajamas to your school clothes once you get there. I guess it will be embarrassing, but you'll just have to find a way to handle that." This may sound extreme, and most parents are unwilling to carry it out. But for those who are, it works after just one trial.

Problem Area 4: Picking Up Toys

"Picking up toys is a big problem at our house. The children play all day, and the playroom and their bedrooms are a wreck. When I ask them to pick up, they cry, "It's too much! I can't! I don't know how to!" After arguing with them, I usually end up doing it myself. I've threatened to throw them away, but the kids know I would never actually do that."

Picking up toys is a family problem unique to the affluent. Parents are often shocked to hear this. Very few middle-class families view themselves as affluent. However, by most of the world's standards, a child who has more than one toy that has been commercially made is affluent. I believe children when they say, "It's too much to pick up," and use that as a starting point for environmental changes. Remember, always consider an environmental change first, as your first and best option is to prevent the problem before it develops.

A simple environmental change is to give children less at birthdays and holiday celebrations. A few carefully selected and well-made toys will last longer and be more highly valued than a sea of poorly made, readily expendable toys. There are fewer broken pieces and less to keep track of. Overindulgent parents lament, "But I want my child to have a happy childhood, and that means wonderful holidays and birthdays she will always remember." A happy childhood is a wonderful thing to want to give a child; even small children, however, are smart and perceptive creatures. They measure a parent's devotion by much more than the amount of toys they have.

A second environmental change is to "rotate" toys. The novelty value of toys wears thin for children after just a few days or weeks. Parents are often astounded at how quickly the excitement over a new toy wears off for a young child. The gift the parent agonized over and hoped the child would be enthralled with for days and weeks is often left on the floor after an hour. Again, this is a problem of affluence. We buy a new car perhaps once every five years. The thrill of the new car lasts weeks, perhaps a few months. Suppose we got a new car every week and the cars accumulated in a huge parking lot behind our house? The "newness" would still be there, but it would probably only last an hour as well. To rotate toys, simply gather them into bins and rotate some bins every week or two. Put a bin or two in the attic. Take a bin or two downstairs. It is amazing how the "newness" comes back after a toy has been put away for a couple of months.

A third environmental change is to make some of the toys relatively inaccessible. Put them on high shelves or in closets. By doing so, your child has to enlist your help in getting them down. Clutter takes longer to accumulate this way. Also, your presence serves as a regulating factor. Example: "Mom, can I get down those puzzles?" "No, not now. We're about to leave. Put away your crayons and paper before we go. Then, when we get back, we'll get down the puzzles." Or "Mom, can I get down those puzzles?" "Well, let's talk about it first. The last time I got them down for you, you took apart five puzzles and spread the pieces all around the floor. Then you complained the puzzles were too hard to do and there were too many pieces to pick up. Then we got to arguing about it. Before I get them down, let's figure out what to do so that doesn't happen again."

If you've gone as far as you can go with environmental changes and you're still stepping in clutter, it's time for rational and logical consequences. This is a form of discipline, developed by Rudolf Dreikurs in the 1960s, which is more difficult to grasp than it seems, yet powerfully effective. The object is to set consequences for a problem that seem logically related to the outcome and that are as close an approximation to real-world outcomes as we can make them. Obviously, we avoid the outright dangerous, abusive, or excessively harsh consequences. In this way, our home life mirrors that of the larger society in which we live.

All behavior problems and consequences are dress rehearsals for adult living. In the picking-up-toys situation, we believe the child when she says, "I can't handle it." Example: "You're right. I believe you when you say you can't handle all these toys and that this is just too much. Somehow I've let you accumulate too much stuff. We'll just have to take some of this stuff out of here and put it away. Then you'll have less to keep up with. I'll start with this stuff on the floor that seems to always be on the floor, since that seems the hardest to keep up with. I'll get this big garbage bag and gather it up and put it away. Then, when you've been keeping your room picked up and you've been missing it, we'll talk it over and think about getting it down again." The emphasis here is on being calm, straightforward, matter-of-fact, reasonable, not angry, not punitive, etc. We'll be coming back to this approach in more examples as we go on.

Problem Area 5: Picky Eaters

"My problem is my preschooler, who is a picky eater. I'm at my wits' end. Every day, I put together a nutritious lunch for her and she responds with, 'Yuck!' Many times she won't even taste the food she is refusing. She doesn't like the look of it or the feel of it, I guess. I'm very concerned about her losing weight. I offer her something else instead, and she says she'll eat it, but then she turns her nose up at that, too. It's exasperating trying to please her. I get especially angry when she asks me to cook her favorite food, spaghetti, and then rejects that, too. Sometimes I've yelled at her."

Young children are known to pediatricians for being picky eaters. Much of the problem here is developmental. Young children do not come into the world prepared to eat three nutritious meals per day. Their appetite varies widely throughout the day and from one day to the next. Their taste buds are not very refined, and they cannot appreciate subtle tastes, blended tastes, or unusual textures. They enjoy very simple, strong favors, and they enjoy them singly, not mixed together. Their interest in vegetables is slow to develop. The parent who understands this—that eating habits are likely to be bizarre in young children—can lower her expectations and her frustration level.

It is much more reasonable to expect a young child to eat one good meal and one poor meal each day and to skip the third meal. It is also more reasonable to hope the child eats several items from each food group each *week*, not each meal.

The overindulgent parent makes the mistake of assuming it is her task to be incredibly creative and provide an ingenious array of food items, one from each food group, that will intrigue her youngster at each meal. Failing this, when the child has rejected everything, she becomes angry and frustrated. Yet she is concerned that her child may be going to bed hungry, and she is likely to let the child have some small something, even cookies, so that he does not go to bed on an empty stomach. The next morning, they start all over again. She tries to please. He says everything is "yucky."

This problem, too, can be looked at as one of affluence. A child who is presented with various foods and who does not want to eat them is simply not hungry. After all, a child in a poor family who gets only one meal a day does not have the problem of a power struggle with a parent over her refusal to eat. Experienced parents know that when a child is hungry, she will eat.

Furthermore, a child who is presented with too many choices is like the child with too many toys—he is overwhelmed. Having too much can be as stressful for children in some ways as having too little. Make simple rules about eating, but give a few simple options, to allow for some individuality. Example: "I will put a small amount of each food on your plate. If you eat, fine. If you don't, that's okay, too. If you want to make a simple substitute, say a raw carrot instead of the cooked beans, or a piece of cheese instead of the chewy meat, and you're willing to go to the kitchen and get it yourself, that's okay. I don't mind if you do the work. [It helps to keep simple finger foods such as carrots, pickles, crackers, cheese slices, apples, etc., on easy-to-reach shelves.] When we're all through, we'll clear the table, and that's that. If you didn't finish everything, then I know you're not very hungry today, and we won't be having any snacks till the next meal."

Problem Area 6: Noncompliance

"My problem is my six-year-old. He will not take no for an answer. Everything has to be on his terms. If I ask him to do something he doesn't want to do, he argues with me. If he asks for something, and I say no, he has a fit. He wears me down with 'Why can't I?' If he is doing something he enjoys, and I ask him to stop and do something else, like come to dinner, or get ready to leave to go somewhere, he gets angry and refuses to cooperate. I have a full-time job and a three-year-old to contend with. I can't do battle with him on every little thing. I know I'm not being consistent with limits, but who can be with a child like this?"

What to do? First, you must understand that the frequency with which children are noncompliant, or refuse to do what they're told to do, has a great deal to do with temperament, or innate personality traits. As any wise grandmother can tell you, some children are "stubborn" by nature and some are "yielding," and they were just born that way. The yielding child is rarely a problem in this area, but the noncompliant child will seek limits and test limits constantly. If the limits are fuzzy, vague, and inconsistent, he will take advantage of this uncertainty to get his way. If he gets his way only occasionally, the thrill of victory is sweet, and the memory of it is powerfully motivating. Even if he doesn't get his way in the end but merely delays complying with you through arguing, the postponing of the negative outcome is in itself reinforcing.

Many overindulgent parents don't set limits because they don't know what they feel really strongly about in any given situation. Example: "How important is it that she turn off the TV right now? Would another half hour of television hurt her?" "How important is it that she go to bed on time? Maybe it really wouldn't hurt her to stay up a little later." "Should I make her wear a jacket outside? Or should I just let her get cold?" In other cases, part of the problem may be that they may feel strongly about some things that seem trivial to the other parent.

Some of these issues about which they feel strongly may have more to do with how they grew up than with what is good for their child. Example: "I was made to sit at the table until I ate everything on my plate, and it was horrible, so I don't care what my child eats. We're just not going to fight over food. On the other hand, I hated going to school in ragged, mismatched clothes, so I'm determined that my child go to school looking great." For others, the problem may be that their feelings about a particular issue may fluctuate with their mood and fatigue level at the time. Example: "I know he needs a bath, but he really fights me on washing his hair, and I'm just not up for a fight tonight."

For the parent who is having trouble with where to set limits with a noncompliant child, it may help to do this exercise. First, get out a sheet of paper and make a list of all the typical problems you have with your noncompliant child in the course of the day. Don't be surprised if you come up with thirty to fifty, or even sixty items. I have read that young children have to comply with a request about every five to seven minutes. Next, take out four sheets of paper and title them thus:

Page 1: Those situations where I can make environmental changes that will allow us to avoid, prevent, or sidestep a battle.

Page 2: Those situations where I can just let it go because it really isn't all that important.

Page 3: Those situations which are moderately important but in which I can let logical and natural consequences take their course.

Page 4. Those situations which I feel are so serious and so important that they are worth doing battle over.

The next obvious task would be to start entering your long list of items onto these sheets of paper. But before doing that, consider how often you reward compliant behavior. Rewards can be hugs, kisses, verbal comments, "bragging on him" to the others in the family, putting stars on a chart, poker chips in a jar, allowing special privileges that are not usually granted or that are usually granted only to the other children. If you're not rewarding him for cooperative behavior ten to twenty times per day, stop here. Do not do the next exercise yet. Put yourself on a reward-only program. Set a goal of ten to twenty rewards per day, choosing a variety of rewards from the reward menu. See how much improvement you can get in a week's time, just using a potent mix of desirable rewards for good behavior. Be attentive. Small acts of cooperation, such as turning off the television when asked, often go unnoticed.

Next, start entering your items on the four pages, checking your lists with those of your partner or spouse if you have one. Some examples of the first category have already been given. Under the second category, do some rigorous analysis and make some tough choices. Be as flexible as you can be. It probably does not matter if she goes out without a jacket on a cold day. If she gets cold, she will come back in and get one. It does not really matter if she goes to school with disheveled hair and mismatched socks. When someone she cares about notices and makes a comment, then she probably will make a change. It really does not matter if she eats standing up or in which order she eats her food, as long as she eats it and shows respect for others at the dinner table. It really doesn't matter if she bathes at night or in the morning, provided she bathes.

Under the third category, be creative. Put as many items as you can here. Some have been suggested already. Put toys away if they are misused or abused. Put items away if they can't be managed and organized in any reasonable way. Take the child to school half-dressed if it comes to that. What about dawdling in the bathtub? Have your child bathe right after dinner. Let him know he can have dessert, some television or video time, bedtime stories, etc., when he has bathed. If he dawdles, he will lose all of these. If the timer on the bathroom shelf goes off and he still hasn't gotten out of the tub, follow through. Pick him up, set him on his bed with towel and pajamas, and turn off the light. He can dry himself and dress himself on the bed in the semidark room. If he refuses to rinse his hair? "Then you can go to bed with soap in your hair." If he refuses to dry himself? "Then you can put your pajamas on over your wet body and have damp pajamas." If he refuses to use the toilet before bedtime? "Then don't call me in the night if you wet the bed. I'll let you handle that problem yourself." If he refuses to brush his teeth? "Then you can go to bed with dirty teeth. But no one will go near you—no kisses, no hugs, no sitting next to you—because of your bad breath. And you will not be allowed any sweets, because they will give you cavities."

Thinking of logical and natural consequences can be fun. The possibilities are endless. If she won't make her bed? "If you won't take care of your bed, then you can do without a bed and sleep on the floor." If she refuses to eat a reasonable meal? "Then you can pass on dessert and snacks because you certainly aren't hungry." If she uses bad language at the dinner table or does repugnant things with food? "If you can't consider other people's feelings at the dinner table, then you can eat alone in your room." If she won't help set the table? "If you don't want to participate in preparing the meal, then you don't get to eat it. You can make yourself a snack and eat it in your room." If she won't help with grocery shopping and putting the food away? "Here are some things you can help with: bread, chips, cookies. You can carry these inside and put them away. If you don't want to, that's your choice. We'll put a sign on the pantry door that says you've given up bread, chips, and cookies this week."

Now we're down to the fourth category, the really important stuff. Here, you must draw your line in the sand. Choose five or six absolutely important rules and make it known that you will do battle on these. Announce ahead of time what the consequences will be, and be prepared to follow through with those consequences on a very consistent basis. Some examples of these are: "You will not do dangerous things like run in the street, handle knives, turn on the stove, and so on." "You will not bite, hit, or kick others." "You will not say abusive things to others, like 'Shut up,' or 'You are stupid,' or 'You are ugly.'" "You will go to school." "You will take your medicine." "You will go to bed when it is your bedtime." If you have done your work in the first three categories, then these category-four showdowns will be minimized.

Be prepared to remove the child from the situation for serious noncompliance. "If you can't play safely in the backyard and be trusted to stay there, then you'll have to stay in the house with me, until I can take you outside and watch you." "If you can't play with each other without fighting, then you'll have to play alone in your rooms, until I have time to play with you and supervise you." "If you can't cooperate with me on shopping trips, then I'll have to get _____ [Mom, Dad, Grandmother, or the sitter] to watch you at home while I go by myself." "If you cannot be trusted in the kitchen not to do dangerous things, then you will not be allowed in the kitchen to cook with me, until you show me you are ready."

Problem Area 7: Tantrums

"I'm concerned about my four-year-old's tantrums. Sometimes she will stand there and scream if something doesn't go her way. I have put her in her time-out chair, but she gets out of it and comes right back, yelling at me, 'I hate you.' I have put her in her room but she just opens the door and comes out yelling again. I have tried ignoring her, like the parenting books suggest, but she yells even louder, even kicks things, in order to get my attention. When all else fails, I spank her. Sometimes that works, but then again, sometimes it just makes her angrier and more agitated. We find ourselves trying to avoid situations that might set her off. There's just nothing we can do!"

Almost every parent faces the problem of tantrums. They aren't limited to two-year-olds but can begin as early as eighteen months and last through adolescence. The child's problem here is one of poor emotional control when dealing with frustration. Tantrums, like noncompliance, generally follow one of three "trigger" situations: being asked to do something the child doesn't like to do, being told "no," or having to make a transition from one activity to another. We expect simple tantrums in the very young child who is two or three years old. Their capacity for adventure and their curiosity far outstrip their sense of caution and good judgment. They are being told "no" constantly. They don't have the verbal skills yet to bargain, wheedle, and cajole. They have almost no internal controls on their emotions yet. They are fiercely asserting their independence in a world that seems to be throwing up constant barriers. Throwing themselves to the floor for a good cry is a natural outlet for this frustration. In these cases, ignoring the tantrum and letting it pass usually works.

What I see more often, however, is the problem of an older child—four, five, or six years old—who is still having tantrums that involve verbal abuse, defiance, throwing objects, etc. Ignoring these tantrums does not work. Paired with this, I often see parents who have had a pattern of setting poor limits and who are now feeling at the mercy of this four-year-old. In fact, their helplessness with this child has given him an inappropriate level of power in the household. While they may know that to give in to the child who is having a tantrum is taboo, they may go to great lengths to placate the child with poor controls in order not to provoke a tantrum.

The noncompliant child with poor emotional controls who has escalated to a tantrum needs to be first offered to put herself in time-out. For example: "You're losing control. Do you need to put yourself in time-out?" By asking the question, the child has the opportunity to self-monitor. By "self-monitoring," we mean paying attention to her own behavior and beginning to take control before a tantrum develops. ("Gee, I really am losing it. Maybe I'd better go to my room before I get in trouble.")

If the child refuses, it is time to pick her up and carry her to the time-out corner. Preferably, this should be a hallway or a corner of an empty room that is unstimulating. By being put in an unstimulating and uninteresting place, the child really does have more of an opportunity for regaining her composure. Set a timer for five minutes to begin. Let her know, "If you kick the wall, make noise, yell, or do anything but sit quietly, I will ask you to be quiet and I will restart the timer again. You must be still and quiet for five minutes."

If your child is clever, she will say, "I have to go to the bathroom. I really do." Let her go, but also let her know that you will restart the timer to five minutes again when she comes back. If she plays in the bathroom, you will take her out of the bathroom, put her back in time-out and lengthen the time-out to ten minutes. If she handles the brief time-out, yet has a tantrum again within an hour, lengthen the time-out to ten minutes. If it happens a third time, then lengthen to fifteen minutes, and so on.

Still, many children will challenge the time-out procedure and refuse to stay in the corner or attempt to grab, hit, bite, or kick. Intervene with, "I can see that you've lost control altogether and can't sit in time-out. I'll have to hold you until you get control again. I won't let you lose control like this." Most parents can hold a young child in their lap, facing forward, facing a wall or corner, with not much difficulty. Put your arms around her arms, your leg over hers, if you need to. Talk to her calmly, patiently. Say very little. Emphasize her getting control again. Keep asking, "Who's the boss?" until she's ready to say, "You are."

Problem Area 8: Tantrums in Public Places

"We can handle tantrums at home. It's public places that render us helpless. Our child has tantrums at the grocery store, in a restaurant, at Grandmother's house. I think he can sense how embarrassed we are. Sometimes we do give in to head off a struggle. But what else can we do, go home? That would punish everyone."

Children do know that they have a kind of power in public places that they don't have at home, and they are wise to its use. Parenting books suggest ignoring these tantrums, but children know that if they escalate their behavior, the parent can't help but do something in a situation where other people are watching and listening. Parenting books typically do suggest leaving the situation, but parents are right in stating that this unfairly punishes the other members of the family, especially the other children.

When you anticipate trouble, because this situation has occurred before, it helps to "preview" the event. By "previewing," we mean discussing with your child the behaviors you are concerned about just minutes before you enter the situation. Also, rehearse what it is that you will be expecting in the way of good behavior, the rewards for that good behavior, and the consequences that you are ready to apply if a problem arises. Try to select consequences that will be troublesome to the child who creates the problem, sparing the others. Don't be afraid to use a time-out procedure in a public place. Anyone who has had children will understand and sympathize. Enlist the child in the previewing as a partner in the problem-solving process. Once you're in the situation, provide cues for self-monitoring.

Example: The family is about to go out to dinner, and you have had past experiences with disruptive behavior in a restaurant. Previewing: "We're about to go into the restaurant. This has been a problem for you in the past. Let's discuss it here in the parking lot for a few minutes while the others go on inside. Do you remember how we've had trouble before with you getting out of your seat and running around the restaurant? When I tried to get you to sit down, you got angry and began to fight me. What do you think we can do this time to prevent that from happening? How long do you think you can stay in your seat before you need to get up? I'll be willing to let you get a dessert if you do well in the restaurant today. If you begin to get out of control, I'm ready to take you out to the car and put you in time-out there. You will stay there while the others eat. First I'll watch you, then your Mom will watch you when she's finished eating. If you continue to give me trouble in the car, I'll start adding time to a time-out when you get home."

Once in the restaurant (or store), remember to use your self-monitoring cues. Example: "You're starting to get out of control. Do you need to put yourself in time-out? Where can you go for a time-out? Do you remember our plan? Are you following the plan? Can you think of a way to stop before I have to take over with the plan we talked about?"

Once you're in a shopping mall, the car is too far away to be a resource for a time-out. You may have to use the corner of a room, a public bathroom, or the side of a counter. Stand the child there, facing the wall or counter, and have him count as high as he can several times until he appears to be calm and in control again. Or, he can sit on a bench in the mall as a time-out while the others shop. Again, remember to preview ahead of time with clear expectations and clear rewards and consequences. Once the situation begins to escalate, be sure to give the child an opportunity to self-monitor first. Always, always, shower your child with praise if the disruptive behavior does not occur. If he stops the disruptive behavior with the self-monitoring cue, give him hugs and announce his accomplishment proudly to the other family members. When this occurs, you've begun to turn the corner on the control problem, as he's begun to develop his own internal controls.

9   Middle Childhood—Ages Seven to Twelve: What to Expect in the Way of Maturity and Responsibility

Psychologist Sheldon White of Harvard University first coined the term "five-to-seven shift" to describe the dramatic and qualitative changes that occur in children at this age. There is a speeding up of growth in height and weight at this age that makes children more capable of taking on serious household tasks and responsibilities. Also, there are dramatic changes going on in the development of neuronal pathways in the child's brain that permit greater and more rapid learning.

In less developed cultures, it is at about age seven that children begin to work in the fields, care for young children, cook meals, and tend sheep and goats. In our modern Western culture, it is at about age seven that children rapidly develop their skills in reading, writing, and mathematical calculation. In either culture, it is around this age that the child becomes, as Melvin Konner writes, "a vessel into which knowledge, skill, and tradition—in short, culture—can be steadily and reliably poured."

Because overindulgent parents are unclear about what to expect from children in the way of independence and responsible behavior, we will outline the developmental milestones for this age group.

Ages Seven to Nine

Between seven and nine, children's self-help skills mature to the point that most nine-year-olds are completely self-sufficient in terms of their everyday care. Seven-year-olds are typically pretty good eaters who can handle their spoon, fork, and knife adequately, though their manners may not be up to what parents would like. Eight-year-olds can usually use a sharp knife for cutting and should need little or no help cutting their meat. Most nine-year-olds are completely independent at the table. They can handle a knife well when cutting meat away from the bone, prepare a baked potato, and peel a hard-boiled egg. Manners are improving and are apt to be pretty good when away from home.

Though sevens are capable of dressing themselves completely, they often don't. They may dress sloppily and leave shoes untied, though they know how to tie them. Most parents say that it is when children are about eight that they begin to notice what other children are wearing and become interested in brand-name clothing. Nines begin to take a little pride in their appearance and are more apt to hang up their clothes spontaneously and put dirty clothes in the hamper without being reminded.

Grooming habits at this age follow a similar course. At seven, most children don't want to be bothered with hair combing and don't have the patience for it. At eight, they may begin to take over the process and comb or brush their own hair pretty well. Most eights can cut their nails on the nondominant hand. At eight, most children can finally bathe independently. Many prefer a shower at this age to playing in the tub with toys and are capable of handling the whole process, from running the bathwater to shampooing. At nine, most children can take over the whole bathing, dressing, and grooming process independently. At most, they may need a reminder to brush teeth or wash hands before dinner.

Besides bathing, bedtime routines change a great deal in the span of seven to nine also. Most sevens have given up their favorite blanket, and only a few still need a stuffed animal to take to bed with them. They like a "reading together" time and a tucking-in. At age eight, most children need about ten hours of sleep. They can get ready for bed completely on their own and have given up special blankets and stuffed animals. They may read to themselves but enjoy being tucked in. By nine, the average child needs only nine hours of sleep. He may stay up a little later to read to himself. Most nines can organize their homework and clothes for the next day and set their alarm clock.

Children from seven to nine develop such good self-help skills in large part because their fine motor coordination (control of the small muscles of the hand) is so much more advanced. By the age of eight most children have become tool-using creatures. They can use tools such as a hammer, saw, screwdriver, and many garden tools. Girls, more so than boys, express an interest in sewing, knitting, and stringing beads, as they can now make these very controlled movements. Both girls and boys enjoy cooking at all ages, but at age eight they can use can openers, mixers, blenders, and microwave ovens. By the time children are nine, their skills with tools are more refined. They can hold and swing a hammer well, saw easily and accurately using their knee to hold the board, and unscrew a bolt. Many girls and boys can cut out and hand sew simple items.

Between the ages of seven and nine, not only are children's fine motor and gross motor coordination more established, but their attention span is longer and they are capable of staying with a difficult task for a concentrated period of time. All these skills come together to make them more capable of taking on responsibilities at home. They are capable of picking up their room and putting items away independently. In fact, many children by age eight or nine take a great deal of pride in their room and in their possessions. Children at this age are capable of fairly intensive household tasks such as dusting, light vacuuming, cleaning the bathroom sink and tub, washing dishes, and running a load of laundry. Outdoors, they are capable of weeding a garden, taking out the trash, raking leaves, and washing the dog.

While this may seem strenuous to many parents, recall, from chapter 2, that in agricultural and nonindustrial cultures, it is not unusual to find children at this age hauling water from a well, carrying vegetables to market, or taking the goats up to the hill to graze. While we disparage this activity as child labor, most such children feel proud to make a direct contribution to the well-being of the family. Children in our culture derive esteem from performance in the classroom, an activity in which only a few will excel and which has no material bearing on the well-being of the child's family.

In our culture, reading and writing are emphasized, and children make a dramatic shift from ages seven to nine. At age seven, most children still enjoy being read to endlessly but many have begun tentatively to read to themselves as well. They enjoy reading signs on the highway, advertising, and labels on store items. Many can look up words in pictorial dictionaries. By age eight, most children read on their own initiative, though what they read may be fairly short. They may read the TV listings, comic strips, notes from friends, magazines, instructions, simple stories, and short books.

By the age of nine, reading is a smooth process for most children. Reading to learn has replaced learning to read. Many nines enjoy a half hour or more of reading to themselves every night at bedtime. They can use dictionaries to find simple words and can use an index, glossary, and table of contents.

The progression of writing skills follows a similar course. At age seven, children have usually mastered the numbers and letters and have stopped making reversals. Their writing is smaller and more even in size than at age six. By age eight, some children are beginning to write in cursive. They often write to amuse themselves, writing poems, letters, and simple stories. By age nine, most children are fully capable of writing a letter to a relative or friend, addressing it, and mailing it. They usually prefer to write in cursive. They enjoy writing notes or instructions, putting signs on their door, or cataloguing their collections of things. Some may keep a diary.

Because of an advance in their understanding of numbers, most sevens are fully capable of understanding an allowance chart on which their jobs are posted along with how much they will be paid for each job. As with sixes, most sevens are fully capable of taking over the earning of all money necessary to buy the toys they would like to have. They are capable of understanding the cost of inexpensive items and saving up their money over a span of time.

Age eight or nine is a good time to begin having children keep two banks: one for spending and one for saving. The fact that a separate bank is designated for "saving" begins to bring home the idea that money is enjoyable to have but it must at times be conserved and not spent. In fact, rather than define a set amount for the child to put in savings each week, have your child come up with a savings plan or goal of her own that includes setting aside a certain amount and not spending it.

This facility with numbers and number concepts leads directly into greater independence and responsibility for children from seven to nine. Sevens can usually tell time to the hour and half hour and sometimes to the quarter hour. They can make use of time to know when mealtime is or when their favorite television show comes on. They may express an interest in a watch but rarely use it. Most eights can tell time to the minute. They can look at a clock and tell if they need to hurry up in order to catch the bus on time. By the time they are nine years old, most children are very conscious of time and use time to organize and plan their day. They usually enjoy wearing a watch. A nine-year-old is capable of setting his alarm clock and waking up by it, even setting it back a bit in order to get up early and finish some reading. A nine-year-old can and often will phone home from a friend's house if he sees he will be late.

Along with the development of reading, writing, and math skills comes the child's increasing ability to locate herself in time and space. A seven-year-old can usually tell where she lives by her house number, street, and city. She can say her phone number and can phone home. She can usually say today's date by month, day, year, and season.

An eight-year-old can do all the above and usually tell the day, month, and year of her birthday. She can usually write her phone number and address, though with a little difficulty. Eight-year-olds are beginning to understand how large the world is and have a general sense of what geography is about. They like to make maps and to read maps. Eight-year-olds are capable of locating where they live on a map of the United States and a map of their state. They may be able to draw a simple map of their neighborhood. Saying and writing personal information such as the above should come easily to the nine-year-old. Also, nine is a good age to begin asking the child to help locate a destination on a map of the city. Another possibility is to begin a hike, turn the map of the trail over to the nine-year-old and ask her to direct the group.

All of these skills come together in shaping the nature of children's play at this age. Seven-year-olds have a much longer attention span than six-year-olds and can play some games that require simple reading and adding, such as checkers, old maid, go fish, Parcheesi, dominoes, and Junior Monopoly. Because they have the attention span to persist on a task for an hour or two, they often enjoy painstaking projects such as Legos, airplane models, jigsaw puzzles, and paint-by-number sets. These tasks are preparation for the kind of lengthy academic projects that they will soon be required to do.

By the age of seven to nine, separation should no longer be a problem for children. Most seven-year-olds are allowed to cross streets and to ride their bikes a short distance from home, though this varies widely with the type of area in which the child lives. Most have no trouble spending a few nights at their grandmother's house, and a few will spend the night at a friend's house.

By age eight, most children are actively seeking out opportunities to have a friend over for the night or to spend a Friday or Saturday night at a friend's home. This occurs more naturally around eight because most children at this age have given up special blankets and stuffed animals, and they are confident that they can handle eating, dressing, bathing, and bedtime routines independently. At age eight, many children are ready to go away from home to summer camp for several nights.

By age nine, most sleepovers, vacations with an aunt and uncle, or a stay at summer camp are no longer a problem. Nine-year-olds, by being able to read and write adequately, use a phone, tell time, handle money, and so forth, are confident that they can handle these situations on their own or with little help. Most nine-year-olds are trusted to roam around their neighborhood without close supervision (provided it's a safe neighborhood) and to walk alone to school. Most nine-year-olds can handle a house key and let themselves into the house. Though many parents would be reluctant to let a nine-year-old supervise himself alone at home in the afternoon on a regular basis, most feel comfortable allowing him to be alone occasionally for up to an hour.

This widening independence and further venturing out from home base puts children in this age range in increasing contact with danger, with the possibility of accidents, and with strangers. For this reason, seven to nine is a good age to begin reviewing with children good problem-solving skills to use when faced with difficult situations. Two particularly good books are *Playing It Smart: What to Do When You're On Your Own* by Tova Navarra, and *What Would You Do? A Kid's Guide to Tricky and Sticky Situations* by Linda Schwartz. These books cover everything from medical emergencies (what to do if you're cut, on fire, choking, etc.) to being approached or followed by a stranger or touched inappropriately. Children at this age thrive on this kind of information, as they seem to have an awareness that they are going farther and farther away from home base and are less able to be protected by their parents. Some parents worry that giving children this kind of information may make them more anxious and afraid of the world outside home and cause them to worry about things they had previously not known about. Children seem to show increases in confidence and decreases in anxiety, however, as they learn how to handle difficult situations.

In school, children make broad transitions from ages seven to nine also. At seven, most children are still learning to read and manipulate numbers. They find it difficult to copy from the blackboard. Most sevens need a teacher nearby in the classroom and are very emotionally attached to their teacher. Many are easily distracted, talk a lot, and dawdle. At eight, most children really begin to function independently in the classroom. There is less daydreaming and goofing off. Eights are capable of copying from the blackboard with just a few oral instructions. They begin to take pride in their work and enjoy sticking with it until they get it right.

At age nine, not only are children expected to work independently at their desks, with few or no prompts, but new demands are made of them to think abstractly and solve complex problems. Most nines are expected to write down homework assignments, bring books home, do the homework, and bring it back the next day. Many children, particularly those from overindulgent homes experience particular problems in the third and fourth grades as they are not prepared for this transition. Most nines are capable of working for an hour or more on difficult academic tasks. Many work even longer, refusing to stop unless they've completed a project and are satisfied with what they've accomplished. Nines are challenged by intellectual and academic problems, preferring those that are more difficult. Most nines prefer to solve problems on their own and refuse help when it is offered.

Eight- and nine-year-olds can use logic and deductive reasoning to solve problems. They can classify items. They are able to picture a sequence of activities. Such "means-end" thinking skills can be put to good use by including children at this age in everyday projects such as washing a car or buying groceries. Eight- and nine-year-olds, because of their ability to use tools, can be included in small repair projects around the house or small building projects. They can do a major part of the repair of their own toys or bicycle or dollhouse. Eight- and nine-year-olds can do a large part of the assisting in cooking a meal or even cook a very simple meal themselves. Many can be responsible for organizing one dinner per week by selecting a menu, listing the foods needed and their amounts, seeing that they are purchased, and following a simple recipe.

Between the ages of seven and nine, children also undergo a major shift in their thinking about themselves and about others. They move from a focus on self to a concern for others and the beginnings of a system of a values and a conscience. They move from a focus on surface qualities of themselves and others to deeper and less obvious qualities. At six or seven, a "friend" is the child she sees most often at school or in the neighborhood. Friends are liked because they have "neat toys to play with." A friend is described in very global terms, such as "fun," "nice," "good," "bad." Friendships are very fluid—easily established and easily ended. They have little awareness of the stable personal traits of the other child.

By age eight, most children have a "best friend" and they strive to maintain that friendship. Eights are upset when a friendship falters or is disrupted by conflict. Beginning at around eight, children begin to describe their best friend in terms of stable personal traits, psychological characteristics, attitudes, values, and ongoing behavior. Children begin to conceptualize a friend as one who helps them and shares things with them, who responds to their needs and has mutual interests with them.

Eights are very attached to their parents (and teachers) and tend to idealize them. By age nine, however, children begin to turn to their peers. A nine-year-old may be more likely to quote his friend as an authority rather than his father or mother. A nine-year-old is likely to worry about a friend who is in trouble and will stand up for or protect a friend. He can see that his friend is separate from him and has needs and feelings and rights of his own. If he hurts a friend, he feels guilty and wants to set the matter straight.

This move away from egocentricity takes place in the child's sense of values and ethics as well. The seven-year-old tries to tell the truth but doesn't always do so. He is upset by lying and cheating, especially by others, but is prone to rationalize it as okay for himself. He is likely to have ready excuses for his own lapses and to blame others for his own mistakes or wrongdoing. Fairness is important to him, though he doesn't always play by the rules.

The eight-year-old views group rules as a good thing and shows a sincere desire to play by them. She understands that rules make things run more smoothly and that everyone benefits by sticking to them. She wants to be good. She thinks in terms of right and wrong and makes her own value judgments. The eight-year-old is thinking about the world around her and what is right and wrong with the world. Eight-year-olds still occasionally blame others but, for the most part, they are beginning to own up to and take responsibility for their mistakes and wrongdoing.

Nine-year-olds still are likely to blame others for small mistakes but are more likely to own up to important problems. They rarely steal and rarely lie. If they do, they usually quickly confess and get the consequences over with. Nine-year-olds want rules and want things done fairly. They accept discipline if it is "fair" and if it follows logical rules. Nine-year-olds work together well as a team because of their acceptance of group rules. This is an age where forming clubs is popular.

When listening to a story about a child their age, six-to-eight-year-olds can imagine what the child in the story might be feeling and also that someone else in the story might be feeling or wanting something different. Even so, their own needs and views tend to take precedence over those of others. Eight-to-ten-year-olds are capable of realizing that not only do the other characters have different thoughts and feelings but each person in the story may be aware of the other person's feelings and may make judgments of that person on that basis. Children at this age begin to be more aware of their impact on other people. They start to realize that others form opinions and make judgments about them on the basis of their behavior.

Ages Ten to Twelve

During the preadolescent years, from ten to twelve, children are consolidating much of their earlier gains in abstract thinking, independence, and social skills and getting ready for the push away from parents that comes with adolescence. Ten is often described as a fairly quiet time for children, a harmonious time between parent and child—possibly for the last time. The beginnings of rebellion against parental authority and the preference for one's peers over one's parents often begins as early as ages eleven and twelve. Most girls will show the first physical signs of adolescence, such as the beginnings of breast development and pubic hair, between the tenth and the eleventh years. Most will begin to menstruate somewhere between the twelfth and thirteenth years. Boys, at eleven, begin to experience some increase in genital size and the beginnings of pubic hair. Some boys are beginning to be more aware of girls and may make remarks at them as they walk by. Their interest in girls is there from time to time but is usually fleeting.

As far as self-help skills, these have all been mastered, though many ten-to-twelve-year-olds may not do them independently or without prompting. Preadolescents usually decrease their sleep time from about ten hours per night to nine hours, but they may need prompting to go to bed and may argue about the enforced bedtime. Most are certainly capable of taking over all grooming, such as taking baths, brushing teeth, dressing, and combing hair, though they tend not to and need to be reminded. Most are capable of choosing their own clothes in the morning, though some may not always choose clothing that is appropriate for the particular event or the weather that day.

Often, by age twelve, the interest in the opposite sex begins to operate its subtle pressure toward increasing the child's independence in this area. By twelve, most children are very sensitive to what the other children think about their teeth, hygiene, clothing, and hair and begin to take responsibility for this area. At ten, most children express a preference as to what kind of clothes they like to wear but may let their parent take a lead when making purchases. By twelve, most children are insistent on what kinds of clothes they will and will not wear and most parents give up the battle to assert their will over what the child will wear.

Most children at ten to twelve are capable of doing a great deal to help out in the household, though they may still need reminding and may be somewhat more rebellious about helping out than at seven to nine, complaining that they have too much homework or that they would rather be with their friends. Most children in this age range set the table, do dishes, make their beds, clean their rooms, take out the trash or garbage, mow the lawn (if it is small and level), weed the garden, shovel snow, sweep, dust, feed the dog or cat, clear out the garage, wash the car, rake leaves, vacuum a few rooms, and do simple cooking and easy ironing.

Because middle childhood is a time of growing awareness of the child's impact on others and her awareness of social rules, this is a good time to use "team approaches" to getting many household jobs and goals accomplished. To do this, take a job such as straightening up the family room, getting dinner on the table, getting the family ready to go on an outing, and delegate various parts of the job to each child. Let it be known that the family doesn't eat, or leave the house, until each phase of the job is done. Put the responsibility of getting the oppositional child to conform on the group as a whole. Handle the situation matter-of-factly and unemotionally.

Example: "What? Jeffrey didn't do the salad? He's still watching television? Gee, I guess we don't eat. I'll turn off the stove. Let me know when you've worked it out." Another example: "What? Sarah won't take the dirty cups and plates out of the family room? Then I guess we may not make it to the movie on time, or maybe not at all. You all have ten more minutes to work it out."

Not only does this approach take the overindulgent parent out of the role of doing everything for everyone, but it puts the problem of what to do about refusal to comply back on the children themselves. It lets peer pressure do the work of the parent at a time when peer pressure is beginning to exert its influence. Children at this age are playing team sports and working in teams in class, and understand that many goals in life are accomplished only through each member of the team doing his or her part. Keep the goal important by making it dinner, a movie, going shopping, out to play, etc.

Along with the team approach to household jobs and goals, this is a good age to hold family meetings on some regular basis. Many children naturally will groan if the meeting is really an excuse for the parent to complain about unmade beds or lecture them about their table manners. Use the meetings to solve problems that are relevant and meaningful to them. Children in middle childhood want to have a say in what goes on in the home and often have very good ideas to contribute. At this stage, most have developed a clear sense of right and wrong, a sense of fairness, and an ability to view a problem not just from their own viewpoint but from several viewpoints. Problem-focused meetings give them a real chance to air grievances, resolve conflicts, take a stand, and demonstrate leadership skills. Example: Anna, who is twelve, spends a lot of time on the phone with her best friend, Erin. Nine-year-old Chris likes to pick up the extension and make gross noises. Another example: Eight-year-old Adam complains that eleven-year-old Brandon is eating all the snacks and sodas and he's not getting any. As you direct the meetings, try to follow a simple three-step process. (1) What's the problem? Let's define it clearly. Let's discuss the upset feelings it causes. (2) What would be a rule we could make that is fair (as far as possible) to everyone? How do we take age into account? (3) What would be an appropriate consequence for breaking the rule? It may even be helpful to put on poster board a list of Household Rules and Consequences with your family name at the top. They might be very specific, such as the following:

THE BAXTER HOUSE

Rules	Consequences
1. No one changes the television channel while another person is watching.	Lose choice of TV show for rest of day.
2. No one opens anyone's door without knocking first.	Make restitution by doing one of their chores.
3. No one picks up the extension to listen in or interrupt while someone's on the phone, unless they've been talking for more than twenty minutes.	Lose phone privileges for rest of the day.
4. No one drinks more than ____ sodas a week without asking.	Must give their soda ration to the others for following week.

Recall from chapter 4 that the skill that most distinguishes competent children from those who are not so competent socially, even as young as age four, is that they can generate alternative solutions to problems. Brainstorm with the children in these meetings. Encourage them to come up with all manner of solutions, household rules, and creative consequences. Let them have their say, no matter how outrageous, knowing you will reserve control over the final outcome. Recall also from chapter 4 that it is the authoritative parents—the ones who allow democratic participation in decisionmaking—whose children were the most responsible and capable and had the highest self-esteem.

If you're not so task oriented, you may want to use the meetings for general discussions of conflicts in the home and how everyone feels about them. You may want to discuss these as ethical dilemmas. The meetings can be a good time to discuss values as well as specific solutions to problems. The ages ten to twelve are thought to be the most important years in the child's life in terms of shaping his values in the years to come. You could put on poster board as well, or instead, a Code of Ethics for the household. Here is a sample from *You Can't Sell Your Brother at the Garage Sale: The Kids' Book of Values* by Beth Brainard:

- Treat steps (parents, brothers, sisters) the same way you treat the rest of the family.
- Share
- Don't tease
- Don't make people wait, be on time
- Don't do or say things that you know will hurt someone
- Admit when you're wrong and apologize
- Pick up after yourself
- Do your share of the household chores
- Take responsibility for your things
- Always use good manners; say please and thank you

Linda and Richard Eyre, in their book, *Teaching Children Responsibility,* suggest using the meetings to hand out awards—certificates or banners to hang on the child's door that say PRIDE (for a job well done), HONESTY (for owning up to a mistake when it was particularly difficult), LEADERSHIP (for taking charge of a problem without any external reminders and directing the work of others), CARING (for thoughtfulness that is beyond the minimal day-to-day level of civility), or DEPENDABILITY (for always being ready to go before everyone else is, or never losing hat, mittens, or boots). You can tailor the banner to the needs of the individual child—toward what she's good at already and what you'd like to see more of.

Ten to twelve is also the age when children first begin to be responsible enough to earn money outside the home. Girls and boys may begin to do some simple baby-sitting at eleven and twelve, watching children for a few hours while a parent works in another part of the house. Many children do house-sitting at this age and pet-sitting while the owner is away. Some, particularly boys, will rake leaves, mow small lawns, or wash cars for neighbors to earn money. If encouraged in this direction, children often come up with novel money-making ideas. Some might grow a vegetable garden in the spring and summer, harvest the produce, and sell it to the neighbors. (You might encourage this by helping with the start-up costs). Some will buy candy in large quantities and re-sell it to their friends at school. Still others might try the old stand-bys of a paper route or a lemonade stand in the summer time. As a take-off on the lemonade stand, I have seen older children in a big city park nearby selling soft drinks and ice cream bars out of a cooler to the joggers and roller-skaters.

If your child has been earning her own money for toys since the age of six or seven, this is a good time to expand this responsibility with money to cover all toys (outside of birthdays and special holidays), snacks, drinks, recreation, movies, and special clothing wants (i.e., designer sneakers). If children have established a pattern of earning money and saving for special purchases for several years, this should be an easy and smooth transition. The ten-to-twelve-year-old's allowance can be increased significantly, too, since she is capable of making a greater contribution to the household. Set a budget for these items based on what you might spend if the money for them came from you. Then outline an allowance that is high enough to cover these expenses, but can only be earned through a good effort on the child's part to accomplish the goals on her allowance chart. (Most parents set an allowance of five to ten dollars per week at this age.) These need not be specific household jobs. The allowance chart may also include desired behaviors such as helping out with a younger child, being generally cooperative when asked to do something, picking up one's clothes without reminding, etc. Also, keep in mind that she is capable of generating some creative schemes to market her services to the neighbors.

Thirdly, I strongly support paying children handsomely for good report cards. Most parents stress education to their children and do so on the basis that "you can get a better job that pays more money." The implication is that there is a direct relationship in our society between knowledge, academic achievement, and money—which there is in large part. Highly refined skills, innovative ideas, and the ability to persevere at tedious and complex tasks all command high prices in our society. The link is a very tenuous one for children, however, in that they cannot see that the tasks they master in school at the age of eleven will benefit them at twenty-five. By rewarding academic excellence with monetary gain when children are young, we not only establish for them in a visible way what our priorities are, but we in fact mirror the values of the larger society.

Once the ten-to-twelve-year-old is generating more money through a variety of methods and is handling money responsibly, she should now divide her money into three banks—one earmarked for "everyday use," one set aside for "savings for a special purchase," and a third for "church or charity." Even children ten to twelve years old have a growing awareness of the economic disparity among people in the world. If they have been putting small amounts of parents' money in the basket on Sunday or donating old clothes or discarded toys to a charity, it comes as an easy transition. Parents might want to review with the child how much of their income they donate to their church, synagogue, or charitable causes and suggest the child set up a plan to donate a similar amount—3 percent, 5 percent, or 10 percent. In doing so, the child has still another opportunity to feel that she makes a contribution to something outside herself, that she has importance, and that what she does counts.

Children in middle childhood can also feel useful and important in many other ways. Certainly, some of the suggestions from chapter 8 can be applied at these ages, too, if they haven't been already—such as involving your children in recycling efforts, going with you to donate furniture or food to shelters and charitable organizations, going door-to-door in your neighborhood distributing notices about a rezoning meeting or a vote on the school bond referendum. The older child can do even more. The ten-to-twelve-year-old can write letters to a congressman or congresswoman about an issue that is of concern to him. He can write a letter to the mayor about the peeling paint at his school, or to the head of a corporation that advertises cigarette smoking to young people. The older child can accompany the parent who volunteers to spend the night at a shelter for the homeless, serving meals and putting out bedding. He can accompany his parent to the voting booth and read the choices for a particular referendum or candidate and punch the card. He can read to his grandmother in the hospital or nursing home and go with a parent to take meals to the shut-in, the handicapped, or the elderly. All these activities give him a sense of having an important place in the world and a chance to role-play what it is to be a responsible adult.

The ten-to-twelve-year-old is capable of independence at a level far greater than the younger child. This is the age when most parents first trust a child to stay alone in the house after school. However, it is not an age that is capable of parenting younger children who are also in the home after school. The eleven-year-old has no direct power over the eight-year-old, and the eight-year-old is unlikely to take orders from the eleven-year-old. Fighting among siblings and lost keys are likely to be the biggest problems among working parents.

Because ten-to-twelve-year-olds are capable of more complex means-end thinking, this is a good time to involve them in even more complex projects around the house. They can help plan the menu for the household for the week. They can compare food prices at the grocery store, taking along a calculator for multiplying and dividing. They can help change the filter and the bag in the vacuum cleaner, help take the dog to the vet, do small repairs on their bicycle or on the lawn mower, bake a cake, and help paint their bedroom. In all of these projects, it is best to involve them in a leadership role, asking questions, giving tips, and staying out of the way. Ask her, "What supplies do we need to have on hand before we start?" "How long will the job take?" "Do we need special tools?" "Do we need to read the instructions?" "What are the safety tips we need to keep in mind?" "What's the first thing we do?" "What's the last thing we do before we leave?" Remember how you felt when you were twelve and your father asked you to help, but all he really did was make you stand there and watch? Didn't you feel useless? Keep this in mind as you let your twelve-year-old take over the activity.

This is a time of intense bonding to the peer group. At ten, the interest in playing team sports is very strong, and children form and reform clubs and loose "gangs" of friends. The loose clubs of age eight and nine are now more organized, more cohesive, and more structured. They last longer and have rules for membership and special rituals for conducting meetings. Interest in formal organizations such as athletics and Boy Scouts and Girl Scouts is at its highest point. By age twelve, most children are spending more time with their peers than they are with their parents.

During late middle childhood, ages ten to twelve, friendships deepen and become more important to the child. Friends become confidants and holders of secrets, people whom the child trusts with private information, perhaps more than they do Mother or Father. Friends at this age help each other with psychological problems such as loneliness, sadness, and fear, and avoid doing things that may hurt the other person. These same-sex friendships are often intense and stable over time and are the dress rehearsals for heterosexual relationships in adolescence.

Along with this intenseness in friendships, most preadolescents suffer a drop in self-esteem between age nine or ten and their entry into middle school, usually around age twelve. For the boys the drop is mild, but for girls it is a major drop. Psychologist Emily Hancock, in her book, *The Girl Within*, writes that a woman's best years, in terms of feeling good about herself, may be over by the time she is eleven or twelve. It is at this age that girls no longer base their self-esteem on their competencies and skills in athletics, music, school, and friendships, but come under the subtle social pressure to measure themselves by standards of physical beauty, by popularity in their peer group, and by what boy might be interested in them. Parents who are concerned about this shift are wise to insist that girls not drop out of the activities they participated in in elementary school but maintain some reasonable involvement in church activities, sports, music, drama, school clubs, Scouting, dance, gymnastics, etc., all the way through high school.

Along with these changes in the valuation of the peer group, and the breaking away from the influence of parents, comes a shift, too, in the way preadolescents conceptualize authority. Researcher William Damon found that by age nine, children think obedience to authority is essentially voluntary and cooperative. Parents and children, bosses and workers, are seen as having equal basic rights, but the authority is seen as having a responsibility toward the subordinate. Authority figures are viewed as people with more knowledge who can be helpful to them. But complying with a parent and teacher simply because "they ought to" is a thing of the past.

By age eleven or twelve, the authority relationship is considered fully cooperative, established by mutual agreement, and related to specific situations. In other words, preadolescents will comply only with teachers whom they respect and only in areas in which they feel the teacher should have authority or is more knowledgeable than them.

The twelve-year-old believes that if he knows more than the teacher about some area in particular, the adult should defer to him. The same goes with parents. Preadolescents pick and choose among parental commands, depending upon the situation and whether the command is felt to be reasonable.

This is a predictable and normal developmental stage and calls for a different kind of parenting style from Mom and Dad. Parents cannot simply give commands that are to be obeyed. They must work toward agreements with the child that are negotiated in a democratic way and based on mutual trust and respect.

It is at this stage that children in overindulgent families become particularly rebellious, as they now are able to view their parents more critically. They often view them as unsure of themselves, not very knowledgeable, inconsistent, and unpredictable. They often describe their parents as serving their own agendas, as overreacting and being overly emotional, and as taking things way too personally. Now more than ever, parents must work toward establishing guidelines that balance the needs of the preadolescent against those of the family, that balance freedom against safety, and that are perceived as fair and reasonable.

10 Middle Childhood—Ages Seven to Twelve: New Approaches to Common Problems

Problem Area 1: Pets Not Cared For

"Our twelve-year-old had a pet turtle. You would think he would be capable of caring for such a small animal, but he's so forgetful that the turtle has become the responsibility of the whole family. Sometimes he just doesn't feed it, or he doesn't change the water. One night, the turtle escaped and crawled under the house. We were all out there with flashlights trying to find it. I hate to just let the animal starve. On the other hand, I really don't want to take over the turtle. I inherited the fish and the dog from him already."

We can see that this parent has made one mistake by repeating mistakes of the past. Something went wrong with the fish and the dog, but yet another pet was brought into the house with no plan in place as to how it would be cared for and no consequences for not doing so. One approach to the problem of pets is to explain to the child that pets are fun but that they require much more maturity than the child is aware of and must be tried out in stages. Explain to him that he didn't ride a bike at the age of two. He first got around on a three-wheel toy with no pedals, then he learned to pedal a tricycle, then he rode a bicycle with training wheels, and finally, there came the day when he rode the bicycle alone with no training wheels at all. Put pets on a hierarchy of difficulty: houseplants, turtles, fish, cats, hamsters and gerbils, and finally dogs. Explain that the child must demonstrate good responsibility with a simple pet before he can advance to a more difficult one.

One ten-year-old I worked with wanted to get a gerbil to start a pet collection, but mother was consistently saying no. His mother was an overindulgent parent who had had difficulty setting consistent limits and using logical and natural consequences. In the past, she had let him have cactuses and fish, all of which had died from neglect. A hamster had to be given away. Rather than give in, she was now saying no to all requests for pets and being sharply critical toward him as well.

I suggested we turn the problem over to him to solve. "Stephen, your mom is frustrated with the experiences you've had with pets in the past. Now she doesn't want to give you a chance. Somehow you must find a way to show her that this time, things will be different. Also, you must find a way to show her how very badly you want this gerbil." To give him a hint, I told him the story of how badly I wanted piano lessons when I was ten. I carefully constructed a paper keyboard with scissors and tape, checked out a book from the library called *How to Play the Piano*, and would sit down on the floor in the living room each evening humming to myself as I played my make-believe music on my make-believe piano. Stephen came up with the plan to begin taking over care of the houseplants at home to show Mom he was ready. He also spent his allowance on a book on caring for gerbils, read the book, and would discuss it at the dinner table. His mother was finally so impressed, she did buy him the gerbil, and he did take care of it.

When the Adams family ran into similar problems with twelve-year-old Chris, we held a family meeting to discuss pet care and real-world experiences with neglect of creatures we have committed ourselves to caring for. I explained that in real life, when parents fail to care for a child, the child is taken away by the social worker, who places the child with a foster family. Then the parents have to come before the judge, who will tell them what to do to get their child back. Often they have to pay child support to the foster family, improve the quality of their home, take parenting classes, and be subject to periodic monitoring and inspection of their home once the child is returned.

Applying this to the pet problem, the family decided that Mom would be the pet social worker who would review the pet's home periodically for evidence of neglect. Chris's nine-year-old sister, Emily, would be the foster parent. If Chris failed to care for the turtle, he would have to give it to Emily temporarily. Then he would have to go before Dad, the judge, at a family meeting and hear what his conditions would be for return of the turtle. Dad said he would probably require Chris to read a book on turtle care and review it with the family. He would also have to pay Emily two dollars per week in pet support. Afterwards, Mom, the pet social worker, would monitor the pet's care briefly for any further signs of pet neglect. The family liked the plan, as it put the burden of work on Chris and also provided some educational information about how our society handles child neglect as well. After following the plan, they had no more problems with pet neglect.

Problem Area 2: Fighting

"My problem is fighting. I have begun to let my two boys, nine and eleven, stay alone at home in the afternoon. They don't do any of the chores they're supposed to do, however, instead they fight over every little thing, and they're on the phone to me constantly with their squabbles. I am a single parent. I can't have these constant phone calls to my office. When I get home, it's more of the same. Each has a complaint about the other. I guess they're vying for my attention. Maybe they're just angry over not having a father who cares about them. I know I've tried to make it up to them on the weekends by taking them shopping, out to eat, and to the movies. But they still fight."

This vignette illustrates several problems. One is that most parents intervene in children's fights as mediators and arbitrators. They take it upon themselves to solve the problem for the children. There is some value in this. It is possible that the parent can teach them some rules of fairness and justice. By ages nine and eleven, however, most children have already internalized some rules about fairness and equal rights and rely on those rules when they are out on the ballfield or playing in the woods behind the house. What is going on here is that the overindulgent parent is allowing them to become dependent on her to resolve their disputes far past an age where they could do so themselves if they chose.

Secondly, out of her own guilt about the children's lack of a father, she is offering too much of the wrong kind of attention at the wrong times. They may be genuinely sad and angry that their father is not more interested in them, but her guilt and overindulgence further interfere with their learning to deal with everyday problems.

We learned in chapter 4 that children as young as four can learn to solve their own disputes. When adults continually use the approach of "dialoguing," children can come up with solutions. By "dialoguing," we mean asking the child to come up with solutions, for example: "When you're mad at her because she's taken your toy, what can you do besides fight? What's a better way to solve this problem?" Dialoguing works, and if a parent uses it consistently, it will become less and less necessary over time. If you haven't begun to use it by age seven, then start now. Put the burden of solving the problem on the children themselves. Show very little interest in who started it, who's right or wrong, and who's to blame. Show much more interest in innovative solutions. Example: "It looks like you're fighting over the television again. This seems to happen a lot. What can you do about it? Can you come up with a plan that would minimize some of this fighting?"

If they are completely out of control, separate them briefly for a time-out and a cooling-off period. Be calm, matter-of-fact. Example: "It looks like you're both too angry now to solve this problem. I'll turn off the television, and you go to your rooms and cool off. While you're in there, be thinking of a plan to solve this problem."

If they come out of time-out still angry and accusatory, send them back for another time-out. Let them know they can't come out of time-out till they have each come up with some kind of reasonable plan. Example: "Oops. Looks like you still haven't cooled off. Let me give you ten or fifteen more minutes to calm down and think. Use your time well."

When they have finally come up with some sort of plan, have them sit down to negotiations. Example: "Good. You've been doing some thinking. Now, sit down at the table and work it out. Let me know what you come up with." If the situation erupts in a fight again, send them back to time-out in their rooms for another cooling-off and rethinking.

As children mature and move from the seven-to-nine age range into the ten-to-twelve age range, I have found it effective to move to the "work-it-out-but-settle-it-elsewhere" approach. Frame the problem this way: "Your fighting at the dinner table is making dinner unpleasant for all of us. You two need to step into the basement [or garage or spare bedroom], where we can't hear you, and work it out. You can rejoin us when you've settled the dispute." In this way, not only do they work it out, but the possibility of missing dinner puts pressure on them to do it quickly. Explain that this is only logical, inasmuch as if they were in a restaurant fighting like this, the owner would ask them to leave.

Another example is this: "Your fighting during the television show is making it hard for any of us to hear. You're going to have to step outside and settle this where you won't bother anyone." You'll get cries of "But Dad, we'll miss the show! It's cold out there! We're in our pajamas!" That's precisely the point. Explain that if they had a loud fight in a movie theater, the manager would ask them to leave and wouldn't care if they missed the movie, if it was cold outside, or if they were embarrassed.

Problem Area 3: Alone in the House After School

In the above example, the single parent was faced with two boys who fought constantly and could not handle the after-school-alone situation very responsibly. As children in the ten-to-twelve age range are tried out with this new freedom, fighting is a strong possibility, but parents also face the problem of the children's breaking any rules that have been set down. They might invite inappropriate friends over, leave the house and roam the neighborhood, not do chores or homework, watch television and play Nintendo instead, or leave food and dirty dishes scattered through the house.

A good way to ease children into after-school independence is to ease them into it a day at a time. When they begin to complain that they are too old for day care or too old to have to go to a neighbor's house every afternoon, explain to them that perhaps they are and it may be time to try them on their own one day a week. In this situation, the mother might try the oldest child on his own on Friday afternoons, if he has demonstrated maturity and responsibility around the house that week. If he does not understand what this means in everyday terms, break it down for him with at least three concrete illustrations.

"I think you might be ready to be on your own on Friday afternoons, but I'm just not sure. You will have to be trusted to come straight home and not stop somewhere else on the way. For me to trust that you will do what you promise to do, I would need to see that you take out the garbage when you say you will and that you do your homework when you say you will.

"Also, you will need to keep a house key. For me to be sure that you won't lose a key, I would need to see that you keep track of your shoes, your coat, your gloves, your homework, little things like that. If you can't keep track of your shoes, then how could you keep something much smaller, but more important, like a house key?

"And I will have to be able to trust you to use good judgment when it comes to answering the phone or the door or letting friends come over. In order to trust you with that part of it, I would need to see that you take phone messages correctly, that you can play with your friends without getting into mischief, that you stop your friends if they are about to do something here that we disapprove of, things like that. Why don't we go over this at the Sunday family meeting for a couple of weeks, and you tell me how you think you're doing."

In the above example, we are bringing several important principles to bear on the situation. First, we allow more freedom to those who demonstrate that they are responsible enough to handle it. Secondly, there is a logical connection between responsibility in one area of life and responsibility in another. (We'll come back to this again when teenagers ask to drive.) Lastly, we are suggesting that the child *self-monitor*. By "self-monitor," we mean that the child takes over the task of measuring his behavior against a standard, asking himself, "How am I doing? Am I doing what I said I could do? Am I living up to the promises I made?"

As you build in the expectations and phase in more time alone in the afternoon, you need to plan for some rational consequences for the child's lapse in adhering to the plan. The most reasonable consequence would be more supervision. Supervision costs money, and the money has to come from somewhere else in the family budget. Example: "I know this is a big responsibility, and I hope you will do well. When we go to full-time on your own at home in the afternoon, however, we'll lose the slot that is reserved for you at the day-care center (YMCA, Boys Club, etc.). If you can't handle it well, then I'll have to find someone, a baby-sitter, to watch you in the afternoons. I'll have to get a high school boy or girl, or the neighbor, Mrs. Rowan, to watch you. Now, I'll have to pay four or five dollars per hour, so that will be sixty or seventy-five dollars per week that will have to come out of our budget for movies, dinners, allowances, and so on. Think it over. The choice is yours for us to use that money on fun things or on baby-sitting."

Many overindulgent parents are reluctant to hire a sitter to supervise their preteenager in the afternoon, or to put them back in day care briefly. They fear it is "too humiliating" for the child. When parents have gone back to baby-sitting, however, they have generally had to do so only once and only for a week or two, and the problem was resolved. The elegance of this approach is that it takes the problem out of the realm of criticism, threats, and emotional interchanges and puts it in the context of a choice the child has made. Example: "This place is a wreck. Well, I can see by the look of this place that perhaps we started this too early. You've made the choice to go back to baby-sitting for two weeks." Preteen says: "What do you mean I made a choice?!" Response: "When we discussed the rules and you knew the consequences, and you chose not to stick to the rules, you chose to accept the consequences."

Problem Area 4: Complaining

"I am exasperated with my ten- and twelve-year-old daughters. Nothing I do seems to be enough for them. They complain that they don't like the way I cook. They complain that I don't buy the foods they like. They complain that they don't have nice enough clothes. They complain that they don't get enough allowance. They even complain that I nag them too much about their complaining. Sometimes I lose control and yell at them about how ungrateful they are. I keep thinking that if I cook a really nice meal or buy them that extra outfit they wanted, they will be happy, but it just doesn't happen."

As we saw earlier in the discussion on developmental changes in this age group, the preteen (and the earlier teenager) begins the process of separating by finding fault with her parents, seeing them as inadequate and out of touch with today's trends. This is an age also when self-centeredness reaches a peak, along with extreme self-consciousness about appearance. Complaining and negative moods do intensify in this age group. In overindulgent families, this developmental problem is compounded by the parents' efforts to satisfy the child's complaints in order to bring about a more positive mood. This overinvolvement with making the child happy increases the child's dependency on the parent at a time when she is trying to become less dependent. This conflict intensifies and, especially with preteen girls, often erupts in hostile interchanges between mother and daughter.

If the parent has been able to give the child reasonable expectations for independence and problem solving, much of the complaining is greatly reduced. For example, if the twelve-year-old is involved in selecting her own clothes, the accusation that Mother is not getting her the "right" clothes is moot. If the two daughters above were involved in grocery shopping and preparing dinner, the complaints about meals would go by the wayside. If they had been earning allowances and earning money outside the home, the complaints about not enough money would seldom be heard.

It may well be the case, however, that you are the parent of a preteen who is "underdeveloped" and a confirmed complainer. Nothing you do is enough for her. You have tried and failed. You have nurtured your daughter with a romantic ideal of parental love, at the expense of independence and problem solving. Now how do you get out of it?

You begin by formulating a response that puts the burden of the solution on the child. And you determine to repeat yourself and persist in the face of all challenges.

Even when you feel you are getting nowhere, you persist and you repeat yourself like a broken record. Remember that your goal is to get your child to generate "alternative solutions." Do not give advice. Whatever advice you give will be criticized as "dumb," "old-fashioned," "just not done nowadays," "too hard," "not good enough," etc. You must stick to only two types of statements: questions and feedback.

Example: "So you don't like what I buy at the grocery store. That's good. I expect you to have your own likes and dislikes at your age. You two put together the grocery list for the next four weeks. Keep in mind you will have to list foods that are healthy, nutritious, and within our budget."

Example: "So you don't like the meals I've been cooking. That's great. I'm getting tired of them too. From now on, each of you will be responsible for dinner one night a week. You plan the menu, I'll assist you in the kitchen. What would you like to cook first?"

Example: "It's rough not having the money you feel you need. How can you earn some more money? What can you do to cut down on expenses? Can you think of some ways we can all save money around the house?"

Problem Area 5: Homework Not Done

"My nine-year-old boy has always given us trouble when it comes to homework. Every day, we ask him if he has any and he says no. Then, at the end of the grading period, we find out that he got very low grades for failing to turn in homework. For a while, we tried having him bring home a paper that all his teachers had to sign every day and that had his assignments written down. But then he just 'forgot' to bring the paper home."

The "forgotten" homework and the "forgotten" assignment sheet are common problems with underdeveloped children at this age, particularly boys. Doing homework is far more tedious and less fun than playing Nintendo or playing outside. If the homework can be avoided in order to play, then there is all the incentive in the world to do so. Parents must devise a plan that provides incentives for remembering to bring the assignment home and complete it.

One effective way is to set up a firm study hour approximately one hour before dinnertime. (For many two-career families, the homework hour can only be supervised either right before or right after dinner.) Let your child know that this is his study hour. If he fails to bring home any homework, you will assign him an hour of "makeup work." This work might involve doing numerous pages of math from a math workbook, copying words and definitions from the dictionary, copying a science article out of the newspaper, etc. Of course, if he brings home his homework, he can do that instead. He cannot come to dinner until the work is completed. If he is still working when the family is eating, he will miss dinner. If he completes the work after dinner, he can fix himself a sandwich. If he is in his room all evening, and the work is never completed, the only reasonable thing to do is to go to bed hungry.

Though the approach may seem harsh, it works well. Nature is on your side. The appetite of a preteen boy is enormous. When overindulgent parents have been willing to enforce the study hour, the makeup work, and the no-work-no-dinner rule, I have seldom seen a boy this age miss more than two meals. If the homework continues to be "forgotten," parents can increase the amount of makeup work until it is such a burdensome amount that the child is highly motivated to bring home the much shorter daily assignment he was given at school.

Problem Area 6: Chores Not Done

"Our problem is not one of being too easy on our kids. They have chores to do. They just don't do them. Oh, I guess we could make them do their assigned chores by yelling at them and standing over them to see that they finish them. But it's easier to do them myself. We used to give them an allowance. But it didn't make sense to give them an allowance for doing nothing. So we stopped giving them money. It doesn't seem to have made much difference. They don't seem to care about not having any money."

This is a very common problem in overindulgent families. There is a perception of limits in the home, because chores are assigned. But there is no real limit setting because there are no meaningful consequences for not doing the chores. The parents in the above example used money as an incentive, but when money failed to work, they failed to substitute any more meaningful incentives. Money is usually an incentive to children in this age range, especially if they have to provide for all their recreational needs out of their allowance. Money is often no incentive in these families, however, because the parents provide whatever small amounts of money are necessary to rent a videotape, go roller-skating, buy some fresh batteries, etc.

It is a good idea with children this age to let them select which chores they will do, since they are old enough to participate in a democratic process. Hold a "jobs auction." Let them bid on jobs, with the low bidder getting the job. Let the more unpleasant jobs be paid at higher rates than the more pleasant jobs. Let them rotate or trade jobs as the need arises.

Once jobs are assigned, let them know that you will pay a "minimum wage," or base rate, for the completion of that job with only one reminder. Offer a bonus for doing the job on one's own initiative, with no reminders, explaining that highly motivated workers get bonuses in the real world. Also, explain that if you have to give two reminders or do the job yourself, they will get no pay. After all, poor workers are let go with no pay in the work world. If money is the incentive you are using, be sure that you give no money at any other time for any optional need, such as for gifts, snacks, toys, movies, camera film, and so on.

In order to gain the child's participation in doing the chores, the incentives must be important and meaningful to the child, and the consequences of not doing them must be dramatic and high-impact. Some children have such modest needs that money may not be much of an incentive. If so, parents need to be creative and come up with alternative incentive plans. The parent might assign a number of points or give out a number of tokens for particular chores. The points can be used to purchase television time, telephone time, or Nintendo time if those are more sought after than money. Example: emptying the dishwasher is worth five points, straightening up the family room is worth three points, cleaning up his room is worth four points. Each half hour of Nintendo time (or TV time or phone time) costs three points.

If money and points do seem to work, the parent may have to go to "dramatic and high-impact"—though logical and rational—consequences.

Example: "What a mess! You two were supposed to empty the dishwasher and take all your dirty dishes to the kitchen before I came home from work. If you won't do your job, then I'm not going to do mine. I'm not cooking tonight. I'll fix myself something to eat (or take myself out to dinner), and you can fix yourselves something."

Example: "I'm tired of trying various ways to get you to hang up your clothes and put the dirty clothes in the hamper. I give up. They're your responsibility now. If you're not going to do your job, then I'm not going to do mine. I'm not going to wash any of your clothes or buy any new ones for you until you're ready to do your job. If I find them around the house, I'll presume you don't want them and throw them away or give them away."

Example: "I'm tired of telling you to take out the trash. Nothing seems to work. You say you keep 'forgetting' to take it out. From now on, we'll put the trash can next to your bed every night. That way, maybe the smell will remind you to take it out."

Problem 7: The Child Who Is Disorganized and Forgetful

"We are frustrated with our ten-year-old. He is so forgetful. He can't find his shoes in the morning. I got him special notebooks to write down his homework assignments, but he still forgets. I help him with his homework every night, and we get it done, but then he forgets to bring it to school. He leaves tools out in the yard overnight. The floor is littered with clothes, a bookbag, or whatever he has come in contact with. We come home from work and there are Coke cans and half-eaten sandwiches lying around. He thinks his bicycle is down the street at a neighbor's house, but he's not exactly sure that's where he left it. And his room! It's a disaster. I only go in there to put away his clean clothes. I don't want to think about what organic creatures might be growing in some mildewed pizza crust pushed under the bed!"

The boy described above is a type of child commonly seen by clinicians in private practice. The presenting problem when the parents call for help, however, is often not the disorganization and forgetfulness, but poor academic performance and declining grades. The parents have learned to tolerate a burdensome amount of forgetfulness over the years and provide the structure and organization that the child seems to lack. They have put up charts, bought multicolored dividers, called the teacher for the child's assignments, written out a daily schedule, rounded up the clothes in the morning, etc. When the school calls to say the child isn't turning in homework, doesn't know how to work independently, doesn't get his work done, and may make some failing grades, parents realize the problem is serious and is beginning to have an impact on the child's performance outside the home.

Naturally, some children are simply more organized than others. In fact, the boy described above might be labeled as having "attention deficit disorder without hyperactivity." Others might call him "immature" or an "underachiever." Whatever the label, the problem behavior is the same. The disorganized and forgetful child seems to create a vacuum that sucks others into doing things for him. It is an easy mistake to make. He seems truly sincere when he says, "I didn't mean to leave my spelling words at school. I just forgot." He is truly regretful when he says, "I'm sorry I left the electric drill out in the yard overnight and it got rained on. I didn't mean to." We figure that with just a little bit more structure from us, he'll take charge and get it together. But he only seems to continue being disorganized.

Many teachers and school counselors recognize these overindulgent parents and stress to the parent that by the late elementary grades to early middle school, they need to back off and let the child flounder. Parents are loath to do this, however, because these underdeveloped children not only flounder, they sink—at least a little. They do not have the skills to swim alone.

A more workable plan is to first help the child develop his own plan to get organized and then back off and let the child flounder and finally swim. By "help the child develop a plan," we mean to continually ask questions and to assign the child the task of coming up with a plan.

Example: "You still seem to be forgetting to bring your assignments home. Can you come up with a plan that will help you to remember? Go into your room and work on a plan for the next hour. Bring your plan to the dinner table and we'll discuss it. But don't come to the dinner table without it."

By "let the child flounder," we mean to let natural and logical consequences occur. Natural consequences are those that would occur naturally without your intervention.

Example: Your son leaves his lunch at home. You do not bring it to him. He is left to solve the problem himself of how to find some food at lunchtime.

Example: He cannot find his shoes in the morning. He is left to solve the problem himself, and he decides to wear old shoes that are too tight or dressy shoes that look funny with blue jeans.

Example: He leaves his completed homework at home. He receives a zero for that assignment. He is upset about how it will affect his final grade.

Example: He forgets to take a jacket with him on a cold day. He gets cold. He wishes he had remembered to take his jacket.

With other problems that center around disorganization, you may have to engineer some creative logical consequences. By "logical consequences," we mean consequences that you provide but which make some logical and rational sense to you and to your child. They are consequences that are similar to real-life situations.

Example: Your son leaves his backpack on the living room floor, his bicycle in the yard overnight, his Legos spread all over the basement floor. You respond: "You know, if I left my car by the side of the road and walked away, the police would find it and impound it. They'd haul it off to a big lot and put a ticket on it and the meter would start running. I would have to pay a fee to get it back, and the longer it's there, the higher the fee. Eventually, if I didn't claim it, they would assume ownership of it, sell it, and keep the money. How about it if I impound your possessions that I find lying around? I'll put a price tag on each one, and you have you pay me to get them back. After thirty days or sixty days, it becomes mine. Of course, if you then wanted a new jacket or bicycle, you'd have to buy it yourself. After all, if the police impounded my car, I couldn't just go to them and ask them to buy me a new one."

Example: Messy rooms are a problem with many children, and especially so with children in overindulgent families. You say: "Our arguing with you to pick up your things in your room is getting old. We're tired of it. From now on, we'll just take everything you don't put away and store it in the basement. We'll pretend it's a lending library. When you want something, you can check it out like a library book. You'll have to turn in each item to the library before you can check out another item. Maybe you can keep track of your things that way—one at a time. If this works for a while, we'll gradually let you have more than one thing in your room at a time."

Problem 8: Lying

Lying is often a concern with young children, but it is a problem that usually resolves itself over time. This is because lying, especially lying to escape the negative consequences for some misbehavior, is a short-term, simple solution to a problem. It is a solution that fails to take into account long-term consequences, such as other people losing their trust in you, disappointing family members or friends, hurting their feelings, making them angry or frustrated, or causing oneself to lose privileges in the future. In overindulgent families, evasive lying may still be a problem in middle childhood, because children in these families have often been prevented from experiencing the negative consequences of lying. Naturally, lying is still having some payoffs, and there is little perception yet of long-term consequences.

We have already looked at the problem of lying about homework and have discussed one approach to the problem—the approach of giving more "makeup homework" than the amount of homework the child would have had if he had brought home the original assignment. Another common problem with this age group is lying about having done a household job. Again, a solution might be to double the amount of household jobs as a consequence, in order to establish an incentive for being truthful. Ultimately, it is the parents' responsibility to provide penalties for lying and incentives for truthfulness. Older children have stated to me that if they think their chances of getting away with a lie are 50 percent, they'll go for it, because the risk is worth it. If the parent is providing few penalties other than a "talking-to," then most children perceive themselves as getting away with it. A parent is thus providing incentives to continue lying.

Another approach is to use the burden-of-proof method. By this we mean that if untruthfulness becomes a chronic problem, the parent must stop doing the work of tracking down every story and instead put the burden of proof on the child. For a period of one week (or two or three), absolutely nothing will be believed without supporting evidence. Evidence of tooth brushing, bathing, and hand washing must be provided. Every homework assignment must be initialed by every teacher every day. Before going to another child's house to play, the child must get the other child's parent on the phone to verify the plans in detail. If the child is out playing, he must come home and check in every thirty minutes and verify what he has been doing.

Another common problem with this age group is the problem of concealing bad grades. Some children will forge them, destroy them when they come in the mail, or say they were never sent out. Here is one burden-of-proof method that worked well with Will, the boy we met in chapter 2:

"We're disappointed that you forged your grades [or failed to bring them home, or hid them]. Now we can't trust you. In order to put the burden of this problem on you till we can trust you again, we're going to ask you to get out half a dozen envelopes, stamps, and sheets of stationery. We want you to address the envelopes to us at our work address and, of course, pay for the stamps. Then we want you to write this note on each piece of stationery. 'My parents and I have agreed I have a problem with truthfulness about my grades [or my behavior at school, etc.]. Therefore, I would like you to write notes to them on the bottom of this paper or send my grades to them in these stamped, addressed envelopes. Thank you.'"

11 Adolescence—Ages Thirteen to Eighteen: What to Expect in the Way of Maturity and Responsibility

Adolescence, as we know it today, is a concept that came into being only around the beginning of the twentieth century. Prior to that time, children began to take on heavy manual work in the factories or on the farms by the age of ten or twelve. Most left school by the age of fourteen or fifteen and married by sixteen or seventeen. The transition from childhood to adulthood occurred at an early age, and there was no time for an "in-between" age. Social philosopher David Bakan asserts that it was new legislation enacted around the beginning of this century to protect children that created a time for adolescence. Specifically, these laws prevented child labor until the age of sixteen, required compulsory schooling (usually to the age of sixteen as well), and brought about the juvenile court system. The new court system protected adolescents from harsh judicial consequences and segregated them from adult offenders, usually until the age of seventeen.

This new legislation then created a time for children from thirteen to sixteen to grow and mature without having to take on the responsibilities of adulthood. The age of sixteen is still a marker event today in that most laws on the books still require adolescents to be sixteen in order to drop out of school, to work a full-time job, to drive a car, or to marry. At seventeen, adolescents can, under certain conditions, declare themselves "emancipated" and move out of the parental home to be self-supporting and can join the military. At eighteen, they can vote and make their own health and financial decisions. These marker ages, however, are only the earliest legal age allowed in our society. In reality, most adolescents remain financially and emotionally dependent on their families until the age of eighteen to twenty-one. In many cases, they remain so until well into their mid-twenties (more about this in chapter 13). Adolescence has come to mean a special in-between age in which youngsters have an opportunity to enjoy life while putting off adulthood as long as possible.

These social changes over the past one hundred years have brought about a now very extended period of time, perhaps as long as ten years, in which children are physically and sexually mature yet financially and emotionally dependent on their parents. It has become a time of increasing freedom and experimentation with adult privileges at increasingly younger ages. Children today, in fact, are maturing physically faster than they did at the turn of the century, reaching puberty about two years earlier than they did in 1900. Some researchers suggest that teens are experimenting with sex about two years earlier than they used to because of this downward trend in physical maturation. Along with this earlier maturation, teens are first experimenting with alcohol and drugs at earlier ages as well.

Many social researchers have noticed a trend toward increasing "social segregation" for adolescents. Whereas in the past, teens spent most of their time in integrated groups where there were people of all ages (such as extended families, apprenticeship work, and family farms), they now spend almost all of their time only with other teens. This lengthening of adolescence, combined with increasing segregation of adolescents, has come to make them a subgroup of society. The term "youth culture" has been coined to describe what is now not just simply an age but a segment of the population that has its own taste in clothing, hairstyles, music, television, and movies. This group has its own language, its own values, and its own heroes, apart from mainstream adult life. In fact, advertisers direct their products toward this narrow subgroup, which is known to have the highest per capita amount of expendable income in the nation.

This lengthening of adolescence, combined with earlier puberty and experimentation at earlier ages, greater affluence, and the separateness of the youth culture, has led to unique problems for families of adolescents in the 1990s. For the majority of American teenagers, the protective legislation that created adolescence and the social trends that have lengthened it have been a great boon. Adolescents now have eight to ten years in which to finish their education, train for a career, and develop a sense of identity before entering adulthood. More adolescents than ever are completing high school and pursuing a college education. Because of their increased affluence, adolescents now have a degree of freedom and material comfort that was unknown in the 1950s and 1960s. For example, owning a car has come to be an expected event among middle-class adolescents. In fact, many middle-class teens expect to have a private bedroom, a personal stereo, a personal television, and a personal telephone as well—possessions that were unthinkable forty years ago. And, finally, the emergence of the youth culture has provided opportunities for adolescents to socialize and identify with peers for several years, establishing a strong support network for themselves before they leave home.

For overindulgent families, however, the problems seem compounded. The increased dependency of underdeveloped teenagers makes separating from their families very difficult. Conflict escalates in these families. It seems that only by rejecting the parent can the adolescent assert that she does not need her parent. Yet adolescents in these families cannot face the responsibilities and the tasks of young adulthood either. John Conger has written, "The overindulged child as he approaches adolescence may find the society's unwillingness to provide a like degree of indulgence frustrating." Not only do they meet with frustration in this way, but their poor coping skills do not prepare them for mature ways to handle stressful situations or make difficult decisions. They vacillate back and forth between seeking dependency on parents and fighting with parents to try to separate from them.

The wealth of material possessions these teens have (even in lower-middle-class families) makes the prospect of enduring the relative poverty of college life unappealing. In addition to this, the increased affluence and freedom of adolescents in overindulgent families is seldom tied to increased responsibility, as it is in more well-adjusted families. Expectations and standards of behavior are particularly hazy in these families, which only adds to the confusion of the adolescent who now lives in a society where there is virtually no moral compass to serve as a guide. This array of choices and opportunities that are not tied to future consequences is bewildering and at times overwhelming. The possibilities for the adolescent to make poor decisions that carry life-altering negative consequences, while great in all American families, is even greater in overindulgent families.

Even more so than in middle childhood, parenting teenagers calls for an authoritative style of parenting. Conger cites a large body of research that indicates that adolescents in authoritative homes are seen as more active, outgoing, socially assertive, and independent, as well as friendly, creative, and less hostile toward themselves and others. Teenagers in families who allow democratic participation in rule making and who promote autonomy are far more likely to consider their parents to be "fair and reasonable" in their rules than teenagers in authoritarian or permissive families.

Other studies have found that when parents express strong interest in and knowledge about their teenagers' opinions and activities and promote independence and active participation in family affairs, their adolescent children develop very high confidence and self-esteem. While the adolescent's peer group is often a powerful force in her life, the relative importance of peer group influence varies from one teenager to another. Studies show that adolescents are much more influenced by their peers when the quality of the relationship with parents is poor, when self-esteem is low, when they feel criticized and rejected at home, and when they feel there is little encouragement and support at home. Typically, in these same unsupportive homes, discipline and control are low, and the parents' own values and behaviors are inconsistent, unrealistic, or hypocritical.

It is not surprising, therefore, that teenagers from overindulgent families—who are less autonomous and whose relationship with their parents is often a tumultuous one, shifting back and forth between dependence and hostility—are much more vulnerable to the negative influence of their peer group. In fact, these teens often choose for a peer group that group of teens who are like them—unhappy, angry, dependent on peer approval, and unsuccessful at school and at home.

Since early psychologists (G. Stanley Hall, for one) coined the term "adolescence" around the beginning of this century, they have been seeking to describe that pattern of psychological change that makes up adolescence as well. We know that a child begins adolescence as a twelve-year-old and very much a child, but somehow emerges from this period an eighteen-year-old, or a twenty-one-year-old, who is psychologically an adult. But what, exactly, goes on in between? What are the developmental tasks of adolescence? The parent who knows will not only survive the child's adolescence with a bit of equanimity and objectivity but can also facilitate this process by nudging the adolescent toward accomplishment of these tasks.

First, there is the adjustment to the physical changes of puberty.

This is probably the most universal task of adolescence, and the least dependent on culture. Physical puberty is accomplished by most girls by the age of fourteen and by most boys by fifteen. Adolescents continue to grow in height and weight, however, until the age of eighteen. Boys continue to grow facial hair as well. All parents know that these changes are awkward and full of opportunity for embarrassment. Children who physically mature earlier have higher self-esteem and are looked up to more by their peers. They often have positions of leadership among their peers. Those who lag physically often lag emotionally and socially as well. Both situations present problems for teenagers, in that the early-maturing girl may not be emotionally ready for male attention, and the late-maturing boy may be harassed and bullied by stronger males. Somehow, over the course of adolescence, things even out. Late maturers catch up, teenagers become accepting of their physical changes, and they learn to cope with the changes in how other people view them as well.

A second developmental task of adolescence is the achievement of an increased sense of control over inner states. The adolescent's sense of control improves on two levels. One is impulse control. Children from the age of two are learning to control impulses, beginning with such primitive impulses as urination and hitting and biting. Learning to control impulses sometimes continues throughout a person's life. Adolescents are expected to anticipate not just the short-term consequences of their acts but the long-term consequences as well. The ante is raised for teenagers because the stakes are higher as well. The results of a casual sexual encounter in the nineties include not only pregnancy and disease but dying of AIDS.

On another level, adolescents are expected to gain better control of strong and powerful emotions. This expectation comes at a time when, due to complex hormonal and emotional changes, emotions are running at an all-time high. Frustration is intense. Rejection is devastating. Wants and needs are overwhelming. An adolescent boy called our office late one night years ago, feeling suicidal because he failed to make the basketball team. An anorexic teenage girl said to me recently, "I just have to be a model. I would starve myself, do anything, to be a model." Somehow the adolescent must go from being dominated by powerful emotions to having them effectively under control by adulthood. And by controlling emotions, we mean not suppressing them but being fully aware of them and taking action to express them in appropriate and socially acceptable ways.

Psychologists call the third developmental task "separation and individuation." By this we mean that an adolescent comes to see himself more as an individual and less as an extension of his family. He no longer relies on his parents for help with every problem, for direction in making every decision. He no longer views his parents as confidants. Instead, he places more value on the opinions of his peers and the opinions of other adults outside the family. He is selective about what he shares with his parents and seeks their opinion on only those issues where he feels they have special knowledge. In many cases, hopefully, he comes to rely on his own ideas or plans to choose a course of action. He decides he's ready to be left home alone at night when his parents go out and that a sitter would be ridiculous, even though he's a little nervous about it. He is no longer interested in going to restaurants with his parents—it's embarrassing. It makes him feel as though he's his parents' child and has no friends of his own. He'll go to the movies with his parents, but only if he and a friend can sit apart from them.

The separating adolescent maintains a "secret" life apart from his parents. He's involved in activities that they don't know about and in many cases are better off not knowing about. Privacy is sacred to the individuating adolescent, and the sanctity of his private room is inviolable. Not only must his room decor diverge from family standards, but he demands that no one go in there. Private phone calls are highly valued as well. Mom's or little sister's listening in on the extension is grounds for all-out warfare.

A fourth developmental task is that of establishing effective and meaningful relationships with peers. This occurs in two phases. First, the adolescent must learn to establish intimate and enduring friendships with same-sex peers. Adolescent same-sex friendships are qualitatively more intense than those of middle childhood, and they should be. This intensity and commitment to a friendship is a preview of the kind of intense and committed bond one makes in a marriage. She may be willing to break family rules to help a friend, even get into trouble to show her loyalty to a friend. She will put her own needs aside and cancel her plans to study for an exam, for example, in order to spend three hours on the phone with a friend who is upset. While this may irk parents and seem misguided, it is normal and healthy to a degree 'and needs to be understood for what it is. Overindulgent parents who have a codependent relationship with an adolescent, as we saw in chapter 5, have an especially hard time coping with this developmental task of adolescence.

The second phase of this task is the development of an intense and intimate relationship with an opposite-sex peer. Many adolescents view this attainment as a mark of social status and seek to eliminate the first phase of this task by going directly into phase two—steady dating—at age thirteen or fourteen. While it may yield some immediate status within a peer group, especially for the early-maturing girl who is getting interest from mature older boys, there is much that is lost in bypassing the same-sex bonding. She needs to first learn with her best friend how to cope with rejection and jealousy, when to trust and when not to trust, what to share and what not to share, when loyalty is in the best interests of one or both people, and when loyalty is ultimately self-destructive to both.

A fifth task in adolescence is the development of a sense of identity. While many have written about this, it is somewhat difficult to describe just what an "identity" is. We know that when we ask a sixth grader to describe himself, he is more likely to relate rather superficial aspects of his lifestyle—from to his appearance to his activities—than he is to describe internal qualities.

For example, a sixth grader might say, "I'm in Boy Scouts. I like to go camping. My friends are in Scouts, too. My dad takes us on canoeing trips. I like baseball, too. I collect New York Yankees cards. School is okay. I like some of the teachers. History is pretty interesting."

An older adolescent, when asked to describe himself, might say, "I'm pretty quiet actually. I have two friends who are real solid, but I don't talk to just everybody. I have to get to know you first. But once I trust you, then I'm really loyal. I'm really good in science and math. I like them because they have practical applications. You can do things to help people or make their lives better with science and math. I have a ham radio and I like to talk to people late at night. I guess it suits me, because I'm kind of a loner and it involves electronics. I've been thinking about joining the Coast Guard. I like the idea of patrolling our coastlines and aiding boats in distress."

Related to the development of a sense of identity is the task of preparing for an occupation. By tenth or eleventh grade, most students have made some decisions about whether they're interested in and capable of doing college work or whether they're more interested in learning the practical skills involved in learning a trade. In healthy, well-adjusted adolescents, these decisions are made realistically and based on the evidence at hand. A sixteen-year-old who is bored with school but enjoys working summers in the building business with his uncle knows he is destined for a trade. A girl who relishes writing term papers for English class and whose idea of a good time is hanging out at a bookstore knows she would probably be a good college student and enjoy college life. Parents facilitate this process by providing diverse opportunities for adolescents to experience many kinds of paid and volunteer work or to excel at a sport or musical or artistic talent. In this process of trying out new skills, being around other adult role models, and getting constant feedback about how they are doing, adolescents derive a sense of vocational identity. They also gain a sense of the persistence they will need and what obstacles lie ahead.

Overindulgent parents hamper this process in a number of ways. They tend to have unrealistic goals for an adolescent, goals forged out of love and concern but lacking in any realistic basis. For example, the parents may say, "She's going to a college and we can pay for a good one. We want her to have the best chance at a good education," when their daughter has a C-minus average and has no interest in college work. In fact, their daughter may have no idea what she is good at or what she wants to do. Her parents have set a goal for her that is based more on what will make them feel like good parents than upon her abilities and interests.

Furthermore, overindulgent parents, by setting goals for their children, typically take over the tasks of achieving the goal for them as well, and the adolescent does not know how to get from A to Z. The seventeen-year-old girl may say, "I'm going to be a nurse. Mom says they make good money and you can always get a job as a nurse," when in fact, she has D-minus in Biology, hates science, and does not know what kinds of prerequisites and SAT scores nursing schools require or where to get an application. Overindulgent parents have often pro-tected adolescents from these problems, choosing to view adolescence as a special time that should be free of worry and strain, a time for having fun and getting a little wild, a last hurrah before adulthood.

These six tasks of adolescence have been grouped in roughly

chronological order. The parent of the early adolescent does well to recognize that the fourteen-year-old is struggling with the issues of coping with his new body, separating from his parents, bonding with his peer group, and controlling strong emotions. The healthy parent not only allows this process but facilitates the fourteenyear-old's emotional growth in just these directions. The seventeen year old, on the other hand, hopefully has mastered some of these tasks. She, most likely, is trying to establish a sense of identity apart from her peer group and her family, is preparing for a vocational identity, and is learning to establish an intimate loving relationship with someone. Hopefully, she is looking ahead to the future and trying out different pictures of who she is and will be.

Ages Thirteen to Fifteen

Early adolescence is a time that many parents compare to the "terrible twos." Not that twos are terrible, nor are young teenagers. But many parents recall the time when their toddler learned to walk and was full of energy and enthusiasm for life. Early teens are like those toddlers in that they do have this tremendous need to venture out and explore, with very little sense of the danger of what they are exploring. They do see themselves as more separate now from Mom and Dad, more able to function on their own away from home, more capable, and more independent. They swing wildly from ridiculously defiant bids for independence to childlike dependency. I'll always remember one defiant thirteen-year-old who insisted she be able to move out and get her own apartment. When her mother insisted she couldn't, she countered with, "Then can I have a hamster?" She may demand to date an eighteen-year-old boy one day and ask her mom to braid her hair for her the next.

Edward Martin writes about his experience as a teacher—first of high school students, then of junior high students. The first difference he noticed was the increased energy of early adolescents. This energy, he writes, was not a controlled sort of energy but a general "twitchiness," an impulsive kind of energy that was seen in wiggling bodies, turning heads, bouncing, jiggling, and squirming. He found them to be intensely enthusiastic. They embraced causes and new interests immediately and intensely, then lost interest just as quickly.

Martin also describes the "discontentedness" of early adolescence.

Young adolescents begin to question and challenge all manner of adult authority and social institutions. They want to know why they have to take certain courses, why the school makes rules against gum chewing, why they can't go to the mall unsupervised. They are often rude, sullen, unhappy, and out of sorts with everything and everybody.

Physical fights are common in middle school or junior high school, among girls as well as boys. Rude and defiant stances toward teachers reach a peak among this age group. Children band together in tight groups at this age, and they can be merciless in taunting and teasing some boy or girl they've selected for harassment. In fact, having a knack for cruelty may give a young teen a measure of social status in his peer group. Because of this, skipping school or getting a stomachache in order to avoid going to school is more prevalent at this age than many parents realize.

And, finally, fear is a strong component of life for early adolescents. Much of it is hidden and never expressed to parents. There is the undeveloped boy's fear of taking a shower in front of other boys in gym class. There is the girl's fear of getting her period at school and everyone knowing about it. There is the general fear of going in to the lunchroom and having no one to sit with. Most would rather go hungry than take the risk of appearing to be a social outcast. There is the fear of not understanding a dirty joke, or not knowing how to kiss, and being a "total geek." This intense fear may manifest itself in an irritability and grumpiness that may seem inexplicable to parents.

This sudden demand for independence and older-adolescent privileges, along with this angry defiance and irritability, makes new demands on parents. They will have to formulate some general approach to these issues that will make sense to the young teenager, though it may never make her happy. Also, the parent will have to hold the line on these issues with a firmness and consistency that will tax the best of parents. This is no time for a parent to be overindulgent, overly emotionally involved, or unable to set limits. The early adolescent whose moods shift wildly from one day to the next needs to know that the adults in charge will hold the course. She needs to see that there are firm yet reasonable boundaries, beyond which she cannot go. The steadiness of her parents will help her to achieve some measure of internal steadiness.

Because she will challenge authority and demand explanations, her parents must be ready to provide simple, straightforward explanations yet not get bogged down in defending themselves under an onslaught of verbal attacks. They must be able to demonstrate a link between increasing responsibility and increasing freedom. When the young adolescent abuses a freedom or a privilege, it must be revoked—but only temporarily. The parent who screams, "You'll never be allowed to see those kids again," or "You're grounded forever," loses all respect. Not only will she not be able to enforce these consequences, but she will look foolish and overly emotional to her teenager. After a few days, her daughter will ask her mother to give her "just one more chance" to prove she can handle a situation. She may ask her father to give her friends "another chance" to show that they're basically good kids. Parents do well do anticipate this and to provide a means for the young teen to dig herself (and her friends) out of the hole she has just dug for herself.

In terms of self-help and independence, young teens should be quite self-sufficient in a wide variety of ways. Remember that in preindustrial nations, children at this age do nearly all the work the adults do. That is not necessarily good, but it does give the parent something to think about. Young teenagers should be capable of doing almost all household chores and, in fact, should be able to do them without having to be told. They should be able to clean the bathroom, run the vacuum, and mow and rake the lawn quite adequately. They should be able to do some simple shopping errands for the family and cook a simple meal once a week. They should be able to run the dishwasher, the washing machine, and the dryer adequately. In fact, fourteen or fifteen is a good age for an adolescent to be in charge of his clothes altogether.

Bedtime should not be an issue, as young teens should know by now how much sleep they need and go up to bed on their own. Similarly, getting up should not be a problem. They are fully capable of setting an alarm clock and getting up on their own. Having to make them turn off the television and get to bed and having to harrass them to get up in the morning is a sign of immaturity and should be dealt with.

Hygiene should no longer be an issue, since the self-consciousness of adolescents is a strong incentive to bathe often and care for one's hair and fingernails. While some adolescents may take great pride in their room and put a lock on their door to keep everyone out, for others the room becomes a visual manifestation of the internal confusion that they feel. It may be littered with once-worn clothes, Coke cans and snack wrappers, and half-finished homework not turned in. A parent might want to link the care of the room with ownership of a television or a stereo or new clothes. Example: "If you can't take care of the clothes you have, then I can't see buying you any more new clothes. Clearly, you've got more than you can handle." Example: "Your room is a disaster. Yet you want a stereo for your room, and next year you want us to get you a car. Frankly, I can't see that you'll be able to take care of a stereo, much less a car, when you can't take care of what you have already."

Homework should not be an issue at this age. Young teens should be capable of keeping up with homework and studying for exams that are scheduled weeks in advance, as well as projects that may take a month to complete. Some parents of children this age still feel they must monitor all homework, organize their fourteen-year-old's projects by putting the due dates on a calendar, and have her bring home an initialed assignment sheet from each teacher each week. While it may work, the young teenager who is pushing away from parents resents this supervision deeply.

Instead, it makes more sense to have periodic discussions about her failure to organize her time well, stay on track, and get work completed. Ask her what she is doing with her free time. Explore with her in an interested way the whole issue of getting organized, planning in advance, and budgeting her time. Example: "I've noticed you watching TV a lot lately and putting off homework till the last minute, then staying up late to finish it. Then you don't get enough sleep and you nod out during biology. So you come home and take a nap and call up Deanne to find out what happened in biology. Then you and Deanne end up talking for two hours. It seems you've lost control of the whole homework thing along the way. Where do you think you need to make some changes? I don't want to put you on some kind of schedule. You're too big for that. But I would like to see you work this out. In fact, I'll help you. Tonight will be a no-TV night and a no-phone night so that you can concentrate on working up a written plan. You can call it 'Getting Control of My Homework and My Time' or 'My Homework

Plan for the Next Thirty Days' or something like that. We'll start phasing in the TV and phone use when it seems like your plan is starting to work for you."

Young teenagers should be able to take on a position of leadership with younger siblings and be willing to help them with small tasks such as getting dressed, picking up their room, and putting away their toys. They should be able to monitor younger children at home after school to some degree. Taking on this leadership role should be noted and rewarded by parents. Continue to hold family meetings from time to time. Be willing to give the young teen a stronger vote than the younger children. Be willing to allow him to chair the meeting from time to time. Encourage his participation in a church youth group that performs a community service for younger children. Suggest he tutor a younger or disadvantaged child at the elementary school. Some summer camps may have junior camp counselor positions for fourteen- and fifteen-year-olds.

Many parents are willing to pay a fourteen-year-old to supervise his nine-year-old sibling after school, figuring it's better to keep the money in the family than to pay an outside sitter. If they do, this may create resentment on the part of the younger child. To compensate for this, the parent might suggest the teenager pay the younger child a small portion of his baby-sitting income in return for good behavior. Other parents strongly object to paying a teenager to do what they feel he should do out of obligation to the family. While this viewpoint has some merit as well, these parents have to be prepared for the teenager to feel angry and exploited unless they compensate the teenager in some nonmonetary way for the valuable contribution he makes to the family through his free baby-sitting.

Money is an area for expanded opportunities for responsibility as well. Because the teenager is doing more around the house and yard, he should be entitled to a higher allowance. He also now has some limited opportunity to hold down a job outside the home as well. Many fourteen- and fifteen-year-olds are permitted to work as long as they are not around alcohol, do not work late into the night, and work a limited number of hours. It is important, however, to provide guidelines for the use of this increased wealth. If you did not do so in middle childhood, now is the time to insist that the teen use this money to provide for his own books, records, movies, recreation, and special clothing needs. Insist that he have a plan for saving a portion of this income for later use. This is not too early to begin saving for a portion of the cost of a car. You may want to begin now, if you haven't yet, to insist that he put aside a portion of this money for a church or other charitable donation.

Early adolescence is a good time for a young person to open a checking account or a savings account at the bank. Many banks now have minimums on these small accounts, and you may want to help with the start-up. It is a good way to familiarize the adolescent with concepts such as service charges, interest rates, and monthly statements. It gets across the idea that she can't just write a check whenever she wants something—penalties are stiff for being overdrawn. This is a good time also for helping her to invest in the stock market. Help her to buy a small amount of shares in her favorite consumer stock, e.g., The Gap or Burger King or Time Warner, and track her stock in the newspaper. Both these activities offer lessons in delay of gratification that parents find impossible to get across to teens through lecturing and arguing.

Early adolescents are capable of abstract thinking to a degree greater than that of children in middle childhood. In fact, it is because of this, some theorists say, that they are more rebellious. They are capable of imagining things they've not yet encountered. They are capable of grappling with abstract ideals. They are able to conceptualize what a perfect parent would be, compare their parents to that standard, and find fault with them. They are capable of arguing an issue from several points of view. Thus, they are able to come back at the parent with an argument for almost everything.

Because of this ability to grapple with abstract ideas, this is a time when values are being formed in a more independent way, and when moral concepts become interesting. Young teenagers enjoy arguing about what is right and wrong, however misinformed or limited their information is. Rather than resent this endless debating or resort to preaching, parents do well to encourage and facilitate the development of moral beliefs at this age. From time to time, have your teenager get out a sheet of paper and write down, "My Code of Ethics." Have him list ten points and be prepared to explain and justify each one. If he can't think of any, give him a few to get started. Examples: "Don't lie to a friend. Don't talk about a friend behind their back. Don't do things that abuse your body." Ask him to give examples of decisions he's made which demonstrate how he is living up to these principles. When he disappoints you, have him get out his Code of Ethics and think about where he went wrong.

Another exercise, suggested by Linda and Richard Eyre, is to have her periodically sort out what her priorities are. For example, you might, through discussion with her, list some areas of importance in her life, such as the following:

1. Have a lot of friends, be popular

2. Have money.

3. Be healthy.

4. Have a boyfriend.

5. Be really good at something.

6. Make good grades.

7. Get along with my family.

8. Look good.

9. Be honest and loyal to my friends.

10. Have nice clothes and possessions.

Put these on note cards and have her sort them from number one in importance to number ten. Ask her to explain why she sorted them in the way she did. Ask her what situations have been tough lately because they put two priorities in conflict with each other. How did she solve it? Did she like the way she solved it? If not, why? How would she handle it next time?

Because early adolescents are challenging parental authority and separating from parents, much of the struggle between them centers around bids for independence. As was stated earlier, independence must be linked to responsibility and to natural and logical consequences. Teenagers will not respond to an authoritarian stance of "This is the rule and that's that." As we saw in the previous chapter, children begin to question authority and respond selectively to authority figures around the age of ten. This is not rebellious or disrespectful but is a sign of emotional and cognitive growth and maturity.

Ages Sixteen to Eighteen

Middle adolescents, those finishing high school, hopefully, and about to leave home, are typically a happier and more contented group than early adolescents. Some of the extreme sensitivity about their body, the painful awkwardness is gone, and they seem at home in their body. Some have actually acquired a level of poise and sophistication about how they carry themselves. While they may be shy and tentative about dating, most feel secure with their peers and have established a group of friends with whom they feel comfortable.

Middle teenagers, as a group, are less angry, less irritable, and less moody. They are more introspective and thoughtful. They have established their ability to function independently of their parents and to get around in the world on their own. Their thoughts are focused more on the world outside the home. What will my life be like? Will someone love me? Will I be a success or a failure? Do I believe in God?

Like the thoughtful fours and fives who follow the terrible twos, these older adolescents are more aware of danger, are more cautious. They chafe under rules but, by and large, see the need for them and are willing to accept them if they see them as reasonable and well-intentioned. Many have figured out that the angry outbursts, the defiant stances, and the acting out really got them nowhere. Whereas a fourteen-year-old will say, "My only problem is my mom. She won't get off my case. She's always got to know where I am. It's my life," a sixteen-year-old who is mature will say, "My mom always has to know where I am. I could argue with her, but it's easier to just call her and tell her. Really, I don't mind it too much. I know she cares about me."

Mature teenagers in this age range also show a greater ability to exert control over their emotions and sort out coherent, well-planned solutions to problems. Cindy Hanson, a researcher in San Diego, investigated coping skills in teenagers with diabetes. She found that teens who coped poorly with their diabetes were those who used "ventilating feelings" and avoidance to deal with stress. Randall Jorgensen and Jerome Dusek of Syracuse University found very similar results in their study of 331 late adolescents. They found that students who coped poorly with stress were those whose coping efforts seem to come under the heading of "stress palliation." Both sets of researchers defined "ventilating feelings" as yelling, swearing, blaming others for their problems, saying mean things, and complaining loudly. Avoiding problems was described similarly by both authors as using drugs, alcohol, overeating and binging, and escaping into music or fantasy to escape one's problems. On another level, it also included denying or minimizing their problems, daydreaming about the way things ought to be, and avoiding people or situations that caused strong uncomfortable emotions—e.g., not doing homework, skipping classes, withdrawing from school altogether, quitting the team, watching the soaps in the afternoon instead of trying to get a job, running away, and, ultimately, suicide.

These poor coping styles are characteristic of underdeveloped teenagers who are immature and functioning more like early adolescents. Mature adolescents are more likely to use the ten healthy coping methods listed by Hanson. These are:

1. Seeking diversions
2. Developing self-reliance and optimism
3. Developing social support
4. Solving family problems
5. Seeking spiritual help
6. Investing in close friends
7. Seeking professional support
8. Engaging in demanding activity
9. Being humorous
10. Relaxing

For example, an eighteen-year-old girl is diagnosed with petit mal seizures. She is told she may not be able to drive a car or go swimming for the forseeable future. She might develop self-reliance and optimism ("I guess I'd better plan to live in a big city where I can get around on the bus"). She might invest in close friends ("I guess I'll try to find friends who have cars"). She might seek spiritual help ("Somehow I feel a spiritual kinship with all people who are handicapped in some way"). A sixteen-year-old boy is anxious about taking his driver's exam because he has had trouble with parallel parking. He might seek a diversion (play his drums to get his mind off it), be humorous (watch some cartoons on the morning of the exam), or engage in a demanding activity (play some tennis afterward to unwind). A fourteen-year-old girl finds it painfully difficult to tolerate being alone. She might write in her diary, talk to her mother about it, call a friend in another state, or ask for professional help.

In summary, you can expect your older adolescent to have accomplished the earlier developmental tasks of adolescence: coping with a changing body, controlling her emotions, separating from the family, and finding a peer group. At this stage of development, she should be investing more energy toward the later tasks: developing a coherent identity, preparing for work or career, and falling in love in its earliest and most faltering forms. The authors Phyllis York and Ted Wachtel of *Toughlove* have written that adolescence is a time of emptiness, a time of clearing away the trappings of childhood to make room for the self that is to come. But what will the new self be? This emptiness, this longing to be something, to have something of one's own, is a natural feeling for this age. Mature adolescents can tolerate it without an excessive amount of ventilation and avoidance. They go out into the world to experience it, and it is by experiencing it, by working, taking courses in school, participating in clubs, and having friends, that they gradually acquire a self that is coherent and understandable.

This is an age when parents lament, "They're never home. When he turned sixteen and got a car, he left. We hardly see him now. This has become a hotel where he comes back to sleep at night." Hopefully, he is gone because he is going out to encounter the world and define himself.

Because middle and older teens are looking forward to what they will be and do out in the world, it is important to discuss with them, from time to time, their plans for the future. Many overindulgent parents put little pressure on their adolescents to make future plans, figuring, "He's so young still, he's got plenty of time." Yet when their teenager gets into trouble, they often will say, "He just gives no thought about his future at all. I guess he figures that after high school, something will just magically happen."

Most parents, even overindulgent parents, eventually try to make some attempt at helping the teenager plan for his future. Many parents go about this by starting out with, "Why don't you..." or "I've been thinking over what you should do after high school, and I think you should..." Generally, this goes over poorly. The teenager will resist someone else imposing their ideas on him as to what he should do with his life. An approach that works better is to begin early with your adolescent to help him set goals for himself and to review those goals with him on a regular basis.

Approach it this way: "It's been a while since we talked about your goals. Let's go out for a pizza Friday and talk. I want you to be ready to tell me what your one-year goals are, your one-month goals, and your next two weeks goals. Better yet, have them on paper and you get to make the selection on dinner." This method conveys interest on the part of the parent, shows respect for the teenager, and lets him know that you have the confidence in his ability to set his own goals. Discuss with him examples of your own goals. Offer examples. Point out what you feel he excels in or where he shows a natural ability. Be willing to have him come to work with you or go to work with a friend of yours. Be ready to assist wherever you can, but be careful not to take over or to criticize unnecessarily.

Examples of one-year goals:

a. Bring my grade-point average up to a 3.0.

b. Decide which college to go to.

c. Save up $1,000 for college.

d. Buy my own car.

e. Get a music scholarship.

Examples of one-month goals:

a. Bring my biology grade up from a D to a B.

b. Visit one college.

c. Put $100 in my bank account.

d. Go with mom to some used car dealerships.

e. Completely learn a difficult piece on the piano.

Examples of one- or two-week goals:

a. Study biology one hour each day.

b. Call my cousin at college and ask about spending a weekend with her.

c. Put twenty-five dollars in the bank.

d. Read a *Consumer Reports* article on used Toyotas.

e. Practice piano one hour every day.

Lastly, encourage or provide incentives for your teenager to get involved in community service. Middle and late adolescence can be a somber time, and teenagers who are maturing and leaving home in the 1990s are more gloomy and pessimistic than teenagers were in the fifties and sixties. David Elkind has written that a major shift in our national outlook has occurred in the last twenty years. While we used to feel that progress was good and life was getting better, we now feel that progress for the most part is bad, science has failed us, life is getting worse, and the future looks doubtful. Teenagers who are on the brink of adulthood feel this gloominess acutely. Job prospects are poor, pollution is ruining our planet, crime is worsening, and "if you have sex, you'll die of AIDS," as one sixteen-year-old said to me recently.

It is the commitment to community service, perhaps more than anything else, that can give a teen a sense that people are basically good, that they care about each other, and that one teenager can make a small difference somewhere, somehow. It also provides a counter to some of the natural narcissism to which teenagers are prone. Beginning with the 1988 graduating class, students in the Atlanta, Georgia, public high schools must provide seventy-five hours of volunteer service to their community before graduating. Parents do well to make this a requirement also, if it is not already required by their local school system. Shelters for the homeless, hospitals and nursing homes, the YMCA and the YWCA, the Boys Club, and government-subsidized day care centers are examples of some agencies open to teen volunteers.

12 Adolescence–Ages Thirteen to Eighteen: New Approaches for Achieving Responsibility

Problem Area 1: Getting Up in the Morning and to Bed at Night

"Our problem is our seventeen-year-old son. He just can't get up in the morning. I guess it's because he stays up so late, watching TV or talking to his girlfriend on the phone. I go in his room to wake him in the morning for school and he's downright surly and rude. I have tried to pull him out of the bed, and he shoved me. I have to drive him to school when he's late and I really resent it. Still, he had an excessive number of *Tardys* on his report card this semester. For a while there, he had his girlfriend calling him in the morning, but he argued with her when she would call, and wouldn't be ready when she came to pick him up, so she gave up on him. On the weekends, he is supposed to be at McDonald's at six o'clock to open up, and he has slept through that, too. I'm afraid he'll be suspended from school or lose his job."

A key phrase in the statement above is "I have to drive him to school when he's late." This is a signal that a parent is overindulgent. Often the first step is getting a parent to listen to the language they use and to change their language. Parents do not "have to" rescue a teenager from his irresponsible behavior. Parents may choose to rescue their teenager out of:

- A need to feel needed by their teenager
- The sense of importance they get when their teenager is dependent on them
- Discomfort with their teenager's strong negative emotions

Teenagers are capable of going to bed at a reasonable time and getting up in the morning at a reasonable time. If they choose not to do these simple things, then it is up to the parent to provide some sort of reasonable consequences. A parent can choose to drive the teenager to school but charge a taxi fee. A taxi fee would be whatever a taxi driver might charge. Better yet, the parent, who might well be a working parent, can write down the phone number of a local taxi company, post it on the teenager's door, and go on to work.

Underdeveloped teens will try to blame the problem on the parent. Example: "It's your fault. You didn't wake me up. You know I can't get up to an alarm clock." Or they might blame the problem on someone else. "It's Angie's fault. I told her to call me at six-thirty, to wake me up, and she forgot." In order to cope with this avoidance strategy, you must frame the responsibility for the problem in an appropriate manner. Whether it is getting up in the morning, getting the dates and times for the SAT, or finding out how much summer school costs, your stock response needs to be, "Who owns the problem?"

Faced with ownership of the problem, your teenager may sleep through and get there late or not at all. He may get an excessive number of *Tardys* and may even get suspended. When he complains, keep coming back with, "Who owns the problem?" When he complains that because he was suspended, he'll have to go to summer school in order to graduate on time, keep coming back with, "Who owns the problem?" When he is upset because the only way he can pay for summer school is to miss a car payment, you know what to say. You might also add, from previous chapters, "What's your plan?" The point is that it is best to avoid arguing, justifying, or apologizing. Stick with these two stock phrases to emphasize that he is the master of his destiny and you have faith that he can solve the problem.

Problem Area 2: Excessive Use of the Phone

"Our problem is our daily battles with our fifteen-year-old daughter over the telephone. You'd think her link to her friends was the very breath of life itself. Our calls don't come through, and we can't get to the phone to call out. We installed call waiting, but when our calls come in, she just tells the person on the other end to call back later. When we ask her to get off the phone for a while, she is rude and sarcastic to us. She says she will get off in 'just a minute,' but that minute takes half an hour. Some friends of ours just gave in and installed a private phone line in their daughter's room to solve the problem, but then they rarely ever saw her again. She stayed up in her room with the door shut, on the phone, all night. As bad as it sounds, we're considering that as our next option."

Many parents of teenagers go about the phone problem in the same way they handled simpler problems when the children were younger. They wait awhile, then order, "Get off the phone so your mother can use it," then expect immediate compliance. This method—giving orders and expecting immediate obedience—will not work with teenagers. Parents need to establish "contracts" with them around the phone and many other areas of conflict in order to gain their compliance. They need to run many aspects of the household in a democratic, participatory manner by this age if not before. I have seen many so-called contracts parents have worked up with teenagers that were not really contracts at all. They were lists of rules and consequences that the parent wrote and gave to the teenager, something like the following:

Rule	Consequence
Household members age 13 to 15 can make 2 phone calls and can receive 2 phone calls per day.	If teenager exceeds this limit, phone usage will be revoked for the following day.

A contract is an *agreement* between two parties as to what each is expected to do. Both parties must participate and have a voice in setting the terms. It must be seen as fair and reasonable to both parties. Both parties must feel that they are getting something they want out of the deal. The following is a phone contract:

Teen	Parent
Teen will keep phone calls to 30 minutes and will politely end call if family member needs to use phone. Teen will limit calls to 4 per day and end calls by 9 P.M. If fails to do so, will apologize and forfeit phone use for 2 days.	Parent will allow teenager privacy when using phone. Parent will be courteous to teen's friends when they call and take messages when the teenager is away. If fails to do so, will apologize.

While some parents may see the second contract as catering to the teenager, the second contract is far more likely to be adhered to and much less likely to generate conflict. It is an agreement based on mutual reciprocity that incorporates respect for both parties. The parent gains access to the phone and an avoidance of arguments. The teenager gains some privacy and a guarantee of access to her friends.

Problem Area 3: Use of the Car

"We are concerned about our son. He is fifteen and a half and is eager to be driving soon. In fact, he has told us what car he expects to get on his birthday. All his friends got a car on their sixteenth birthdays. But, frankly, he's so immature and irresponsible, that we're scared to death for him to have a car. I think his getting a car soon would be a disaster, but we just don't know how to say no to him."

One area of struggle for parents of middle adolescents is naturally going to be the car. It has become a rite of passage in our society now to obtain a driver's license on one's sixteenth birthday, and in many places, it has come to be seen as a right as well to receive the first car the same day. This is a measure of our growing affluence that would have been unthinkable twenty-five years ago. In fact, in many suburban areas, just any old car won't do, it must be a new car and a nice one. Over-indulgent parents, in their eagerness to see an adolescent's face light up over her first car, may go quite into debt to provide a really nice car on this birthday.

Often, however, the glow fades in time, and the parent is dismayed when the car is not cleaned, is not maintained, and is driven by irresponsible friends. When this happens, the overindulgent parent is crushed by the lack of appreciation and responsibility shown by his adolescent and explodes in a tirade of verbal abuse. After a while, the anger subsides and the parent resigns himself to the situation with resentment. When the car is damaged or wrecked through irrespons- ible driving, he grumbles and criticizes, yet pays for repairs or another new car. The teenager can't understand "why Dad is always so down on me and doesn't think I can do anything right." Dad can't understand why his daughter can't be more responsible.

Looking at it from a distance, we can see it is only natural that something given freely with no conditions and without having to be earned has little value. Those things we as adults have most treasured were most likely those things we acquired through work, effort, or long and patient sacrifice. It makes more sense to look at the use of a car as a privilege that precedes ownership of a car. Use of the car can proceed gradually through several steps. Progressive use of the car can be earned through demonstration of the maturity that is needed to successfully handle this responsibility. If several behaviors can be directly linked to concrete situations that may arise with the car, the teenager can see the connection and see that it is reasonable. I have yet to have a teenager object to this system.

For example, here are some analogies you might use:

1. Your room is a mess, you lost your sweater, and you can't find your baseball shoes. I don't see how you can take care of a car if you can't take care of these inexpensive things. You might leave the car windows down in the rain or ignore the warning light when the car is low on oil.

2. You forgot about this paper until the last minute, and now you don't have time to do it. I don't see how you can plan ahead well enough to manage a car if you can't manage to do your homework. You might forget to put gas in the car, forget to take money or a gas card with you, or forget to check the map before you head off somewhere.

3. You don't seem to feel a need to follow rules that others set down if you don't like them. That worries me. You may go through a stop sign or a red light because you don't see any point in it. You may ignore the speed limit, feeling it is a waste of time because it just slows you down. I want to see you work harder at following rules, even rules that you think are dumb. This is a necessary but inconvenient part of being a good driver.

4. You've had such poor control of your emotions lately, I don't think you're ready for driving alone. When you argued with your girlfriend on the phone, you got so mad you put your fist through the door. I'm concerned that you may get mad at a driver that passes you or cuts you off, and just blow up and lose control. I want to see you work on better emotional control before I'll feel comfortable letting you drive alone.

Problem Area 4: Irresponsible With Money

"Our sixteen-16-year old son is always needing money and lots of it. He has expensive tastes in clothes, and a lot is going into the upkeep of his car. He doesn't seem to want to save any or spend it on necessities. We put pressure on him for a while to get a job so that he could earn his own spending money, but he doesn't keep them very long. He gets tired of the low-level jobs that teenagers are given. However, we're concerned that if he did keep a job and do well at it, he would increase his hours and his grades would suffer. He might eventually drop out of school. We're between a rock and a hard place—between giving him money outright or seeing him work too much."

Money—how it is earned and how it is spent—is often a large source of conflict between teenagers and their parents. Teenagers work outside the home in larger numbers than in the past, and virtually all the income they earn is "expendable" income—that is, it is spent on nonessential material goods and pleasurable activities. David Elkind, in a 1989 article in *Parents*, cites a study which found that only about 30 percent of high school seniors regularly put away money for their education or for long-term savings. Only about 18 percent of working high school students contributed any money for family expenses. On the other hand, 75 percent of them used all their money for personal expenses—typically clothing, entertainment, and records.

For this reason, the lure of work and money quickly comes into conflict with the need to do well in school. After all, school is not much fun, and it doesn't pay. Studies show that teenage work is not all that beneficial to teenagers. Elkind, in a recent talk about his book *Adolescents in the Post-Modern Age*, stated that teenagers, while they may acquire a work ethic from after-school jobs and earn some spending money, also suffer many negative consequences. The work they do tends to be routine, montonous tasks and they don't learn skills that are useful to a future career. They learn to steal on the job and learn unsavory business practices. Once they work more than fourteen hours per week, their grades begin to suffer. Once they work more than twenty hours per week, they become exhausted and burned out.

If caught in this cycle—school is a waste of time, and I need to earn more money in order to keep up the car payments on my nice new car and my nice wardrobe—students tend to do poorly or even drop out of school in order to work more. As all their income goes into car, clothes, and recreation, however, they are forced to live at home well past eighteen, as their low-paying job will not allow them to live independently. They realize then that they need more education in order to make more money, but are unable to take vows of poverty, even if they are willing to, because they are saddled with debt.

Most experts in the area suggest that parents help teenagers set up a budget for themselves and give them increasingly greater responsibility for managing their own expenses. In chapter 10 it was suggested that children be given the responsibility of earning all the money for their own toys and recreation. By the teenage years, you may want to include all clothing in her budget. By age seventeen or eighteen, you may even want to include such things as car insurance, car repairs, gas, and savings for college. Help your teenager to make a list of all sources of income. Include part-time jobs, money for good grades, gifts, allowance, and full-time summer work. You also exert control over how much allowance you are willing to pay and how much you are willing to grant for good grades.

Then help her draw up a projected list of money needs for the year, broken down on a monthly basis. Be sure to include here a regular savings plan for college or trade school and a donation plan under which a portion of her income is to go to a charitable agency. Neale Godfrey and Carolina Edwards, authors of *Money Doesn't Grow on Trees*, call this the S-O-S plan: spending, offering, savings.

If you are concerned that you are putting too much emphasis on her earning money outside the home, consider providing some incentives or bonuses for those things that you most value. Propose a "matching funds" plan. For example: You will match whatever she saves for a car on a one-to-one or two-to-one basis; you will match whatever she saves for college or trade school on a four-to-one or six-to-one basis.

Parents do well to bring adolescents into the whole process of money management. I often ask middle and older adolescents, "How much money do you think it takes to run your household?" Children of overindulgent parents typically do not know what expenses go into the running of a household, and their answers are usually a gross underestimation of the total bill. Overindulgent parents will often say, "I didn't want to trouble her with these adult problems." It is very educational, however, to give her a great deal of information about the costs of running a household.

A recent study of high school seniors, done by the Consumer Federation of America, found that teenagers have a very poor grasp of money management, even though they spend almost $80 billion a year of their own money. "Financially illiterate high school seniors are not prepared to cope with the world of consumption," said Stephen Brobeck, the director of the study. "Eight million kids own cars, but they haven't the faintest idea about what auto insurance covers," said the study's coauthor. The study found that students earn more than $100 billion a year and spend $79 billion of it, yet the vast majority did not know the difference between a checking account and a savings account.

Godfrey and Edwards have an excellent quiz for teenagers to test their money knowledge. It includes questions such as "Do you know how to balance a checkbook?" and "Do you know what to do if you lost your checks or credit card?" You might begin with this quiz as a takeoff point for teaching your teen the basics of money management. When helping your teenager open a bank account, you might insist she go to three different banks and consider service charges before opening an account. Make sure she does the talking and asks the questions. You might want to open a charge account with your teenager so that she can understand the concept of finance charges. Have your teenager sit down with you from time to time and open the bills. Sort them out in order of importance and due dates. Have her make out the checks to the various utilities (except for signing them, of course), and put them in the mail. Paying the water and electric bills herself may even cut down on some arguments about her using the washer and dryer to clean only one pair of jeans. Review the family budget at one of your family meetings. Ask your teenager where she would suggest you make changes in the budget and where she thinks the family could save some money.

Help her to actually read the fine print on the auto insurance and understand what the terms mean. Have her gather information on comparison rates from other insurance companies. Have her read up on the repair records and maintenance costs of various cars before

buying one. Mature adolescents, ages sixteen to eighteen, will appreciate the fact that you took the time to teach them about these adult
matters. They will grow in confidence as they see that handling adult
responsibilities, which seems so overwhelming at times, is something
that they can learn and can understand and handle effectively.

Problem Area 5: Skipping School, Failing Grades, Wanting to Drop Out

"Our sixteen-year-old daughter has no interest in school anymore.
She just wants to work and make money. Her grades are terrible. She's
flunking most of her courses. The teachers say she sleeps through her
first three classes. I'm sure it's because she works till eleven o'clock and
then goes out with her friends. We want her to quit this job, but she
absolutely refuses. We feel there's nothing we can do."

Virtually all of the parents I have ever seen, in the lower- to upper-
middle-class community in which I work, want their teenagers to do
well in school and go to college. This dream, however, is sadly
disappointing for many. As stated before, the freedom, status, and
affluence of working competes with academic performance for many.

Overindulgent parents seem especially hard hit with this problem,
as their teens appear to have so little ability to set goals and make plans
for their future, to delay gratification, and to demonstrate the kind of
self-discipline that is needed to balance school, work, and social life and
do well in all three areas of competence at the same time.

Parents of younger teens, fourteen to sixteen, have found it helpful
to invoke a "no pass, no play" rule—only in this case, it would be "no
pass, no work." It makes sense to emphasize to a teenager that school is
their main area of work, as it is where they prepare for the future.
Having a job is secondary. By and large, it is where they make extra
money for recreation and for a car. You may want to exercise your
authority as a parent to limit her part-time job to fourteen hours per
week during the school year, and make the job conditional on
maintaining a certain grade point average.

For the older teenager, sixteen to eighteen, the picture is somewhat
more complicated. Teens in this age can drop out of school and may
threaten to. They may refuse to quit their job. They may threaten to

move out if the parent puts conditions on them for holding a job. Often the overindulgent parent sets no guidelines out of fear that the adolescent will act on one of these threats. Yet some guidelines must be set that seem logical and reasonable.

You can continue to provide incentives for staying in school, such as contributions to her car expenses or college savings plan in return for good grades. You cannot, however, ultimately prevent a teenager from leaving school prematurely. Explain that a teenager's primary job is to go to school and prepare for her future. If she chooses not to do this job, by skipping school, flunking school, or withdrawing, then she is choosing to be an adult and must act like one. She must work full-time, do a major part of the household and yard work, and pay for room and board, just like the adults in the house do. Review the family budget with them. Divide it into thirds (if there are now three adults in the household) and indicate to the older teenager how much her third would be. Divide up the household jobs and list her third of the responsibilities. If she complains that she cannot possibly pay one-third of the bills, be willing to compromise, but make sure that her contribution is a large one, and that it is remotely comparable to what she may have to pay to support herself outside the home.

Lastly, if she quits school, do not panic. It isn't the end. Most adolescents who quit school prematurely eventually go back to school to finish their education, as they become aware of how much money it takes to live on their own. You facilitate this process by having them pay room and board. You significantly delay their return to school by allowing them to live with you rent-free and to spend their money on the pursuit of fun.

Problem Area 6: Constant Demands for Greater Freedom and Adult Privileges; Not Enough Responsibility

"Help! We have a contract for the phone, a contract for the car, a contract for schoolwork, a contract for dating....We are overwhelmed with contracts. It's getting too difficult to keep up with."

While entering into contracts is a workable approach for adolescents, the contracts may become numerous and have to be constantly revised. I have also had success with families in developing an overall master plan, called a "levels system." Levels systems have been used successfully in residential psychiatric programs, group homes, and halfway houses for adolescents since the 1960s. These programs present detailed lists of responsibilities and privileges that are posted on the wall for all to see. An adolescent patient or resident begins the program on the bottom level, with absolutely no privileges, and moves up through the levels by demonstrating the required behaviors and mature attitude and being voted on by his peers.

While these programs might seem overly rigid and downright militaristic to parents, I have found that teenagers from overindulgent families embrace them wholeheartedly. It is as if for the first time, living with and getting along with others made sense. They can get what they want, not by coercion, threats, and acting out but by an orderly and predictable means. All the rules are clear. All the privileges are clear. Not only are these teenagers enthusiastic, but their mood improves as well. Shocked parents make comments like "She loves all these rules. I don't get it. At home, she resisted every rule I gave her."

What they fail to see is that at home, the rules were often arbitrary, inconsistent, and made up on the spot, in a moment of anger. Privileges weren't tied to responsibility but were granted inconsistently as well— as a result of manipulation, in a moment of parental weakness, or on the basis of the parent's mood at the time the request was made.

Parents can create a levels system for teenagers as an outcome of family meetings. Begin the meeting with an explanation and rationale. Invite all the children to participate. Suggest some initial guidelines for rights and responsibilities. Always, always, encourage your teenager to participate and voice her opinion. If she chooses not to participate, let her, but remind her that the parents and other children may make up guidelines that will still affect her, even though she didn't participate. From time to time, review the adolescent's adherence to the program and whether she ought to move up or down a level. You may want to have the family give her feedback on how she is doing. You may want to have a family vote on the matter. This could be effective if you give the parents' votes more weight than the children's votes, so that it is clear the parents are still in charge. The following is a rough outline of a two-tiered levels system that might be drafted to cover important issues that are sources of conflict for teenagers.

LEVEL I

(May be suitable for twelve-, thirteen-, or fourteen-year-old, depending on parents' comfort level)

Responsibilities

- I will maintain passing grades in all subjects.
- I will stick to a regularly scheduled study hour as set down by parents, with a minimum of arguing.
- I will bring home all necessary books and materials and have assignments written down.
- I will do required chores when asked to, with a minimum of arguing.
- I will not use obscene language in the house or scream at or hit anyone in the family.
- I will control my temper and not destroy my possessions or those of anyone else in the family.
- I will be truthful at all times about where I am going, who I am with, and what I am doing.
- I will pick up and put away things in my room on a weekly basis.
- I will keep my clothes hung up or folded and put away in drawers.
- I will go with my family to the church of their choice two times per month.

Rights

- I can stay up until nine-thirty P.M. on school nights and ten-thirty on weekends.
- I can choose my own clothes with some parental guidance and within the parental budget.
- I will be allowed to go to movies, parties, and the mall as well as go skating, on my own in the daytime or with remote adult supervision at night.
- My curfew will be ten-thirty P.M. on weekends.

- My allowance will be five to eight dollars per week.
- I will be allowed two half-hour phone calls per night.
- I may close my door at any time and family members must knock to come in.

LEVEL II

(May be suitable for thirteen-, fourteen-, or fifteen-year-old, depending on parents' views)

Responsibilities

- I will maintain grades of C or better in all subjects.
- I will schedule an hour of study time for myself each night and will do so without being reminded.
- I will keep up with all assignments, important events, and appointments on a calendar, without outside supervision.
- I will do required chores without being asked.
- I will wash my own clothes and athletic uniforms whenever needed.
- I will keep my room reasonably neat and orderly without being told.
- I will maintain involvement in at least one athletic or extracurricular activity, such as baseball, ballet, violin, Scouting, etc., without argument or prodding.
- I will participate in at least one family activity per week.
- I will control my temper when my family gives me constructive criticism and will accept responsibility for my actions.
- I will continue to share my parents' faith but will be allowed to choose a youth group activity over church attendance.
- I will continue to be honest and straightforward with family members at all times.

Rights

- My bedtime will be ten P.M. on school nights and eleven P.M. on weekends.

- I can choose my own clothes, within the parental budget. I will be allowed to wear them the way I want to.
- I will be allowed to go to movies, go skating, go to parties, or go to the mall at night for up to three hours unsupervised.
- My curfew will be eleven P.M. on weekends.
- My allowance will be five to fifteen dollars per week.
- I will be allowed to use the phone privately for up to three half-hour phone calls per evening.
- I will be allowed to apply for my learner's license and drive with supervision.
- I will be allowed to work up to eight hours per week outside the home and spend the money as I choose.

LEVEL III

(May be suitable for fifteen- or sixteen-year-old, depending on parents' views)

Responsibilities

- I will continue to make grades of C or better.
- I will take responsibility for getting tutoring or outside help when I need it and work up to the best of my ability.
- I will study one to two hours a night as needed, on my own.
- I will do chores independently and pitch in to help others whenever needed.
- I will be completely responsible for my own clothes, shoes, and personal possessions.
- I will discuss my problems, decisions, and future plans with my family from time to time.
- I will be courteous and helpful with parents, brothers, sisters, and relatives.
- I will make plans in advance, with consideration for other family members, notify my parents where I am, and call home whenever I might be late.

- I will save part of my income for future use. I will show good judgment with my money.
- I will continue to pursue one extracurricular activity.
- I will show good judgment in dating. I will continue to develop good friendships, even when dating someone.

Rights

- My bedtime will be up to me to decide.
- I will buy my own clothes.
- My curfew will be twelve A.M. on weekends.
- I will be allowed to be in a car with drivers aged seventeen and over with good driving records.
- My telephone time is unlimited, but phone usage stops at ten o'clock. I may have a private phone in my bedroom.
- I will be allowed to get my driver's license and make short trips during the daytime unsupervised.
- I will be allowed to make night trips and longer trips with supervision.
- I will be allowed to work up to fourteen hours per week.
- I will be allowed to date someone no more than two years older than me.
- I will be allowed to attend the church of my choice, provided I do so on a regular basis.

LEVEL IV

(May be suitable for seventeen- or eighteen-year-old, depending on parents' and home situation)

Responsibilities

- I will continue to strive to work to my full potential in school or in my vocational training program.
- I will express concern for and interest in the members of my family.

- I will take on a leadership role with kids younger than me, both at home and in the community.
- I will continue to set goals for myself and to develop plans toward reaching those goals.
- I will make a meaningful contribution to the running of the household.
- I will continue to develop friendships with others thoughtfully and selectively, choosing those who are good for me.
- I will not date anyone who manipulates, abuses, or exploits me or who threatens my safety.
- I will continue to be truthful with family members at all times.

Rights

- Bedtime is at my own discretion.
- I will make all my own selections of clothes and pay for them with my own money.
- I will be allowed unrestricted use of the car, provided I ask permission. I will be allowed to own my own car, provided I pay for a portion of it.
- I will have unlimited use of the phone. I will be allowed to own my own phone if I pay the bill.
- Curfew will be at my own discretion, provided I am home at a reasonable hour and discuss all my plans in advance.
- I will be allowed to spend the night away from home, provided I call my family and inform them of where I am.
- I will be allowed to date whom I choose.
- I will be allowed to work as much as I feel I need to.
- I will be allowed to make my own choices with regard to college, trade school, the military, etc.

Problem Area 7: Use of Alchohol and Drugs, Running Away, and Sexual Promiscuity

"It may be too late for us to get help for our seventeen-year-old daughter. She sneaks out of the house at night and runs the streets with a group of kids who are always in trouble. She has been picked up by the police for drinking, being out after curfew, and being in a car with an underage driver. We know she abuses alcohol, and we think she may be using drugs, too. She has run away once, and we brought her back, but we're afraid she'll run again. She has made one suicide attempt, taking some pills. We took her to a therapist, but she said she didn't like her and wouldn't go back. We gave up on school. Now we're just hoping to keep her alive."

Unfortunately, this kind of family is turning up all too often in the offices of psychologists, psychiatrists, and family therapists today. This underdeveloped teen is reckless, totally out of control, and miserable. She sees no way out of her problems. She is escaping life through acting out, substance abuse, running away, and suicide attempts. The parents are frightened, intimidated, and helpless. They fear for her life yet feel powerless to do anything about the situation for fear of the negative consequences.

For these families, their first and probably best step would be to join a Toughlove group. Toughlove is a self-help movement that began in the 1970s to help parents with out-of-control teens. Far more than being about "getting tough" with teens, it is more about parents turning to other parents, to the school, to the courts, to mental health and substance abuse professionals, and to the community at large to get the support they need in coping with teens such as the one above. Through this group, parents make strong ties with other parents who may have been through this crisis already, or who are not so burdened with financial problems or the stress of being a single parent.

Toughlove groups help each other with practical, though often creative, solutions. A teenager who doesn't come home on time for dinner doesn't eat. If she refuses to comply with the house rules, she must move out and live with another Toughlove family until she is ready to cooperate. A runaway who hangs out with his friends' families must have his sources cut off by telling these families that they are legally responsible for him. In order to come back home again, he must earn his way back and agree to abide by a strict contract. A teenager who is assaultive will be physically restrained by other Toughlove men in the program. A restraining order will be taken out and will be served. A teen who is picked up by police and taken to the youth detention center will stay there until he receives a hearing on his case. A teenager who is abusing substances must go through rehabilitation, be totally clean and sober, and abide by a strict contract before being allowed to come home again. A teenager who is suicidal must go into a residential psychiatric program before coming back home again.

Many overindulgent parents are shocked at the mention of not allowing their teenager home, calling the police, using restraining orders, a stay in the youth detention center, psychiatric hospitalization, etc. They refuse to believe that these desperate measures would ever have to be used with their adolescent children. They love them so deeply, they could never do such a harsh thing to them. Yet the consequences of not doing so are far graver. They include violence and death.

Authors Phyllis York, David York, and Ted Wachtel cite a 1983 ABC News study on teen violence which found that a million and a half acts of violence by teens toward their families occurred that year. One psychiatrist predicted that as many as half of these teens could end up in prison. David Elkind cites a recent study that found the suicide rate among adolescents has tripled since the 1950s. Why these statistics are so grave is very complicated. There is no one cause but rather a number of causes that all contribute to the problems of the seventeen-year-old girl described above—a loss of confidence in our society, the loss of a sense that the world is getting better, too much affluence, too much freedom, the high divorce rate, early maturation, poor coping skills, and overindulgent parenting, to mention a few. Author Phyllis York has written, "Young people we know who have been suicidal are not, as popular belief would have it, suffering long-standing depression. Rather they are mostly unrealistic, having expectations greater than life is likely to fulfill. They are kids who like to escape, through fantasy, drugs, and alcohol. They live in their dreams with their wishes, expecting unconditional love and wanting someone to take care of them, to solve their problems for them over and over again."

Now more than ever, families of teens need Toughlove. It is a program that moves from blaming families to finding practical, workable solutions. For overindulgent families of underdeveloped teens, it may make the difference between life and death for the adolescent son or daughter they love.

13 Your Underdeveloped Young Adult: What's Wrong?

If you're a parent of an older adolescent who is underdeveloped, you may have skimmed through much of the last several chapters, musing to yourself, "Yes, these are good ideas, but my son is twenty-two. It's too late to try any of these approaches. Yet he's still living at home. What do I do now?" If this is you, you are not alone. According to a 1987 *Time* magazine article, the U.S. Census Bureau reported that 59 percent of men and 47 percent of women between eighteen and twenty-four were depending on their parents for housing, some living in college dorms but most living at home. This averaged out to 53 percent of all young adults at the last census count. Fifty three percent is more than half—it is a majority. These figures were up from comparable figures of 54 percent for men and 41 percent for women in 1970. In addition, the report goes on to say that 14 percent of men and 8 percent of women aged twenty-five to thirty-four were dependent on their parents for housing. Declared sociologist Allen Schnaiberg of Northwestern University, "This is part of a major shift in the middle class."

Another source suggests that 40 percent of the current population of young adults aged twenty to forty are "excessively dependent" on their parents. While such figures are hard to pin down, since so many young adults move back home temporarily or are in and out, still they are undoubtedly extremely high. The ABC television show *20/20* did a segment in October 1991 on young professional men who remain at home with their parents. They cite a recent census study that found that 33 percent of all single men aged twenty-five to thirty-four still live at home with their parents, the highest rate ever.

How is it that we have this myth that our children will grow up and leave home at eighteen, fully independent and ready to be self-sufficient? There are many demographic reasons why so many young men and women are living at home or are otherwise financially dependent on their parents. The cost of college tuition has gone up relative to incomes, and the cost of sending a son or daughter away to college has become out of reach for a majority of American families. College costs for room and board at a state university more than tripled between 1965 and 1985 and have more than doubled since then. Likewise, the cost of cars, homes, and rent has gone up dramatically, relative to the increase in incomes, making it harder for a young person to buy a nice car or a first home. Rent and food costs increased by 267 percent between 1970 and 1987. During these years, median earnings increased by 250 percent. However, the purchasing power of the dollar fell by nearly 300 percent with inflation taken into account. This has brought about the harsh reality of lowered expectations for a comfortable lifestyle. The headlines of the newspapers have been saturated with articles on bleak job prospects for college graduates in the late eighties and early nineties. While more students are going to college than ever before, there are twice as many graduates as there are college-level jobs. In 1982, the Labor Department found that 47 percent of college graduates twenty-four years old or younger were in non-college-level jobs. Keep in mind that these figures did not include those who were working part-time, going to school full-time, or simply "hanging out" at home. It has been suggested that the figure is realistically over 50 percent.

The divorce rate is likely a contributing factor as well. Between 1970 and 1983, the divorce rate doubled in this country. More than half of all marriages now end in divorce, and the figure is even higher for marriages between those under the age of twenty-five. Many, if not most, of these early marriages yield small children who must be cared for, and child-care costs alone eat up more than the monthly child support check. A great many of these women, and men as well, see no choice but to bring the children back home to live so that they can fall back on the financial help their parents provide and the child care that they don't expect to pay for. In addition to this trend, having a child out of wedlock no longer carries the social stigma it once did. In many areas, living at home with one's parents while having a child alone and working has become quite acceptable.

Lastly, the higher rates of drug and alcohol abuse may also make their contribution to the problem. According to the National Institute on Drug Abuse, the number of Americans abusing cocaine increased dramatically during the 1980s. This problem is most prevalent in middle-class young adults. Even more significant is the large percentage of young people who regularly abuse alcohol. The pattern of regular binge drinking begins in high school and continues into college. These students go to college but soon come back home with the explanation that they "partied too much." Young people with problems of substance abuse who enter the work force right after high school have unstable work histories and often are down on their luck financially. Returning home to "get into rehab" and "pay off my bills" can become a revolving door for many young adults.

This pattern, however, is a direct result of some rather subtle cultural shifts. The encounter movement of the 1970s popularized the notion of intrapsychic exploration as a valid and desirable goal. Terms like "finding myself," "doing my own thing," and "getting my act together" have become part of our everyday vocabulary in middle-class households. Uncle Jack wants to know why Bill hasn't found a job now that he's graduated from college with a degree in economics, why he's a street juggler instead. "He's finding himself," his mother replies. "He says he's got to do his own thing for a while," grumbles Dad over his newspaper. "I'm into juggling," Bill says, "it centers me."

Susan Littwin, in her book *The Postponed Generation*, has developed a fascinating description of the pampered, educated, middle-to upper-middle-class young person who cannot grow up. While many of these young people go back home to "find themselves," still others stay in the college community where they went to school, eking out a meager existence for years and doing "some serious hanging out." In fact, she points out, there are whole towns, such as Santa Cruz, California, where the community ethos is one of avoiding the traditional markers of growing up—a job, a home, marriage, children—and devoting oneself to living in a kind of stastis between childhood and adulthood. No one makes appointments; no one has answering machines. Commitments are déclassé. It is as if young people went into a chrysalis stage in Santa Cruz and simply stayed there.

Another subtle shift is the shift in expectations. Our culture has become so affluent that young people's expectations, in the way of a comfortable lifestyle, have become incredibly high. A car, once a luxury, is now a necessity. Air-conditioning and a stereo in the car are considered necessities as well. An apartment with air-conditioning, a dishwasher, washer and dryer, television, stereo, and VCR is now considered "basic"—not luxurious. Expendable income—income for entertainment and recreation—present at such high levels in high school, is now considered a necessity. On one level, it is testimony to how advanced our nation has become that a lifestyle undreamed of in other cultures has come to be seen as the norm in our culture. And yet, on another level, these expectations for a high standard of living put an unfair burden on young people. The lifestyle carries a price tag so steep that it is virtually unattainable to young people, with the exception of recent M.B.A.'s and law school graduates. The lifestyle that is available to a young person—sharing an apartment with three roommates, having no air-conditioning, washing dishes by hand—seems like poverty-level living by most standards today. Susan Littwin, borrowing from Robert Coles, has described this phenomenon as a sense of "narcissistic entitlement." We'll come back to this later.

A third shift is the deferral of marriage to later years, as well as the decision not to marry at all. In the 1940s, 1950s, and 1960s, premarital sex was forbidden. Since preserving one's virginity was highly valued, getting married was the only way for both men and women to find out about sex. In the seventies, premarital sex became acceptable, and so was separated from the decision about marriage. Both men and women could have sex without marrying each other, so why marry? In 1960, 72 percent of women between the ages of twenty and twenty-four were married. In 1984, only 43 percent in that age group were married.

Not only have young people delayed marriage, but the number who never marry has doubled as well since 1970. For young men, being single and living at home used to carry connotations of being "a mama's boy," of shirking one's duty to have a family and contribute to the community. It even suggested vague implications of being homosexual. Attitudes about singlehood have changed dramatically with the surge in the divorce rate in the seventies and the eighties. One change has been the normalizing of being single. Being single now does not mean being an "old maid" or a man "tied to his mother's apron strings." "Singles" in this era are people with lots of freedom, glamorous lifestyles, and Club Med vacations. They are people who work out at the health club, drive nice cars, and wear trendy clothes. All of that costs money, and staying at home saves money.

Lastly, we are an aging nation. We live longer and are heathier while we are alive. We are retiring earlier. Most of us have comfortable lives by the time we are fifty. Our children are grown by then. Our house is paid for. We may retire at fifty-five and be in good health for the next twenty years. What will we do to fill our lives? For many of us, having a grown son or daughter at home, or even a divorced daughter or son and grandchildren, meets a strong need—the need to be useful while we still feel healthy and productive. When parents typically died at sixty, there was a built-in cultural pressure to get adult children ready to care for their parents by the time the parents were in their fifties. Now that life expectancy is in the seventies, there is no such pressure. In fact, there is a vacuum in older parents' lives that is often filled by allowing as much dependency as a grown child seems to want.

Where do overindulgent parents fit into these broad social changes? While these trends in our society have contributed to young adults' staying at home longer than ever before or coming back home in droves, today's parents, on the other hand, seem more tolerant than ever of remaining in a parent role with them. This is not the parent role of the past—teaching, guiding, and gently pushing them out of the nest. This new parent role is one of caretaking, rescuing, bailing out, "enabling" their adult offspring's dependency. The return back home is not brief, it is prolonged. The search for identity is not moving forward, it has stagnated. Many of these late adolescents seem amazingly unconcerned and complacent about their dependency. Still others are unhappy, often angry at their parents. Some of these parents are complacent as well about their grown son's or daughter's dependency on them, yet just as many are often angry, confused, and guilt-ridden. And yet their enmeshment, their codependency on each other, continues.

Let's take a look at three common scenarios, so that you can get a feel for some of the difficulties these families have in common.

The Never-Left-Homes. There are several reasons why some young adults never leave home. There are those who are simply baffled at how to begin growing up. Nancy Eberle calls these "the future-shocked." Some finish high school and have no idea what to do. Many work a little at some odd job and take a course here or there at the community college, hoping that by meandering about for a few years, they'll figure out what to do. Over time, the job, which they don't like, grows to be full-time. They have car payments and charge cards to pay off. They cannot afford to move out. Then they become "the financially strapped"—those who are too deeply in debt to move out.

Still others of the "future-shocked" variety manage to go to college and get a degree, yet at twenty-two have no earthly idea what to do next. Susan Littwin calls this phenomenon *"The Graduate* summer." These students finish up their schooling and come home to lie around the backyard pool in a funk, trying to sort out what to do with their lives. Their parents stand around anxiously watching and waiting. Their questions are responded to with "I don't know. I've been under a lot of stress. I can't think." "Having had an expensive education and more advantages than any other generation on earth," Littwin says, "they seemed confused, unfocused, and dependent."

Then there are the Peter Pans. This is a term coined by Dan Kiley, author of *The Peter Pan Syndrome*. ABC-TV's Lynn Sherr did a piece on Peter Pans for the show *20/20*, titled "Still Living With Mom," which aired October 4, 1991. In her segment, she interviewed Robert, aged twenty-seven, an assistant district attorney and a partner in a law firm; Kenny, twenty-seven, a dentist; Tommy, thirty, a rehabilitation technician; and Lawrence, a twenty-seven-year-old investment banker. All lived at home with their mothers and were living a very affluent lifestyle. All these young men cited money as the reason they stayed home. While all made good incomes, none could have the affluent lifestyle on their own that they were able to have by staying home. They also cited a dread of "having to struggle" if they were out on their own. The following is an interesting bit of dialogue that depicts the kind of dependency in which these families seem mired.

SHERR: Do you do his laundry for him?

DENTIST'S MOTHER: Yes, but he can do it for himself, but it's no problem.

SHERR: You iron for him?

DENTIST'S MOTHER: Yes, but he can do that himself.

SHERR: But you tend to do it, right?

DENTIST'S MOTHER: Right.

SHERR: Do you cook for him?

DENTIST'S MOTHER: Yes, but he can take care of himself.

SHERR: *(voiceover)* Keep in mind Kenny's mom is doing all this for her son the dentist while also working part-time herself as his receptionist for no salary until he gets established....

SHERR: Does he pay rent?

DENTIST'S MOTHER: No. He doesn't make any money yet.

SHERR: But he's a dentist. I mean, everybody knows dentists make lots of money.

DENTIST'S MOTHER: Right, he just got started.

What is remarkable about these families is how unconcerned they all are about the situation. Tommy, the rehab therapist, says, "I feel I've reached thirty and I feel that's an age that I need to get out. I feel a little dependent now with my parents there."

Dan Kiley, who appeared on the show, made a comment toward the end that is worth remembering if you are like the parents of these men: "Every day your son is here past the day of his twenty-fifth birthday, and lives here when he could...move out, he grows weaker."

The Refuelers and the Wounded Birds. Eberle coins the term "refuelers" for those adolescents and young adults who make it out of the house but later have to come back. Like birds out of the nest, they become wounded and head for home. Typically, they return after crisis and failure. Some partied themselves out of college with drinking and reckless behavior. The tuition and college costs were wasted, as they earned no credits during their stay there. After a period of time to regroup, they decide to reenroll at another college where they think they'll party less. Parents are faced with shelling out still more money for tuition and room and board, which may be wasted repeatedly. Then there are those who managed to get a job and apartment, but their roommate moved out, leaving them with the rent and unpaid bills. There are those who got a job and lost it suddenly. They had no savings or second job to fall back on. All the bills came due, and they could not pay them.

More-troubled adult children run into difficulty with chronic drug abuse problems. They do fairly well until they are arrested and have no money for attorney's fees or rehabilitation programs. They come back home with promises to "get clean" and stick with their rehab program, but little by little, they begin to drop out of treatment. The old "user" friends begin to come by the house again, and it is evident that drug use has begun once more. Parents are faced with continuing the dependency or asking him to leave, fearing that this move "will force him to sell drugs to support himself." Still others, particularly daughters, develop dependent relationships with disturbed young men who abuse them repeatedly. They come back home for refueling, only to leave home again because "he promised not to hit me again."

Still other refuelers are grown sons or daughters who come home with small children. At first, the move seems temporary, a chance to "get back on their feet." Providing occasional child care is no problem. But then child care comes to be expected on a full-time basis. And it is expected to be free. These families run into serious conflict when the parent develops an active social life and expects free baby-sitting for this too. The parent's money becomes expendable income, as no rent is charged. Soon the grandparents are providing transportation for the children's doctor visits and taking them to and from school. Disagreements arise over the parent's care of the children or neglect of them. While the conflicts intensify, the adult parent soon can see no way to survive and raise her children on her own, without her parents' help. The overindulgent parents are afraid to ask her to leave because they are afraid the grandchildren would not be well cared for.

Those Who Left Home but Never Cut the Cord. Lastly, there are those young adults who managed to make it out of the home and establish a separate life for themselves, but it is a life that is often floundering. These young adults have lives that often teeter on collapse, and only a bailout from Mom and Dad will save them from disaster. Sometimes I see these young adults when they come to me as couples seeking marriage counseling. The following is a reworked excerpt from a session with DeAnn, aged thirty-two, and Wayne, thirty-three.

WAYNE: You have got to start writing down the checks in the checkbook. You bounced four checks last week.

DEANN: It's just a little mistake to make. I don't see why you're so upset.

WAYNE: I'm upset because I have to take money from my business to cover them. On top of that, I have to cover all the bad check charges. We can't afford all these things. You're going to have to spend less.

DeAnn: Well, these are things that are necessitites. You'll just have to make more money, or I'll have to call my father and ask for money. He'll help me out, and he'll do it nicely, too.

WAYNE: There you go. comparing me to your father again. He bought you a new car three times when you totaled the one you had. I can't do that. I'm not willing to do that. You have to be more responsible. And you have to stop buying so many toys for Zach. The kid has five times as many toys as he could ever play with.

DeAnn: I am responsible. But I work hard and I can't see denying myself something I feel we really need. I deserve to have nice things. And Zach is away from me all day while I'm working. He deserves nice things, too. If you're going to be mean to me, I'll just have to call my father.

We can see from this dialogue that this thirty-two-year-old adult's continuing dependency on her father to bail her out of her financial problems is impairing her ability to manage her resources wisely. It is also creating a great deal of conflict in her marriage. And the pattern is repeating itself, as we see her taking an overindulgent stance with little Zach.

Still other adults (as old as their mid-thirties) I've worked with are single and on their own, but not really on their own. Their checking account is a joint checking account with their mother's name on the account. This is so their mother can review their account from time to time and put money in it when the checks bounce. Some checks even read, "Mr. _____, guardian of _____." Some of these adults have had homes given to them so that "they might have a roof over their head." Yet the parent's name is on the deed, and the ownership of the house is in question. These adults are reluctant to call their parents for money—to start a business, to pay their tuition so that they can go back and get more schooling, to pay their mortgage—but it's so easy to do when the money is there and freely given. The overindulgent, and now middle-aged, parents see no alternative, fully believing that their son or daughter would be out on the street if they didn't come forth with the money that was needed. "How can we say no and make her suffer," they ask, "when the money is there in the bank and we don't mind giving it? She doesn't need the money after we're dead and gone, she needs it now. We figure we're giving her her inheritance now while she needs it the most to get started, to get settled."

In chapter 2, we listed the twelve traits of the underdeveloped child. These children have poor frustration tolerance, they give up easily, and they are poor at solving problems for themselves. They are reluctant to try new things, to take risks, for fear of failing. They use poor coping skills, preferring to avoid problems rather than face them. They have low self-esteem and are excessively dependent on their parents and their peer group for direction and reassurance. They are unable to manage strong emotion and get easily overwhelmed when faced with multiple problems. They seem unusually self-centered and lack a sense of concern for others. As adolescents, they have a poor sense of identity and no realistic goals for the future.

What are these underdeveloped children like when they become adults? In general, it can be said that they are usually unhappy adults who are struggling to make a successful go at adult life. Some mature slowly, gaining the maturity between the years of about eighteen to twenty-five that they did not get while at home in the overindulgent family. These young people make it because the cord was cut at eighteen or nineteen and they were left to struggle with and solve some of life's problems on their own. But for those whose parents still cannot cut the cord, the pattern becomes more chronic. Many of the above ten traits still characterize their behavior, though several new ones described below, may be added.

Underdeveloped children grow up to have, as young adults, a quality of narcissistic entitlement *that often alienates others.*

This term is borrowed from writer Robert Coles who wrote about the children of the rich in his book *The Privileged Ones*. This is not, however, only a trait of the very rich, as our society has become so affluent that even middle-class adolescents and young adults often carry with them this sense of entitlement. What is meant by "narcissistic entitlement" is that these young people feel "special," "different," and "more deserving" than others. They come into adulthood expecting that others will recognize their specialness, will give them more interest and attention than they do the mass of others, who are not perceived as special at all. They expect to stand out from the crowd, not by virtue of their skills, talent, knowledge, or even personal charisma, but just because they are who they are. It is the Mr. Rogers message, "You're special just because you're you," taken to an extreme. These young adults expect the world to treat them as special, as standing outside the humdrum, workaday existence that others are destined to lead.

These young people have unusually high expectations of the social community around them. Their motto is, "Ask not what I can do for my society, ask what society can do for me." They expect to be rescued when they get into a jam and to have exceptions made for them. They expect the law to be bent for them, for the rules to be applied to others but not to them. They expect to be greatly appreciated for what little they do and to have few if any demands placed on them. Often this sense of entitlement is acted out through their addictive behavior with food, alcohol, and money. As we saw above, DeAnn says, "I work hard and I can't see denying myself something I really need." A "want" becomes a "need." The act of holding down a job is seen as justification for gratifying wants.

We can also see from the above dialogue that DeAnn's reckless handling of money and her attitude of entitlement are alienating Wayne from her. These young adults alienate others as well. They alienate coworkers with their attitude that they should be treated as though exceptions should be made for their lateness, their excessive sick leave, and their refusal to come early or stay late. They alienate friends with their lateness, forgetfulness, or lack of interest in matters outside themselves. They expect others to forgive and forget their transgressions and to love them in spite of themselves. Susan Littwin says, "They put great emphasis on the self, dislike answering to others, believe that things will somehow work out for the best, that their fantasies will come true, and that the world they move in will be strung with safety nets."

They have chronic feelings of unhappiness, frustration, and disappointment.

This may be a natural outcome of their sense of narcississtic entitlement. Underdeveloped children, having become young adults, find the world a much harder place in which to succeed than they ever anticipated. "It all looked so easy" when they were young. "I thought you just went to school and you got a job and everything worked out okay," they say. They never anticipated the possibility of not getting the job they wanted. They never expected to have to do work they didn't want to do, or to ever be laid off or lose a job. They never anticipated having to do without "the necessities." They never gave much thought to how much they were putting on the charge cards and that it would all come due someday. They never anticipated having to live in a place that was less than what they wanted.

These young people find others disappointing, too. Friends don't always come through for them in a pinch the way they expected. Their boss doesn't appreciate them in the way they expected. Everywhere they go, there are demands on them. No one seems to think they're special. Other people their age seem to be having an easier time making it in the world than they are. Why aren't they? Often these young people come to see therapists in their late twenties and early thirties. Their story is one of a series of failures: at getting an education, at long-term relationships, at managing money, at succeeding in the workplace, at cutting the dependency on Mom and Dad. As Littwin says, "These were special children of perfect parents, and they've had little practice in dealing with failure and rejection. But fate has taken these bright, charming middle-class aristocrats and dumped them into a rude, tightfisted world." "This isn't how it was supposed to be," they say, "There weren't supposed to be all these problems. All the things I ever wanted to be and do just seem impossible to me now. My life is all messed up. I don't know what's wrong. It's just that nothing has gone right for me."

They have ongoing difficulties in intimate relationships.

These young adults have difficulty sustaining a long-term relationship with anyone, which is perhaps a second outgrowth of their sense of narcissistic entitlement. They do not view love in a mature way—as an opportunity for mutual growth. They see love as an opportunity to meet their needs, to be finally recognized as special. They view their lover as someone who will take care of them, put up with their moodiness and fits of temper, and forgive them, as devotedly and completely as their mother or father did. They come into a relationship expecting total acceptance, encouragement, reassurance, patience, nurturance, and guidance, with nothing asked in return. It does not occur to them that the other person may have needs that they expect the "special one" to meet as well. They expect their lover to be like their overindulgent parent, an expectation that is never fulfilled. As in work, they are often disappointed in love as well.

And what is happening with the now middle-aged parents of underdeveloped young adults? We saw in chapter 3 that these parents had great difficulty setting limits with their demanding youngsters. They had no framework of realistic expectations for them or standards to which they expected their children to comply. There were no clear-cut consequences for going past the limits or not adhering to family rules. Guilt-ridden and overly concerned with gaining their children's love and approval, these parents tended to give in to the child's demands. We often find that they are still doing so as parents of young adults, though now the costs are even greater. We find them resenting the young adult son who comes and goes at all hours of the night, or resenting the daughter who leaves her children in their care while she goes away for the weekend with her new boyfriend. There are no expectations for these young adults with regard to how they are to live with the family as adults.

These parents are still anticipating their children's needs and rushing forth with well-intentioned efforts to set them on the right track. They search the want ads for jobs and fold the newspaper back so that a particular ad will be noticed by their unemployed son. They buy "just one more" car for their daughter, insisting this is the last time but feeling they have no choice in the matter because she has to be able to get to work. They outfit a whole nursery for the unplanned baby. These parents are still doing for them those things that they can do for themselves. They wash their adult children's clothes, buy them furniture, pay their bills, pick up their dry cleaning, and file their income taxes for them. They still seemed mired in providing "just a little more" for them in the hopes that they soon will be independent, failing to see that they are instead intensifying their son's or daughter's dependency.

They are still "rescuing" their sons and daughters. They come to the aid of the daughter whose husband has left her, ready to blame the husband for the breakdown of the marriage. They rescue the son who has become mired in debt because he and his new wife ran up their charge cards to the maximum in order to establish their new lifestyle with the "necessitities." They are still quick to defend their son or daughter and blame someone else for their difficulties.

"He wasn't good enough for her."
"After all, it was his wife who got them into debt. He had no idea what she was doing with the charge cards."
"The university was so big, she just didn't get the individualized attention that she needed."
"He's so misunderstood."
"He was so smart, but he just never reached his potential. I think the teachers just didn't know how to motivate him in the right way."
"It was so hard on him when his father left us. I hold his father to blame for his anger and for the trouble he's gotten into."
"I blame myself for his troubles. When I divorced his dad, I went to work and put him with a sitter in the afternoons. I just wasn't able to give him the kind of family I wanted for him. I've been trying to make it up to him ever since."

As they did when their children were younger, these parents often feel bitter, hurt, and angry. They come forth with gifts, offers of help, consolation, reassurance, affection, emotional support, money, a home, child care, etc., only to find that it is often unappreciated. They often feel misled, misused, taken advantage of. At times, this resentment may break open into angry arguments and accusations being hurled back and forth. These parents may be verbally abusive, yet quickly feel guilty afterward.

What is new for these parents in middle age is their confusion and bewilderment. Their son or daughter to whom they have given so much is unhappy, struggling, and angry at them. Nothing seems to be turning out the way they expected it would. They expected their adult child would be happy, secure, and self-confident. Instead, he is confused, unsure of himself, moody, and irritable. They expected he would be stable, successful, happy at something. Instead, he is struggling to find his way, not really happy with anything. He received so much love, yet now he is failing at life. He may be abusive to others, and may have problems with addictive behaviors. He may even be self-destructive. What happened?

Love was supposed to be the balm that soothes all ills, that guarantees a happy childhood and a successful adulthood. They have given all the love and affection they could, yet it hasn't been enough. These parents often feel guilty and assume that they must not have given enough love (as they define it), and rededicate themselves to still more giving and more sacrifice, more understanding and more patience. They feel they are to blame for their children's unhappiness, which they may be in part, but certainly not through their lack of giving.

These parents of underdeveloped young adults go through this process of confusion and bewilderment leading to guilt and and self-blame. The guilt leads to more giving, more doing for their young adult children, thus further crippling them emotionally. As the young adult continues to flounder, the parents continue to experience confusion and guilt and continue the cycle. Often it is the young adult who finally sees that this dependency on her mother is crippling her and that it is she who must cut the cord by detaching from her family.

By the time their children reach young adulthood, these parents have come to live in a state of denial about the realities of their son's or daughter's life. Everyone else around them can see that their adult child has a serious problem—with money, maintaining a home or marriage, neglectful parenting, with holding down a job, substance abuse, etc. Yet these parents simply don't see it. They deny the painful reality of the young adult's problems, preferring to see them as minor or temporary. They prefer to see their children through rose-colored glasses and their problems as something Mom or Dad can solve for them with just a "little bit of help," "some love and understanding," or "a small loan to help them get back on their feet." By denying the reality of the magnitude of the problem and refusing to put responsibility for the problem on their children, they are insured a continued role in their children's lives as helper, rescuer, and nurturer. Again, they are acting out of self-interest, under the guise of "love" for their adult child. It is their need to be needed, to be an essential part of their son's or daughter's life, that drives them.

It is the healthy parent who has learned, at least by the time their children are adults, that she does not need to be a superparent, that what is in the best interests of her adult children is for her to be a "good enough" parent—a parent who is conscientiously putting forth her best effort, who is aware of her weaknesses and shortcomings, and who is always willing to make amends for her mistakes. She is able to see that she gave her children their best for eighteen years, now it is up to them to make of their life what they will. She can see that she must pull back, way back, and let them flounder if necessary. She realizes that she is ultimately powerless over most of her children's problems, that problems in living can only be resolved slowly, gradually over time, by trying out solutions and seeing how they work. She knows that her son or daughter must learn about life the way she did, through trial and error, through painful lessons, and through experiencing the consequences of their behavior.

Writer and psychiatrist M. Scott Peck perhaps said it best when he described the deeper meaning of love in his popular book *The Road Less Traveled*. Sometimes what truly nurtures another person's growth is withholding what we could easily provide. True love is often judicious giving—and judicious withholding as well. To act judiciously means to use one's judgment, and judgment requires more than the spontaneous and even instinctual urge to nurture and provide. In some situations, to love one's child is to make a thoughtful and sometimes painful decision not to give when giving will inhibit growth and foster dependency.

14 Your Underdeveloped Young Adult: Helping Him Out of the Nest

Problem Number 1: Leaving the Nest

"Our twenty-six-year-old son, Steve, is working and enjoying life. He has friends he hangs out with. He likes to take trips up to the mountains on his motorcycle. He has a steady girlfriend, but they're not thinking about marriage. He comes and goes as he chooses. I don't mind as long as he calls and tells us he won't be home for dinner. I keep up his room for him and wash his clothes. I really don't mind. He's very sweet to me and always thanks me. I wouldn't dream of asking him to pay any rent.

"In fact, I really don't mind him being here at all. The conflict is with my husband. My husband thinks he should move out, get his own place. He's angry that Steve doesn't pay any bills or help out around here. He says he is ready for us to have the house to ourselves. He says I baby Steve. I really don't see what's so bad about Steve being here. Steve's happy and it feels good to me to have a son to look after. He's just taking his time to grow up."

In this scenario, where the mother is complacent about the adult son who won't grow up but the father is impatient for him to be moving on, it may have to be the father who takes the matter in hand. In chapter 11, several pages were devoted to helping the adolescent set goals and to the need for the parent to offer help in this area. If you haven't been helping your child or adolescent to set goals, now is the time to begin. It's never too late. You must be careful, however, not to take over the job of goal setting yourself and set goals for him that are yours but not his. Focus, instead, on asking questions that are specific enough to gently pressure him to make a commitment to a stated outcome. Here are some examples of how to begin:

"You've graduated and we're proud of you. We understand you

need some time off to unwind. Tell us how much time you need before you start college [or go to work]?"

"What are your plans for the next six months?"

"Tell me why it is that you're not sure. What is it that you're not sure about?"

"Where could you go to get more information on that so that you can make up your mind?"

"Where do you want to be in a year? What are your goals for the next year?"

"What is it you need from us to help achieve your goals?"

"Tell me what you would like to try to accomplish on a month-by-month basis in order to reach that goal."

You may also find it necessary in reducing conflict to state your own personal limitations with the situation right from the start. You can state them lovingly and with care and concern but assertively as well. Examples:

"You can stay here rent-free as long as you're going to college or trade school full-time and making a C average or above. If your grades fall below C average, you'll have to pay the tuition yourself. In order to do that, you'll have to get a part-time job. I don't mind helping you out, but I don't want to get into arguments with you about how you're wasting the money I spent on tuition. If it's your money, then it will be your problem, and I'll stay out of your business. That way, I think we'll both respect each other more."

"We've talked it over and we don't feel that letting you live here indefinitely is good for you or good for us. We'll give you all the help we can for the next six months, then you're on your own. We want to see you happy and secure in your own life and in your own home. I'm sure you've got bigger plans for yourself than just being our kid forever. We've got plans of our own, too."

"We feel we have to have some sort of house rules for children who reach eighteen and over. You have to go to school full-time or work full-time. One or the other. If you go to school full-time and make good grades, your rent and meals are free, though you'll still have to help out around the house just as you did in high school. If you quit school, you'll have to work and pay room and board, just as you would if you were on your own. We'll set your fee at 60 percent of your take-home pay."

Overindulgent parents always have difficulty with this last limit. And yet it is a vital one. It is only by paying something for his keep that the young adult can feel a measure of independence and can take pride in the fact that he is paying his way and not freeloading off his parents. One solution for the guilty parent is to put the money in a savings account at the bank. Use some when you need it, but let it accrue. When your son or daughter finally moves out, give him or her the money back to use as a down payment on a house or apartment or for furniture.

Secondly, it is important not to make the mistake of charging a nominal room and board fee, such as fifty or one hundred dollars per month. Sixty percent may seem steep, yet most adults probably spend easily this much of their income on rent, utilities, food, and home maintenance. In fact, 70 to 80 percent may be more realistic. Keep in mind that charging a nominal fee will keep your son or daughter trapped in a low-income job. Since all her money is available to pay for her car, clothes, recreation, and entertainment, she will have little motivation to earn more, yet always realize that she can't live independently on what she makes. Having little expendable income not only gives young adults a sense of real life, it gives them an incentive to build a better life for themselves.

Finally, set a date, a deadline, a circled day on the calendar for her to move out. Post the calendar where she can see it every day. Ask her every day, as the date draws near, if she has found a place, saved up enough money, and so on. One mother I worked with found these questions falling on deaf ears with her twenty-one-year-old son. Finally, I suggested she get packing boxes and fill up his room with them. He was astounded to see that she really meant it. Even down to the last few days before he was to leave, he had not packed, and doubted she would really ask him to leave. So she began to pack them. He got the message and finished the packing himself, but he still had not found a place. With two days to go, she gave him a list of rooming houses and apartments that were cheap and asked him to turn in his key. This was the final and most dramatic cue. He got on the phone to a friend and arranged, on the morning of the day he was to move out, to stay at a friend's house. Mother made it clear to him he could come back to eat any time he was hungry, and that he could come back for care any time he was ill. In fact, he was invited to drop in and visit or stay for dinner any time he wished, but he could not move back in. And he didn't, and it worked.

Problem Area 2: Coming Back Home After a Faltering Start

"Our daughter Kimberley, who is twenty-two, has come home to figure things out—again. This is the second time. She and her live-in boyfriend broke up again, and she didn't have the money to manage the rent on her own. We really don't like her associating with him, but we're helpless to say she can't see him, since she is an adult. He drinks and has been physically abusive to her. She says they need each other and that she is the only one who really understands him. She is gone all hours of the night, probably drinking with friends and smoking pot. We don't like it, but who are we to dictate to a twenty-two-year-old what her curfew should be? We can't treat her like she's sixteen. Should we simply be patient and wait for her to grow up and 'get it together'?"

Kimberley and her parents illustrate many of the characteristics of the "refuelers" who have come back home. They aren't teenagers; they have been out on their own and have had the freedom to live as they chose to. And yet, they are back home and living in their parents' home again. It must be remembered this is their parents' home, not theirs. Overindulgent parents feel torn between setting down rules, as if their children were still teenagers, and backing off completely, for fear of the conflict they will encounter. They want to treat their grown son or daughter like an adult, yet are dismayed by what they see as a lack of maturity. They want to place some demands on their adult children, yet feel sorry for them because they have been beaten down by life. They have trouble balancing the needs of the wounded young adult who seeks a safe haven, the needs of the younger children who may resent the older child's getting so much freedom and attention, and their own needs for peace and harmony in their home.

The key here is to have a mutually agreed-upon understanding in place before the young adult comes back home. It is necessary to do this ahead of time because it is at this time that the young person is in crisis and is highly motivated to reach the safe haven of home. He may be without funds, without a place to stay, without a car. Once he is settled into the comfort of home, I have found, there is no incentive to cooperate with a contract, other than the parents' threat of asking him to leave. This threat is such a negative incentive that it creates conflict, ill will, and still another crisis in the family. Most parents would rather avoid developing a contract rather than precipitate another crisis.

If parents demand that a contract be in place before the young adult comes home, this allows for two possibilities: the crisis will intensify, her motivation will increase, and an agreement will be reached that will prevent conflict and confrontation later on; or the young adult will see that the expectations placed on her are more than she is willing to accept and that she is better off choosing to live somewhere else instead. This saves a great deal of emotional pain for everyone.

Over the years, I have found the following areas to be the most important ones to be negotiated:

Reason for coming home and goals while there. Probably the most important issue is this one—to figure out what happened and to have some degree of a plan for the future. Again, we get back to goal setting. If their stated goal is "To get it together," persist in getting a more concrete response. Persist in asking tough questions that get your son or daughter actively problem-solving.

Example:

Q: "What mistakes do you feel you made?"

A: "I guess I partied too much and didn't study."

Q: "What do you need to do so that this doesn't happen again?"

A: "I don't know. I guess drink less and study more; maybe stay away from partying friends."

Example:

Q: "What mistakes do you feel you made?"

A: "I don't think I did. My roommate moved in with her boyfriend and left me with the rent. I couldn't handle it. And her checks for the utilities all bounced, and my name was on the bills, so I had to pay them."

Q: "But if you blame it all on her, you'll just feel like a helpless victim. What could you do differently in the future?"

A: "I guess I could ask for references on the next roommate. I could have a savings of five hundred dollars for things that come up that I hadn't planned on. I know, I could require both of us to put five hundred dollars into a joint bank account as a hedge against sudden move-outs. But I'll have to save up five hundred dollars to do that and find a roommate with that much money, too."

Next, pursue the dialogue with questions that narrow down and focus a list of concrete and measurable goals. Examples of goals:
"To complete one year of community college with a grade point average of B or better."
"To be drug-free for one year. To attend ninety Narcotics Anonymous meetings in ninety days."
"To get my car paid off in one year."
"To save one thousand dollars for deposits on an apartment."
"To work two jobs until I pay off all my debts."

The length of stay. It is helpful to all concerned to have an estimated date of departure. It gives the parents a sense of how long their return to parenting will last and when they can expect to have their privacy back again. It also gives the young adult a sense of optimism about the future. He does not have to feel like a failure who has come back home defeated and discouraged, having regressed to the status of a child again, with no end in sight. His enforced loss of status and loss of freedom is a finite circumstance. He can see the light at the end of the tunnel. There is a way out, and the time will be relatively brief. Here are some more examples:

"To stay here and work till Corey reaches school age and I can afford after-school care—about two years."
"To get over the pain of the divorce and get a job paying $25,000 a year—about six months."
"To go to vocational school and learn a new trade—hopefully, in nine months."

The parents' expectations. It is important to clarify the parents' expectations, since their expectations and the young adult's expectations may be quite different. If the goal is "getting a job," the parents' expectations may be that she spend three hours a day at it and take any job she can find. Their daughter's expectation may be that she wait until an opening in retail sales comes up at her favorite department store. If the goal is "going to school and partying less," the parents' expectations may be that he go to college full-time and not party at all. Their son's expectation may be that he go to school part-time so that he can keep his grades up and still party all weekend.

Differences in expectations inevitably lead to conflict unless ironed out in advance. If a young woman comes home because her husband physically abused her, her parents may expect that she will not see him again, at least until he undergoes treatment. They may be dismayed to find out that her expectation was that she would stay there until he apologized and promised not to do it again. A young man may come home with a goal of "not doing drugs anymore," which may be interpreted by his parents to mean not doing any addictive substances. What he may mean, however, is not doing cocaine and not dealing drugs. He may see drinking beer and smoking a little pot at parties as perfectly okay, because he's not doing hard drugs and he has it under control.

The possible need for them to seek professional help or attend support groups. Many of the "refuelers" and "wounded birds" do have significant emotional problems that led to their difficulties. Parents may see the need for professional help, but the underdeveloped young adult may not. Overindulgent parents will promote and encourage treatment once she is home. They will make the initial phone calls, provide transportation, even pay for treatment. Yet appointments are missed and offers of help are rejected. The parents are left feeling helpless and inadequate in the face of what they see is self-destructive behavior.

I have found it important to address these issues very early— before the adult child comes home. The young adult must be willing to make the initial phone call to set up an appointment, to attend a group or therapy session, and to pay for at least 25 percent of the cost. Though it may seem harsh, it is even more effective to require that she begin this treatment as a condition for being allowed to come home. The young adult may protest that she has no money, no car, no place to stay. But if she is sufficiently motivated, she can find a couch to sleep on and a ride to her first AA meeting, or her first battered women's meeting, which is free of charge.

Their contribution to household expenses. As stated before, it is by far best if the parents require a meaningful financial contribution if the son or daughter is working—something on the order of 50, or 60, or 70 percent of their take-home pay. If you feel guilty taking it, put it in a bank account and call it their savings account. Explain that it is a sign of respect to them as adults that they pay their way just as other responsible, mature adults do.

If they have no money and are job-hunting, let some nominal but reasonable amount of debt for living expenses accrue over time— possibly $250 per month, with the understanding that it will be paid back when they get a job. Don't feel guilty. It will give them an extra incentive to get to work soon and not to be too particular about the job they're looking for. If there are big jobs around the house for which you would have to pay a worker, and your child is capable of doing them, let him or her do those jobs for a set monetary value, to be applied against the debt. Examples: painting the house, chopping down a dead tree in the back yard, making new curtains for the living room, helping to finish out the basement, providing a weekend of baby-sitting the younger siblings while the parents get away by themselves.

Payment of bills. Will your adult child have medical insurance? (She cannot be included on your policy unless she is a full-time student.) If she doesn't have health insurance, who will pay her medical bills or the obstetric bills when the baby comes? Who will pay if the dentist says she needs a root canal? We have already touched on fees for psychological treatment and college tuition. What about her traffic fines if she should be pulled over for speeding? What is to happen if her car insurance comes due and she doesn't have the money? And if she needs a new transmission? It is easy to say, "Have her pay for them herself," yet what if she'll lose her job if she can't use that car to get to work? If she gets a DUI, or if she's going through a divorce and needs an attorney, who will pay? And the long-distance phone bills to the boyfriend or the estranged husband that range from fifty to one hundred dollars per month? What about those? Many of these bills must be paid yet are quite steep.

As far as possible, these issues need to be negotiated ahead of time. They need to be anticipated and talked about honestly and openly. The parents must make their position known. Keep in mind that if you take an overindulgent stance and set about to pay all these bills yourself, the consequence is likely to be negative. Not only will you feel taken advantage of, but her self-esteem will be further eroded and her dependency on you intensified. Instead, encourage her to pursue every avenue of financial help she can on her own. Encourage her to pursue help through Legal Aid and to pursue child support through the governmental support-recovery programs. Encourage her to apply for loans, scholarships, and work-study programs. Do not be too proud to let her apply for food stamps, free-lunch programs for the children, or low-cost health care through public clinics and medical schools. Even if she has little money, always require her to pay at least a small portion of the costs herself to allow her a degree of pride and dignity in her attempts at self-sufficiency.

Smoking, drinking, or drug use in the home. "How can I prevent him from smoking?" parents ask, "when he's twenty-two and he's a smoker. He's an adult. He can buy cigarettes whenever he wants." Your son may be an adult, but it is your house. You have a right to give guidelines about what is done in your house. The same goes for alcohol and street drugs. Overindulgent parents have difficulty setting limits with all of these addictive behaviors that they disapprove of but feel powerless to stop.

One mother agonized over her twenty-four-year-old son's abuse of alcohol while living with her. "How can I tell him simply to stop? He's an alcoholic just like his dad. Alcoholics can't just stop drinking. I would like him to get help, but he won't. All I can do is hope and pray that he'll cut down on his drinking." Another mother approached her twenty-year-old son's pot smoking this way: "Yes, he's smoking a little pot, but at least it's pot and not amphetamines. And I'm not sure he is, I just suspect it. I don't feel it's right to search his room. He's an adult now. He just got out of rehab six months ago, and he's been doing so well. I don't want to provoke an argument."

If you know that conflicts over cigarettes and controlled substances will be an issue when your grown offspring moves back home, discuss it ahead of time. Give your expectations, your limits, and the consequences for breaching those limits. It is only fair to your grown daughter to let her know what your terms are, so that she can choose whether she wants to move home under these conditions. If you're already in this situation, you need to attend a support group for family members of substance abusers. Toughlove is a good group for parents, and Alanon is an effective source of support for all members of the family.

Use of family possessions. You must also address the rules for the young adult's use of family possessions such as the car, telephone, television, stereo, etc. Is she to be a family member, just as the teenage siblings are, and abide by the same rules? Or does she have a special status with regard to use of these things because she is an adult? Or is she to be treated as a guest in the home who asks permission to use these things? What happens if she monopolizes the telephone? If she doesn't return the car when the seventeen-year-old needs it to get to work? Is her room her own? Or is the furniture in it yours? Can she keep her room as she pleases because she is an adult? Or is she to abide by your rules for neatness? Keep in mind that she is an adult and that you want to respect that. You do not want to diminish her self-esteem or emphasize her sense of failure by making her abide by the same rules as the teenagers. Yet you also want to be clear that it is still your house and these are still your possessions, and she must be respectful of everyone else in the house.

Comings and goings. Then there is the issue of the hours he keeps and his comings and goings. Is he to be granted the adult status of going out whenever he pleases and coming back at all hours of the night or early morning? After all, if he has lived on his own, can you realistically set a curfew for him as if he were sixteen? But, do you want to go through the apprehension of locking the doors late at night and listening for his car in the driveway? Is he expected for dinner? When do you prepare dinner if you have no idea if he will be there to eat it? Again, it is helpful to respect his adult status and grant him some degree of freedom and responsibility that is beyond that of the younger siblings. Some families have found it reasonable to have a policy that is at least somewhat restrictive and yet courteous and considerate to other family members. Some suggested guidelines might be:

- Always call by five P.M. to let us know your plans for dinner.
- When you go out, let us know where you are going.
- Be back by the time we go to bed [whatever that time is], or call to let us know when you'll be back.

- Be back by the time we go to bed, or call and let us know that you'll not be back till the following morning.
- Have dinner with us every Monday night. The rest of the week, you're on your own.
- If you're staying with friends, call at least once every twenty-four hours, to let us know your plans.

The company they keep. Often a great souce of conflict is the issue of the company they keep. If your grown daughter has come back home because her live-in boyfriend physically abused her, do you say nothing when she goes out on a date with him? If she has left her husband and come to you with her children, do you have a say in the matter when she goes out with her girlfriends to a singles bar? If she's single and you're enlightened, you might not mind whom she dates, but suppose you find out she's dating a married man? What then? And if his "user" friends call the house? Do you take their messages? Your adult son says he's come home to go to community college and pull his grades up, but his old buddies that he partied with in high school come by the house almost every night. Do you allow it? Do you forbid it?

Hopefully, if you set up a contract at the outset, this will not be a major problem. His goals, the reason why he is there, and what he hopes to accomplish was mapped out at the beginning. If the contract was thorough, it also addressed associating with certain people who may have a negative influence on the achieving of those goals. If not, now is the time to work up that contract or add in this element of socializing—how much, when, and with whom. Try to step out of the parental role of giving permission or forbidding contact with certain people. Instead, go back to your problem-solving dialogue. Ask questions that may stimulate him to think about his actions more carefully.

Example:
"We know you went out with Robert again, and we're concerned. We'll never forget how you looked that night he beat you. We care about you. It must be hard to say no to him. What kind of help do you need to be able to say no when he calls? How can we help you to achieve the goal you set when you came, which was to not see him for two months? What kinds of things can you think of to do that would keep you busy and keep your mind off Robert?"

Example:

"We've been concerned about how much time you've been spending with your old drinking buddies. When you came home, your goal was to study three hours a night, four nights a week, to pull your grades up. This past week, you've been home only two nights, and you spent one of those nights on the phone to your girlfriend. You're not keeping your commitment to us and to your yourself. We can't just stand by and say nothing or we're contributing to the problem. Yet we can't stand over you like we did when you were fourteen and say, 'You're not going anywhere till your homework is done.' You're too old for that.

"What do you need to do to stick to your plan? What's not working? Where do you need to make some changes? Is there a way we can help you make those changes?"

Impact on younger children. If your younger son has moved into his big brother's room while he was away, does he now move out again so that his big brother can have his old room back? Should the younger son have to share his room with his big brother after having had his own room for two years? Is that really fair to him?

What happens now that your grown daughter is back home and wants to borrow the car? The old family car was passed down to your sixteen-year-old daughter after big sister left home. Does your younger daughter have to give it up? Should she share it? She will say, "[Older sister] got to be the only one to use it when she lived here. Why shouldn't I? Let her get her own car." If the adult daughter uses the family car, is she expected to provide transportation to the younger, nondriving children? Should she be required to provide baby-sitting for the younger children? You may think, "Of course, she ought to do so as part of paying us back." On the other hand, she may counter with, "Why should I? I'm a boarder here. I'm paying rent. You wouldn't ask a boarder to provide transportation and child care." Discuss these issues ahead of time. Be prepared for how the younger children will react to these changes. Be ready to be challenged by both the older and younger siblings at the same time. Think out your position and be ready to explain it in a simple and reasonable fashion.

Children of the grown child. If your son or daughter has come home after a marriage fell apart and brings young children with him or her, you may welcome them with open arms. He or she will need a great deal of emotional support, and the children may feel emotionally lost and be suffering, too. However, the potential for conflict is great. We will devote a separate segment to this one issue later. Keep in mind that even at the outset, you want to try to anticipate some problems early and discuss them openly.

Housekeeping. Last, and certainly not least important, is the one obvious issue that is a minefield: housekeeping duties. Should your grown son be expected to contribute to the weekly grocery shopping, the cooking, the kitchen cleanup? Why not? He did so when he had his own apartment. What about the vacuuming, cleaning the bathrooms, taking out the trash? Surely, he should at least do his own laundry and take care of his room. Remember the answer of the dentist's mother who was interviewed on the television program, "Yes, he can do it for himself, but it's no problem." If he could, why didn't he? Often the answers overindulgent parents give have to do with love, guilt, and avoidance of conflict.

Example:
"Because I love him. I don't mind doing it, really I don't. I'm glad to be there for him when he needs me."

"Because I feel guilty asking her to help. She's got so much on her mind, and she's so down right now. I just don't want to burden her."

"I feel guilty asking him to help out around the house. He's so busy, going to school and working too. And besides, he is paying us rent. Shouldn't housekeeping come with the rent?"

"I just don't want to ask her. I know what will happen. We went through this when she was in high school. She would have shouting matches with me over these things. She feels I'm too picky, and we never see eye to eye on how clean a bathroom should be. It's just easier to do it myself."

As you walk through these minefields when you're drawing up your contract, keep in mind these points. First, housekeeping does not come with the rent. No landlord will ever come by to clean up the kitchen for them. Housekeeping chores don't go away when you're depressed, or tired, or busy, or have children. They still have to be done. Helping your adult child to learn this now can only help him in the future to juggle the multiple responsibilities that come with adult living. Helping him to handle "all this" when he's feeling overwhelmed is the best help you can give him.

Problem Area 3: Handling Crises From a Distance

"We disagree over how to handle calls for help from my youngest son and his wife. It seems they got in over their heads financially and were about to lose their house. They bought a big house with a swimming pool when they were both working and the money was coming in. Then she got laid off. Harry says, 'Not another penny.' I say, 'How can we let them lose their house?' After all, my grandchildren live there, too. We have helped out our youngest son many times before. When he was in college, he never could manage to live on the allowance we gave him. I don't know why he's having such a hard time getting a handle on his life and his finances. In fact, I've sensed a little resentment from our older two sons because we've never given them any money. But I can't help that. They've always been so self-sufficient and so capable, they haven't had any crises. They haven't needed help. They've never asked for money."

In overindulgent families such as these, the parents scratch their heads in bewilderment and reach for their checkbooks. The under-developed young adult, usually but not always the youngest, often resents the older siblings who "have been so lucky," and the self-sufficient siblings feel deeply mistreated. Often the parents can't understand why they feel mistreated. The older siblings see a pattern going on whereby irresponsibility is rewarded and good judgment and careful living are punished. They become increasingly hostile toward the parents and toward the underdeveloped sibling. The parents, hoping to avoid future crises, take over the job of deciding how the money is to be spent.

Examples:
"I'll buy you a house, but I'll own it and you pay me rent. Then one day when you're ready to buy me out, I'll let you have it back."
"I'll buy you a car, but it will have to be one that I pick out, because my money is going into it."

"I'll get you an attorney, but it will be my attorney, because I know she's good."

Soon the underdeveloped young adult living away from home is angry at Mom and Dad for controlling her life and treating her like a child. She feels insulted and demeaned. The well-meaning parents are embroiled in conflict and confrontation on all fronts.

Before responding to a crisis with a bailout, stop and think. Ask yourself these questions:

• Am I responding to a genuine crisis that came about through no fault of her own? Or is this a problem that she brought about through her own poor decisions?

• How will the other grown children see it? How will it look to them? Will they see this as fair?

• Have I stopped to consider that in sending money for this bailout, I am taking away from what is left for other needs that may arise in the future, such as genuine emergencies, my own future needs, and my grandchildren's college education?

One way to respond to this problem is to call a family meeting, if the other grown children live in the area, or to solicit their advice by phone. Make this a family decision. Work toward a consensus. Your other children may surprise you with the soundness of their recommendations.

Try to develop an approach that rewards hard work and responsibility, something like a "matching-funds" program.

Examples:

"You can go to another, more expensive college, but you'll have to come up with one-third the tuition. Your choices are wide open, and I'll match you three-to-one."

"I'll give you [or loan you] a small amount toward a new car, but only if you put up an equal amount of your own money."

Try to develop an approach that provides for your getting something out of the deal as well. This makes it a "contract of mutual interest" rather than a bailout. You are less likely to feel cheated, angry, and used later on. Consider how the other family members may want to be involved in the decision also. But be sure you do not take over and take control.

Examples:

"We'll go in with you on a new house, but we'll be half owners with you. When you sell it, we'll split the profit between us. We'll work out the details with an accountant."

"We'll put some money into your business, but we'd like to be a voting partner, too. I'll ask my accountant to go over the books with you to see if the business is sound."

"Your brother Tom says he'll kick in one thousand dollars, but he wants you to give him your old computer and printer and show him how to use it. Nancy says she can help out with five hundred dollars if you could keep her kids for three weeks this summer instead of her sending them to summer camp."

Problem Area 4: Grown Children Returning Home With Their Own Young Children

"Our daughter has moved back in with us and brought with her our two granddaughters, ages four and six. At first, we were happy to help out, but it has become more and more of a strain for us lately. We expected her to be here a month or two till she and her husband patched up their marriage, but now she's saying she doesn't want to get back together with him. She's enrolled in a nursing program that will take two years to complete. We didn't mind watching the girls at first, but now it's like we're tied down all the time. And last week we had it out with each other over how to punish the girls. The little one had gotten into my china cabinet to get cups and saucers to have a tea party with her dolls, and I gave her a good spanking. My daughter fussed at me and said, 'I'm the mother, I'll decide how they're to be punished,' and I said right back to her, 'And it's my house you're living in!' She didn't like that at all. Frankly, we just didn't count on all this. We had raised our kids and were through being parents. We want our quiet house back."

This last interchange illustrates the fundamental problem with grown children coming back home with their own children. The parent is the one in charge of the children, yet the grandparent is the one who owns and runs the house. Overindulgent parents often set few limits when these arrangements begin and so are dismayed when the conflict sets in, yet it inevitably does. The single-parent family they welcome into their home arrives with the expectation that they will be provided with an endless fountain of resources that will cost them nothing. The young adult parent has little sense of responsibility or obligation to the older parent and sets few limits with her own children. She expects a great deal from the older parents yet has few expectations of giving much in return. The young children are often demanding and out of control. The overindulgent pattern then extends through two sets of relationships and three generations.

As in a marriage, some clarification of who has control must be accomplished. The older parent can't reasonably take over all the parent's control of the children and completely demoralize her because "it's my home." Nor can she be driven into retreating into her back bedroom by seven o'clock every night, "to escape the noise." In a marriage, a couple may negotiate each and every issue, each time it comes up, and compromise carefully and equitably. Or one partner may give in completely to the other. A third choice is to divide up the turf into "your" area of control and "mine."

Example:
"Look, I think you should be in charge of punishment, because you are the parent. If we see them doing something we think they shouldn't be doing, we'll turn it over to you to handle. We'll accept your decision, provided you mete out some kind of punishment.

"But this is our house and these are our things and we're fussy about them. We think we should say where the girls can and can't go in the house. We'll lock up the expensive things and the breakables. But you must make it clear to them they are not to write on the walls, eat in the living room, or put their feet on the sofa."

If you can negotiate some of these issues ahead of time—how much the children will have to adjust to their new home and how much the new home will adjust to them—you'll prevent many arguments. A parent's emotions about his children are intense and even irrational at times. It will not work to in any way undermine his importance to the children or his sense of being the one who has the last say. Discipline and limit setting may be especially difficult areas where conflicts have to be resolved. Food, clothing, and hairstyles may seem like small issues but can become quite emotional. Television watching, manners, politeness, and bedtimes also need to be worked out. Again, try to seek compromises that respect your son's need to be the parent while respecting your need to have control of your home.

Example:
"Okay, I can see that you have set views about what they should watch on TV and I respect that. We don't mind what they watch as long as they watch the old TV in the family room and stay out of the living room when we're in there. We like the house quiet after eight-thirty, and would appreciate your turning the TV off then and getting them to bed."

Beyond this, child care can be a big source of conflict. As I view the problem, it seems best if the older parent gives the parent set hours when she will provide child care and requests at least a small fee for her time. I have yet to see an older parent do this. Parents who work and pay for child care know that quality, reliable child care is a precious commodity. They pay a day-care center $5,000 or more a year per child for child care, and are accustomed to paying a nanny around $15,000 to $20,000 a year for individualized care. Individualized care, provided by a biological relative, is even more valuable, as it is of even higher quality; thus, it is worth even more.

Parents who pay for child care shape their workday around the care that they have, set aside a large portion of their budget for it, and treat caregivers with respect. What message will you give your adult child if you provide the highest quality of care available at no charge, the hours are limitless, and the caregiver can't quit, no matter how much she may feel mistreated? How will your daughter make the transition to selecting and paying for high-quality care when she moves out? If you feel guilty about charging a nominal fee for the care, do it anyway and put the money in a bank account or buy savings bonds with it. Call it a college education fund for the grandchildren. When the grandchildren are graduating from high school, give the bonds back to them. Say it was money you earned baby-sitting them when they were little.

15 Concluding Remarks

In the three and a half years I have been compiling this book, I have continued to come across articles, programs, and research studies that bolster my assertion that the overindulgent parenting style is common among American families and that the implications of this problem are serious and far-ranging.

The January 19, 1995, edition of the CBS-TV news program *48 Hours* was titled "Discipline: When Is It Too Much?" One of the featured speakers was Dr. Larry Steinberg, a writer and developmental psychology researcher at Temple University in Philadelphia. The following is an excerpt from the transcript of the show:

> DR. STEINBERG: What we're seeing now in research is that children who haven't had limits set for them appropriately along the way—when they're two, three, four years old—are often children who develop discipline problems when they're in the elementary school years. And those are often kids who develop more serious problems during the adolescent years.
>
> *(Footage of Steinberg in his office)*
> ERIN MORIARTY *(voiceover):* Dr. Larry Steinberg is a psychologist who coauthored a four-year study of 20,000 teenagers. What he found is that problems in school, even the use of alcohol and drugs, can often be traced to what he calls indulgent parents.
>
> DR. STEINBERG: These are parents who might be very loving and warm toward their children, but these are parents who don't set very many limits and don't make very many demands of their kids. They let the kids call the shots.

The study Steinberg is referring to was conducted in 1991 with several colleagues and is described in his recently released book, *Crossing Paths: How Your Child's Adolescence Triggers Your Own*

Crisis. Steinberg and his partners interviewed 204 adolescents and their parents in order to explore what effect their children's adolescence had upon their parents' lives. As part of the study, he also looked at indicators of the teenagers' psychological well-being in four areas: emotional adjustment (whether they had high or low self-esteem), their school achievement (good grades or poor grades), their involvement in problem behavior (such as using drugs or alcohol), and their subjective reports of distress (for example, feelings of anxiety and depression).

He then categorized the families in terms of their adjustment to their adolescent's growing independence from them. About 80 percent of the parents fell into one of five categories (most of which should now be familiar to the reader): authoritative, autocratic (authoritarian), indulgent, overly enmeshed, or disengaged.

Steinberg expanded his groups to five in order to better differentiate those parents who were permissive out of a belief in trust, democracy, love, and so on, from those who had disengaged from the responsibilities of parenthood. While the indulgent parents (15 percent of the sample) became more permissive over time, they still maintained their emotional investment in the child. The disengaged group (about 10 percent of the families) pulled back completely, from limit-setting and from emotional involvement, saying things like, "I can't tell her what to do any more," and "He needs to learn from his mistakes." Steinberg's enmeshed group (about 15 percent) were those who were warm and loving toward their child, like the authoritative and the indulgent group, but who became increasingly overprotective and frustrated their child's efforts at independence and individuality. They were overly involved in managing the details of their child's everyday life.

Naturally, the group who fared best in adolescence were—you guessed it—the adolescents from the authoritative homes (about 50 percent). They were confident, socially self-assured, and had high self-esteem. They performed well in school and seemed to be motivated to achieve. They were less likely to get into trouble of any kind—alcohol, drugs, or juvenile delinquency. And they reported the lowest incidence of problems with anxiety and depression. These were the same "superkids" Diana Baumrind described nearly thirty years ago.

Steinberg also found that the adolescents from the indulgent homes were having trouble accepting authority. They were relatively confident and self-assured around their peers but were more likely than the other teenagers to get into trouble and to perform poorly in school.

If you've thought of giving up on your difficult adolescent, note that Steinberg found that the adolescents from the disengaged families fared worse still. Like those with a "neglecting" style, described in chapter 4, these parents (10 percent of his group) pulled back and lowered their level of involvement and investment in the adolescent's life. Like the indulgent parents, they were more permissive, but they lacked the warmth and emotional closeness of the indulgent group. These adolescents scored poorly on all four measures of psychological well-being. They were the most likely to become involved in drugs, alcohol, and crime. Steinberg's advice to parents of teens is clear: Don't be too permissive, but above all, don't disengage from your parental role.

I continue to see these families in my practice as well. I recently completed a custody evaluation on the O'Hara family. The O'Haras were finalizing a long and protracted divorce, including questions as to custody of and visitation with the youngest child, ten-year-old Megan. Father, Dan, was a very successful vice president of a financial services company. Mother, Peggy, was an assistant to the administrator of a nursing home. The O'Haras' marriage had held up well over the years, despite numerous transfers due to Dan's promotions. That is, until the middle child, Robert, hit his teens. He began to act out and rebel against mother and school authorities while Dan was away on his many lengthy business trips. Peggy and Dan quarreled over the next year over how to handle the situation while Robert drifted into drug use and skipping school.

Another move put a further strain on the family. Robert escalated even further and became physically abusive toward his mother and sisters. Dan became increasingly ambivalent about his approach and was sometimes overly harsh, even verbally abusive, and sometimes withdrawing. Peggy responded by sabotaging Dan's efforts, taking Robert out of treatment programs where Dan had arranged admission. By the time Robert entered his second drug rehabilitation center, Dan and Peggy had separated. By the time of the divorce, Dan had disengaged even more and Peggy had become more overindulgent.

When I interviewed him, Robert had stopped using drugs, but he had dropped out of school with a tenth-grade education and was drifting from one low-wage job to anther. He was attending an outpatient drug-free social program, but Dan had stopped attending with him, because Peggy wouldn't follow through with the consequences in the contract Robert had drawn up with his counselor. Dan wanted Robert to finish high school, but Robert said he "wasn't much for school." Peggy was content to have Robert live with her and to have the freedom to come and go as he pleased, as long as he didn't use drugs. She put no demands on him, gave him no responsibilities. Robert, at eighteen, was a lost and drifting young man with a sense of entitlement. When asked what his goal was, he said that he wanted "to take a few courses one day so that I can be able to do whatever I want."

This example, while highlighting some of the problems of the overindulgent and the disengaged style of parenting, also brings up another factor—the role of temperament. While Robert was doing poorly, older sister Aileen was a successful college student in her senior year of a tough premed program. Younger sister Megan, though emotionally troubled about the abuse from her brother and sad about her parents' impending divorce, was a straight-A student in school. What made the difference?

We know from resilience research that temperament plays a big factor in the importance of life events and family variables to adult adjustment. Resilience research incorporates the study of risk factors— those childhood factors associated with poor outcomes in adolescence or adulthood. Robert was male and had an oppositional, rebellious temperament. These factors set him apart from his sisters, who were more cautious and more conforming in their approach to life. These factors, though clearly challenging, would not pose a great problem in an authoritative household with two parents who go about parenting as a team. But a disengaged and often absent parent combined with an overindulgent mother proved to be two additional risk factors.

Over the years, I have observed that some children are at greater risk for behavioral problems in overindulgent households than are others. One group are the children (usually but not always boys) who are oppositional and defiant and continually challenge rules and requests to comply. These children typically respond to stress with disruptive behavior. Oppositional children continually push against the limits, and the limits must be firmly held. Several studies on the effects of divorce on children are now finding that these boys are especially at risk in single-parent homes where the mother is overindulgent.

Another high-risk group are the anxious and often dependent children. These are the children who refuse to sleep alone as young children, who resist separating from Mom or Dad. They are reluctant to approach new people and new experiences. They tend to avoid situations that might make them anxious. Overindulgent parents tend to allow, even foster, a great deal of dependency in these children, hampering their developmental efforts toward separation and independence.

A third group at risk are those children with attention deficit disorder. Some of these children are hyperactive and impulsive. They approach life in a reckless and haphazard manner, their poor judgment getting them into difficulty with parents, teachers, and peers alike. A subset of this group are not overly active but are extremely disorganized and forgetful, often bewildered and usually "off task"—engaged in pointless and irrelevant behaviors. They need clear rules and consistency, and structure, structure, and more structure. The overindulgent style, combined with this risk factor, is a particularly problematic combination. These parents tend to provide too little structure with no consistency, then find themselves in frequent rescue missions when the child is in a jam. These two factors together contribute toward high rates of school dropout, juvenile delinquency, and drug use among attention-deficit-disordered adolescents.

The Pirellis: The ADHD Child
in the Overindulgent Family

The Pirelli family is a case in point. Rita was a thirteen-year-old eighth grader who had already been diagnosed as having ADHD (attention deficit hyperactivity disorder) when the family came to see me. The mother, Barbara, called asking for help not just for Rita but "for the whole family. We're all miserable." Rita was immature and impulsive. She was constantly in trouble at school for not doing her work and for acting out in the classroom, even though she was on medication for her disorder. Barbara had tried making demands on Rita to be more responsible, but Rita's angry

outbursts—her yelling, door slamming, and refusals to comply—
simply wore Barbara down. Harry traveled and was out of town for
most of the week. When he was home, he would explode at Rita in
a tirade of verbal abuse. Then, feeling guilty, he would take her
shopping. "After all," he said, "that's why I work hard all week, to
spend money on Barbara and the girls."

We worked for a while on a behavioral contract, but Barbara
and Harry had trouble sticking to their end of the agreement and
following through with consequences. Then I handed them the
manuscript for this book one afternoon and suggested they might
want to try a little outside reading. Harry took it with him on his
next business trip. Barbara read it, too, and they both reported that
the ideas in the manuscript were starting to click.

The turning point came when big sister Andrea came to a
session. Andrea was a star student and champion swimmer, never a
behavior problem. Again, this family's parenting style was not a
problem for Andrea, only for Rita. Andrea cried as she told the
family how she didn't want to bring anyone over to the house
because of all the yelling and fighting. Everyone was moved. Harry
stopped yelling and went back to following through with consequences. Barbara stuck to her guns and didn't give in. Rita felt
some guilt for the first time, too, as she heard how her behavior had
been affecting the family. Rita resolved to make her bed every day,
do her homework, and comply with her mom's requests. She even
volunteered to mow the lawn. "I started to tell her she couldn't, to
wait for her father to come home, but then I remembered what you
said in the book, to let them try something difficult," Barbara said.
"Rita did a beautiful job. Her dad was so proud of her when he saw
the lawn." The family had had their best week ever the last time I
saw them. Rita formally made amends to everyone in the family,
and they each gave her specific, individualized positive feedback
about her behavior that week.

I recently gave a talk to a group of child protective services
caseworkers on "transcenders"—those children who seem stress-
resistant. The late sixties ushered in a shift toward studying wellness in
our society as opposed to sickness, and psychological research has
followed this trend. Researchers began to study those children who
defied the odds and did well in adulthood despite coming from

unstable families, having mentally ill or criminal parents, or having sustained abuse or trauma of some kind.

In researching the talk, I found much of my reading dovetailing with points that were raised in the previous chapters in this book. One important point was that stress, in and of itself, is not necessarily harmful to children. Dr. E. James Anthony, a psychiatrist at the Washington University Medical School in St. Louis, studied three hundred children born to psychotic parents. After twelve years, he had identified a group of 8 to 10 percent of these children who were doing so well, he called them "invulnerables." Anthony came to the conclusion that not only did these children have good problem-solving skills and many competencies, but that it was coping with stress that made them strong. Low-risk situations (families whose children are sheltered from even moderate levels of stress) may create a false belief that a child is invulnerable, according to Anthony, but the child "has never been tested or tried in the fire of experience." Anthony returns to Greek myths to make the point that rather than being protected from risk, the hero is exposed to it and gains in confidence and competence with each encounter. Anthony advocates that parents take the position of letting the children be the masters of their own fate.

E. Mavis Hetherington, a psychologist at the University of Virginia and one of the pioneers of child development research in the United States, looked at resilience and successful coping in a longitudinal study of 180 parents who were divorcing and the children from those families. She found that most children who had warm, emotional support from their parents actually developed more adaptive skills when stress levels were moderate than when they were extremely low (or high). She concluded that, for the average child, some practice in solving stressful problems under supportive conditions enhanced their later abilities in all those areas that appear so lacking in under-developed children. These areas include the ability to delay gratification, to persist at difficult tasks, and to be flexible and creative in problem solving and in interpersonal relationships. She also found that if the stresses were spread out over time, the children could cope with them more easily.

Both Hetherington and Anthony refer to the work of the eminent British psychiatrist and researcher Michael Rutter, who first developed the concept of "inoculation" against stress. Protection, Rutter has written, "is not a matter of pleasant happenings" but a matter of developing skills that help our children cope successfully with stress. Rutter studied a large sample of children in poor neighborhoods in London whose parents were mentally ill, as well as a group of children living on the Isle of Wight, and he continued to follow them for many years. Immunization against stress, he concluded, lay not in avoiding stress but in the successful engagement with stress. Rutter referred back to earlier studies on alterations in hormonal levels in paratroopers in training to suggest that actual biological changes occur in the body as a result of successful coping. These biological adaptations are a vital part of life experiences, he concluded, part of nature's way of strengthening us.

When I asked for questions at the end of the seminar, one woman expressed surprise that the children who were given moderate amounts of stress, spaced apart over time, were more competent young adults than those who had had low amounts of stress. She asked how she could apply this to her own children—how she could "dose" them with moderate amounts of manageable stress. "Let them make decisions," I told her, "let them assume a little more responsibility than you're comfortable with. Let them set and work toward important goals. Let them experience the consequences of their actions, if these consequences are not life altering. When they fail, calmly help them explore why they've failed and encourage them to make a plan to succeed the next time. Think of them always as developing competencies at handling the myriad of challenging experiences life will have in store for them."

Rutter surveyed the whole field of resilience research in 1987 and concluded there were essentially two protective factors that ensured an emotionally healthy life as an adult. The first was a well-established feeling of one's own worth as a person. Everything we know about this area suggests that secure early attachments to warm, supportive individuals (at least one) make it more likely that children will grow up with high self-esteem and self-efficacy. The second major protective factor is the conviction that one can cope successfully with life. This belief appears to come from the successful accomplishment of tasks important to the individual. These tasks may be interpreted broadly as social successes, the taking on of responsibility, success in artistic skills or athletics, as well as academic successes.

Overindulgent parents already know how to provide secure early attachments. With this book, it is hoped that by giving our children responsibility, setting clear and consistent limits, not rescuing them, and helping them develop good problem-solving skills, these families can then provide the second factor that Rutter describes as ensuring a good life, even amid the hardships that lie ahead.

References

Chapter One

Harris, Marvin. "How Many Children?" and "The Need to Be Loved." In *Our Kind*. New York: Harper & Row, 1989.

Heininger, Mary Lynn Stevens. "Children, Childhood, and Change in America, 1820–1920. In *A Century of Childhood, 1820–1920*. Rochester, N.Y.: The Margaret Woodbury Strong Museum, 1984.

Kagan, Jerome. Chap. 7. In *The Nature of the Child*. New York: Basic Books, 1984.

Kett, Joseph. *Rites of Passage*. New York: Basic Books, 1977.

Konner, Melvin. *Childhood*. Boston: Little, Brown, 1991.

Spock, Benjamin, and Michael B. Rothenberg. "The Parents' Part." In *Dr. Spock's Baby and Child Care*. New York: Simon & Schuster (Pocket Book Edition), 1985.

Stone, Lawrence. *The Family, Sex, and Marriage in England, 1500–1800*. New York: Harper & Row, 1977.

Whiting, John, and Beatrice Whiting. *Children of Six Cultures*. Cambridge: Harvard University Press, 1975.

Chapter Four

Alpert-Gillis, Linda, et al. "The Children of Divorce Intervention Program: Development, Implementation, and Evaluation of a Program for Young Urban Children." *Journal of Consulting and Clinical Psychology* 57, no. 5 (1989): 583–89.

Asarnow, Joan, et al. "Coping Strategies, Self-Perceptions, Hopelessness, and Perceived Family Environments in Depressed and Suicidal Children." *Journal of Consulting and Clinical Psychology* 55, no. 3 (1987): 361–66.

Baumrind, Diana. "Effects of Authoritative Parental Control on Child Behavior." *Child Development* 37 (1966): 887–907.

_____. "Child Care Practices Anteceding Three Patterns of Preschool Behavior." *Genetic Psychology Monographs* 75 (1967): 43–88.

_____. "Current Patterns of Parental Authority." *Developmental Psychology Monograph* 4, no. 1 (1971): 1–103.

Baumrind, Diana, and Allen E. Black. "Socialization Practices Associated with

Dimensions of Competence in Preschool Boys and Girls." *Child Development* 38 (1967): 291–327.

Becker, Wesley. "Consequences of Different Kinds of Discipline." In *Review of Child Development Research*, Vol. 1, ed. M. L. Hoffman & L. W. Hoffman. New York: Russell Sage, 1964.

Camp, Bonnie. W., and Mary Ann Bash. *Think Aloud: Increasing Social and Cognitive Skills—A Problem Solving Program for Children: Primary Level.* Champaign, Ill.: Research Press, 1981.

Compas, Bruce. "Coping with Stress During Childhood and Adolescence." *Psychological Bulletin* 101 (1987): 393–403.

––––––. "Stress and Life Events During Childhood and Adolescence." *Clinical Psychology Review* 7 (1987): 275–302.

Compas, Bruce, et al. "Coping With Stressful Events in Older Children and Young Adolescents." *Journal of Consulting and Clinical Psychology* 56, no. 3 (1988): 405–11.

Coopersmith, Stanley. *The Antecedents of Self-Esteem.* San Francisco: Freeman, 1967

Elardo, P. T., and M. Cooper. *Aware: Activities for Social Development.* Menlo Park, Calif.: Addison-Wesley, 1977

Folkman, Susan, and Richard Lazarus. "An Analysis of Coping in a Middle-aged Community Sample." *Journal of Health and Social Behavior* 21 (1980): 219–39.

Folkman, Susan, et al. "Appraisal, Coping, Health Status, and Psychological Symptoms. *Journal of Personality and Social Psychology* 50 (1986): 571–79.

Hanson, Cindy, et al. "Coping Styles in Youths With Insulin-Dependent Diabetes Mellitus. *Journal of Consulting and Clinical Psychology* 57, no. 5 (1989): 644–51.

Howie, R. "The Relationship Between Interpersonal Problem Solving Ability of Four-Year-Olds and Parental Values and Attitudes." Ph.D. diss. Millersville State College, Millersville, Pa.

Krohne, Heinz Walter. "Parental Child-Rearing Behavior and the Development of Anxiety and Coping Strategies in Children." In *Stress and Anxiety*, vol. 7, ed. G. Sarason and C. D. Spielberger. Washington, D.C.: Hemisphere, (1979):233–45.

Lazarus, Richard, and Susan Folkman. *Stress, Appraisal, and Coping.* New York: Springer, 1984.

Levy, David. *Maternal Overprotection.* New York: Columbia University Press, 1943.

McClelland, David C. Chap. 9. In *The Achievement Motive.* New York: Appleton, 1953.

Platt, Jerome, et al. "Adolescent Problem-Solving Thinking." *Journal of Consulting and Clinical Psychology* 42 (1974):, 787–93.

Rotheram-Borus, Mary, et al. "Cognitive Style and Pleasant Activities Among Female Adolescent Suicide Attempters." *Journal of Consulting and Clinical Psychology* 58, no. 5 (1990): 554–61.

Shure, Myrna, and George Spivack. *Problem-Solving Techniques in Child Rearing*. San Francisco: Jossey Bass, 1978, 8–10.

————. "Means-End Thinking, Adjustment, and Social Class Among Elementary School Aged Children." *Journal of Consulting and Clinical Psychology* 38 (1972): 348–53.

Shure, Myrna, et al. "Problem-Solving Thinking and Adjustment Among Disadvantaged Preschool Children." *Child Development* 42 (1971): 1791–1803.

Spivack, George, and M. Levine. "Self-Regulation in Acting-Out and Normal Adolescents." Report to National Institute of Health, M–4531, Washington, D. C.: United States Public Health Service, 1963.

Spivack, George, and Myrna Shure. "The Cognition of Social Adjustment: Interpersonal Cognitive Problem-Solving Thinking." *Advances in Clinical Child Psychology* 5 (1982): 323–72.

————. "ICPS and Beyond: Centripetal and Centrifugal Forces." *American Journal of Community Psychology* 13 (1985): 226–43.

Weissberg, Roger, et al. *The Rochester Social Problem Solving Program: A Training Manual for Teachers of Second to Fourth Grade Children*. Rochester, N.Y.: Center for Community Study, 1979.

————. "The Evaluation of a Social Problem Solving Training Program for Suburban and Inner-City Third Grade Children." *Journal of Consulting and Clinical Psychology* 49 (1981) 251–61.

————. "Problem-Solving Skills Training: A Competence-Building Intervention with Second- to Fourth-Grade Children." *American Journal of Comunity Psychology* 9 (1981) 411–23.

Winterbottom, Myrna. "The Relationship of Childhood Training in Independence to Achievement Motivation." Ph.D. diss. University of Michigan, 1953.

Youngstrom, Nina. "Develop Coping Skills of Children, Panel Told." *APA Monitor*, Aug. 1991, 23.

Chapters 7 and 8

Ames, Louise, and Frances Ilg. *Your Two-Year-Old: Terrible or Tender*. New York: Dell, 1976.

————. *Your Three-Year-Old: Friend or Enemy*. New York: Dell, 1976.

————. *Your Four-Year-Old: Wild and Wonderful*. New York: Dell, 1976.

————. *Your Five-Year-Old: Sunny and Serene*. New York: Dell, 1979.

————. *Your Six-Year-Old: Loving and Defiant*. New York: Dell, 1979.

Doll, Edgar. *Vineland Social Maturity Scale*. Circle Pines, Minnesota: American Guidance Service, 1965 edition.

————. *Preschool Attainment Record*. Circle Pines, Minnesota: American Guidance Service, 1966.

Dreikurs, Rudolf. *Children: The Challenge*. New York: Dutton, 1964.

Dreikurs, Rudolph, and Loren Gray. *The New Approach to Discipline: Logical Consequences*. New York: Dutton, 1990.

Ferber, Richard. *Solve Your Child's Sleep Problems*. New York: Fireside, 1985.

Galinsky, Ellen, and Judy David. *The Preschool Years: Family Strategies That Work—From Experts and Parents*. New York: Times Books, 1988.

Lipson, Eden Ross. *The New York Times Parents' Guide to the Best Books for Children*. New York: Times Books, 1988.

Mussen, Paul, et al. *Child Development and Personality*, 6th ed. New York: Harper & Row, 1984.

Chapters 9 and 10

Ames, Louise, and Carol Haber. *Your Seven-Year-Old: Life in a Minor Key*. New York: Dell, 1985.

————. *Your Eight-Year-Old: Lively and Outgoing*. New York: Dell, 1989.

————. *Your Nine-Year-Old: Thoughtful and Mysterious*. New York: Dell, 1990.

Ames, Louise, et al. *Your Ten- to Fourteen-Year-Old*. New York: Dell, 1988.

Brainard, Beth. *You Can't Sell Your Brother at the Garage Sale: The Kids' Book of Values*. New York: Dell, 1992.

Damon, William. *The Moral Child: Nurturing Children's Natural Moral Growth*. New York: Free Press, 1988.

Doll, Edgar. *Preschool Attainment Record*. Circle Pines, Minnesota: American Guidance Service, 1966.

————. *Vineland Social Maturity Scale*. Circle Pines, Minnesota: American Guidance Service, 1965.

Dreikurs, Rudolf, and Loren Grey. *The New Approach to Discipline: Logical Consequences*. New York: Dutton, 1990.

Eyre, Linda, and Richard Eyre. *Teaching Children Responsibility*. New York: Ballantine, 1984.

Feldman, Beverly Neuer. "Raise Your Child to Become a Millionaire. " In *Kids Who Succeed*. New York: Fawcett, 1987.

Hancock, Emily. *The Girl Within*. New York: Fawcett, 1993.

Konner, Melvin. *Childhood*. Boston: Little, Brown, 1991.

Lee, Thonnia. "Making Allowances." *Atlanta Journal and Constitution*, Feb. 26, 1992.

Poole, Sheila. "Kids Can Start Early Learning About Money Management." *Atlanta Journal and Constitution*, Sept. 16, 1991.

Chapters 11 and 12

Bakan, David. "Adolescence in America: From Idea to Social Fact." In *Twelve to Sixteen: Early Adolescence,* ed. J. Kagan and R. Coles. New York: Norton, 1972.

Conger, John. "A World They Never Knew: The Family and Social Change." In *Twelve to Sixteen: Early Adolescence,* ed. J. Kagan and R. Coles. New York: Norton, 1972.

Dalglish, Art. "Survey Finds Teenagers Don't Understand Money." *Atlanta Journal and Constitution,* Sept. 12, 1991.

Dinkmeyer, Don, and Gary McKay. *Parenting Teenagers: Systematic Training for Effective Parenting of Teens.* Circle Pines, Minnesota: American Guidance Service, 1990.

Elkind, David. "Money Management for Teens." *Parents,* Nov. 1989, 222.

————. "Adolescents in the Post-Modern Age." Talk given at the opening of the Summitridge Medical Center, Lawrenceville, Georgia, Mar. 25, 1993.

————. "The Facts About Teen Suicide." *Parents,* Jan. 1990, 111.

Eyre, Linda, and Richard Eyre. *Teaching Children Responsibility.* New York: Ballantine, 1984.

Godfrey, Neale, and Carolina Edwards. *Money Doesn't Grow on Trees: A Parent's Guide to Raising Financially Responsible Children.* New York: Fireside, 1994.

Jorgensen, Randall, and Jerome Dusek. "Adolescent Adjustment and Coping Strategies." *Journal of Personality* 58, no. 3 (1990): 503–13.

Kagan, Jerome. "A Conception of Early Adolescence." In *Twelve to Sixteen: Early Adolescence,* ed. J. Kagan and R. Coles. New York: Norton, 1972.

Konner, Melvin. "Metamorphosis." In *Childhood.* New York: Little, Brown, 1991.

Lamb, Doris. *Psychotherapy With Adolescent Girls.* New York: Plenum Press, 1986.

Luke, Robert. "Own a Piece of Disney World." *Atlanta Journal and Constitution,* Mar. 22, 1991.

Martin, Edward. "Reflections on the Early Adolescent in School." In *Twelve to Sixteen: Early Adolescence,* ed. J. Kagan, and R. Coles. New York: Norton, 1972.

Patterson, Joan, and Hamilton McCubbin. "Adolescent Coping Style and Behaviors: Conceptualization and Measurement.: *Journal of Adolescence* 10 (1987) 163–86.

York, Phyllis, et al. *Toughlove Solutions.* New York: Bantam, 1985.

Chapters 13 and 14

Ashner, Laurie, and Mitch Meyerson. *When Parents Love Too Much.* New York: Avon, 1990.

Eberle, Nancy. "The Full Nest Syndrome." *Woman's Day*, July 7, 1987.

Halpern, Howard. "As Long as He Needs Me." In *You and Your Grown-Up Child: Nurturing a Better Relationship*. New York: Fireside, 1992.

Kiley, Dan. *The Peter Pan Syndrome*. New York: Avon, 1983.

Littwin, Susan. *The Postponed Generation: Why American Youth Are Growing Up Later*. New York: William Morrow, 1986.

Martz, Geoffrey. *How to Survive Without Your Parents' Money*. New York: Villard, 1993.

Okimoto, Jean, and Phyllis Stegall. *Boomerang Kids*. Boston: Little, Brown, 1987.

Peck, M. Scott. *The Road Less Traveled*. New York: Simon & Schuster, 1978.

Toufexis, Alexis. "Show Me the Way to Go Home." *Time*, May 4, 1987, 106.

Chapter 15

Hetherington, E. Mavis. "Coping With Family Transitions: Winners, Losers, and Survivors." *Child Development* 60 (1989): 1–14.

Lamborn, Susie, et al. "Patterns of Competence and Adjustment Among Adolescents from Authoritative, Authoritarian, Indulgent, and Neglectful Homes." *Child Development* 62 (1991): 1049–65.

Pines, Maya. "Superkids." *Psychology Today*, Jan. 1979, 53–63.

Rutter, Michael. "Psychosocial Resilience and Protective Mechanisms." *American Journal of Orthopsychiatry* 57, no. 3 (1987): 316–31.

Steinberg, Lawrence, et al. *Crossing Paths: How Your Child's Adolescence Triggers Your Own Crisis*. New York: Simon & Schuster. 1994.

————. "Over-Time Changes in Adjustment and Competence Among Adolescents From Authoritative, Authoritarian, Indulgent, and Neglectful Families." *Child Development*, in press.

Suggested Reading for Children

The following books represent only a very partial list of the many books for young children that portray characters solving problems, facing difficulties, becoming more independent, displaying courage, persevering at a difficult task, and showing responsibility and concern toward others. A good reference work that has recently been published is: *Books That Build Character,* by William Kilpatrick and Gregory and Suzanne M. Wolfe (New York: Touchstone, 1994). This book not only includes fiction works for children, organized by age groups, but also includes book listings from historical fiction, biography, and sacred texts. Also of interest is William Bennett's compendium, *The Book of Virtues* (New York: Simon & Schuster, 1993). Billed as "a treasury of great moral stories," the book is organized around themes such as responsibility, self-discipline, courage, honesty, and faith. Keep it handy for bedtime reading.

Storybooks for Young Children, Ages Three to Six

Andersen, Hans Christian. *The Ugly Duckling.* (San Diego: Harcourt Brace Jovanovich, 1979). A timeless tale of endurance and patience in the face of rejection, unfairness, and mistreatment. It gives children hope that they, too, can triumph over adversity if they discover their true identity.

Babbitt, Natalie. *The Something.* (New York: Farrar, Straus, 1970). A little boy faces a nighttime fear in a creative way.

Brown, Marc. *Arthur's Nose.* (Boston: Atlantic-Little, Brown, 1976). An aardvark comes to terms with his unusual nose. The first of a series about coping. See also: *Arthur's Pet Business.*

Brown, Marc, and Stephen Krensky. *Dinosaurs, Beware!* (Boston: Atlantic-Little, Brown, 1982). A basic guide to household safety.

———. *Dinosaurs Divorce: A Guide for Changing Families.* (Boston: Little, Brown, 1986). Dinosaurs cope with the trauma of divorce.

Brown, M. K. *Let's Go Swimming With Mr. Sillypants.* (New York: Crown, 1986). Mr. Sillypants overcomes his fear of swimming.

Cohen, Miriam. *Will I Have a Friend?* (New York: Aladdin-Macmillan, 1967). The first of three about Paul, who adjusts to kindergarten.

Heine, Helme. *Friends.* (New York: Aladdin-Macmillan, 1982). A story of cooperation and helpfulness between a rooster, mouse, and pig.

Hewatt, Joan. *Rosalie.* (New York: Lothrop, 1987). Rosalie is an old dog but the family makes adjustments for her.

Hill, Susan. *Go Away, Bad Dreams.* (New York: Random House, 1985). Tom learns how to use his imagination to make bad dreams go away.

Hines, Anna. *All By Myself.* (New York: Clarion, 1984). A little girl goes to the bathroom in the dark all by herself.

Hughes, Shirley. *Alfie Gives a Hand.* (New York: Mulberry-William Morrow, 1984). Alfie is shy but overcomes this to help a girl shyer than he. See also: *An Evening at Alfie's* and *Alfie Gets In First.*

Jonas, Ann. *When You Were a Baby.* (New York: Greenwillow–William Morrow, 1982). A book for toddlers and preschoolers. All stories end with "but now you can..."

Joyce, William. *George Shrinks.* (New York: HarperCollins, 1985). George shrinks to a tiny size and has to cope with chores.

Lester, Helen. *Pookins Gets Her Way.* (Boston: Houghton Mifflin, 1987). Pookins is spoiled rotten but learns a lesson about cooperation. See also *Tacky the Penguin.*

Lobel, Arnold. *Fables.* (New York: HarperCollins, 1980). Short fables with contemporary morals.

McKissack, Patricia. *Flossie and the Fox.* (New York: Dial, 1986). Flossie outwits the fox in this Tennessee folktale.

McPhail, David. *First Flight.* (Boston: Little, Brown, 1987). A little boy goes on his first airplane trip to his grandmother's. See also *Andrew's Bath; A Big Fat Enormous Lie; I Want to Be Big;* and *Henry Bear's Park.*

Piper, Watty. *The Little Engine That Could.* (New York: Platt & Munk-Putnam, 1930). The classic story about a little train with perseverance.

Scarry, Richard. *Richard Scarry's Pig Will and Pig Won't.* (New York:

Random House, 1984). Good lessons, well taught, about manners and cooperation.

Seignobosc, Francoise. *Minou*. (New York: Scribner's, 1962). A cat in Paris overcomes his fear of the world beyond his home.

Dr. Seuss. *Horton Hatches the Egg*. (New York: Random House, 1940). A classic story about persevering in the face of trials and tribulations.

Sharmat, Marjorie. *Gila Monster Meets You at the Airport*. (New York: Puffin-Penguin, 1980). A boy moves cross country and copes with his fears.

Steig, William. *Amos and Boris*. (New York: Penguin, 1971). A story about the merits of cooperation and helpfulness.

Tusa, Tricia. *Libby's New Glasses*. (New York: Holiday, 1984). An ostrich helps Libby cope with new glasses.

Vincent, Gabrielle. *Ernest and Celestine*. (New York: Mulberry-William Morrow, 1982). Ernest tries to solve the problem of the lost duck-doll for Celestine. See also *Ernest and Celestine at the Circus; Ernest and Celestine's Patchwork Quilt;* and *Breakfast Time, Ernest and Celestine.*

Watanabe, Shiego. *How Do I Put It On?* (New York: Philomel, 1979). A story about "doing it all by myself." See also *I Can Take a Walk, I Can Build a House!* and *I'm the King of the Castle.*

Storybooks and Early Readers, Ages Seven to Nine

Andrews, Jan. *Very Last First Time*. (New York: McElderry-Macmillan, 1986). Eva, an Inuit girl and her first trip under the sea ice to gather mussels for her family to eat.

Brainard, Beth. *You Can't Sell Your Brother at the Garage Sale: The Kids' Book of Values*. (New York: Dell, 1992). Chapters discuss issues such as taking responsibility, being a good friend, fighting prejudice, and getting involved.

Delisle, Jim. *Kidstories: Biographies of Twenty Young People You'd Like to Know*. (Minneapolis: Free Spirit Publishing, 1991). True stories profile real kids who are doing something special to improve themselves, their schools, their communities, or their world.

Dragonwagon, Crescent. *Always, Always*. (New York: Macmillan, 1984). A little girl copes with spending the school year with her mother in New York and her summers with father in Colorado.

Drew, Naomi. *Learning the Skills of Peacemaking: An Activity Guide for Elementary-Age Children on Communicating, Cooperating, Resolving Conflict.* (Rolling Hills Estates, Calif.: Jalmar Press, 1987). Sixty-six concrete lessons teach specific, essential peacemaking skills: compromise, mediation, and cooperative problem-solving.

Flournoy, Valerie. *The Patchwork Quilt.* (New York: Dial, 1985). Tanya's family works together to complete grandmother's quilt.

Griffith, Helen. *Georgia Music.* (New York: Greenwillow–William Morrow, 1986). A little girl eases her grandfather's dying.

Herzig, Alison Cragin, and Jane Lawrence Mali. *Oh Boy! Babies!* (Boston: Little, Brown, 1980). Preppy boys take a course in infant and child care.

Kurelek, William. *A Prairie Boy's Winter.* (Boston: Houghton Mifflin, 1973). An account of a prairie farm in winter in the 1930s.

Lasker, Joe. *The Do Something Day.* (New York: Viking, 1982). Bernie is burning to do something and sets off on a tour of his neighborhood.

Lobel, Arnold. *Fables.* (New York: HarperCollins, 1980). Contemporary fables for children of many ages.

Navarra, Tova. *Playing It Smart: What to Do When You're On Your Own.* (Hauppage, N.Y.: Barron's, 1989). What to do if: you get separated from Mom and Dad, the electricity goes off in the house, a friend tells you a secret, etc.

O'Donnell, Elizabeth Lee. *Maggie Doesn't Want to Move.* (New York: Four Winds–Macmillan, 1987). Seven-year-old Simon insists he doesn't mind moving, it's his sister, Maggie, who will miss the playground.

Peet, Bill. *Pamela Camel.* (Boston: Houghton Mifflin, 1984). This brave camel prevents a wreck by stopping a train. See also *Hermit the Kermit.*

Rabe, Bernice. *The Balancing Girl.* (New York: Dutton-Penguin, 1981). Margaret is confined to a wheelchair and learns to develop special skills.

Schwartz, Linda. *What Would You Do? A Kid's Guide to Tricky and Sticky Situations.* (Santa Barbara, Calif.: The Learning Works, 1990).

Sample contents: runaway pet, stuck in an elevator, drunk adults, nosebleed.

Steptoe, John. *Stevie*. (New York: HarperCollins, 1969). A black boy copes with the problems a foster brother causes in the house.

Waddell, Martin. *Go West*. (New York: HarperCollins, 1984). Diary of a nine-year-old girl who goes west by covered wagon.

Williams, Vera. *A Chair for My Mother*. (New York: Mulberry-William Morrow, 1982). A wonderful story about a little girl who helps her mother wait tables in order to buy her a chair. See also *Music, Music for Everyone* and *Something Special For Me*.

—————. *Three Days on a River in a Red Canoe*. (New York: Mulberry–William Morrow, 1991). An account of the trip with instructions on how to set up a tent, make a fire, and cook.

Ages Ten to Fifteen

Armstrong, William. *Sounder*. (New York: HarperCollins, 1969). A young black boy must come to terms with racism and his father's imprisonment.

George, Jean Craighead. *Juliet of the Wolves*. (New York: Harper-Collins, 1972). Miyax runs away and finds herself lost in the Alaskan wilderness where she learns to live with wolves.

—————. *My Side of the Mountain*. (New York: Puffin-Penguin, 1959). The author, a nature writer, writes of a boy who builds himself a treehouse, in a story of courage, independence, and curiosity.

Hautzig, Esther. *The Endless Steppe*. (New York: HarperCollins, 1968). The year is 1941. A girl and her family are herded to a Siberian labor camp for five years, charged with being capitalists.

Hipp, Earl. *Fighting Invisible Tigers: A Stress Management Guide for Teens*. (Minneapolis: Free Spirit Publishing, 1995). Proven, practical advice covers everything from coping with stress to being assertive, building supportive relationships, taking risks, making decisions, dealing with fears, using positive self-talk, even growing a funny bone.

Java, John. *Fifty Simple Things Kids Can Do to Save the Earth*. (Berkeley, Calif.: Earthworks Gp., 1990). Wonderful ideas for helping kids feel they can make a difference. Sample items: cut down

on energy use in the home, make a birdbath, write a letter to the
editor of the local newspaper, adopt an animal, write to world
leaders.

Karnes, Frances A., and Suzanne M. Bean. *Girls and Young Women
Inventing: Twenty True Stories about Inventors and Their Inven-
tions.* (Minneapolis: Free Spirit Publishing, 1995). Part I presents
true stories, such as the inventor of the Lectro-Lock and the Pocket
Diaper. Part 2 includes tips on creative problem-solving, making a
prototype, applying for a patent, and developing a marketing plan.

––––––––. *Girls and Young Women Leading the Way: Twenty True
Stories About Leadership.* (Minneapolis: Free Spirit Publishing,
1993). Girls and young women share their personal experiences with
leadership, from earning a Girl Scout badge to organizing a com-
munity-wide event. Includes a "Leadership Handbook" section.

Krumgold, Joseph. *...and Now Miguel.* (New York: HarperCollins,
1953). Twelve-year-old Miguel wants to go with the men in his family
on a long and hard sheep drive to the Sangre de Cristo Mountains.

Lewis, Barbara A. *Kids With Courage.* (Minneapolis: Free Spirit
Publishing, 1992). Stories of young people of all ages who take social
action, fight crime, work to save the environment, and even perform
heroic acts.

––––––––. *The Kid's Guide to Service Projects: Over 500 Service Ideas
for Young People Who Want to Make a Difference.* (Minneapolis:
Free Spirit Publishing, 1994). More than 500 ideas on a variety of
topics: animals, community development, crime fighting, friendship,
hunger, literacy, safety, transportation, government, and more.

––––––––. *The Kid's Guide to Social Action: How to Solve the Social
Problems You Choose—and Turn Creative Thinking Into Positive
Action.* (Minneapolis: Free Spirit Publishing, 1991). Everything kids
need to make a difference in the world: step-by-step directions for
letter-writing, interviewing, fundraising, speechmaking, media
coverage, and more.

Lyons, Mary E. *Letters From a Slave Girl: The Story of Harriet Jacobs.*
(New York: Macmillan, 1993). Twelve-year-old Harriet must tend the
baby, endure the mistress's cruelty, and evade the attentions of her
master (based on a true story).

MacLachlan, Patricia. *Sarah, Plain and Tall.* (New York: HarperCollins,

1985). Sarah leaves her home in Maine to be a mail-order bride to a widower in the plains. Poignantly written, it touches on themes of longing, self-esteem, and raw family needs.

Nelson, Richard E., and Judith C. Galas. *The Power to Prevent Suicide: A Guide for Teens Helping Teens.* (Minneapolis: Free Spirit Publishing, 1994). This book explains what teens need to know about suicide and suicidal people, spells out the warning signs of suicide, guides readers through the critical steps of reaching out to a friend, motivates young people to get their schools and communities involved, and helps them to help themselves when they're feeling stressed, depressed, or overwhelmed.

Neville, Emily Chaney. *It's Like This, Cat.* (New York: HarperCollins, 1963). Dave comes to terms with family conflict.

O'Dell, Scott. *Island of the Blue Dolphins.* (New York: Bantam, 1960). The story of Karana, the Indian girl who lived alone for eighteen years on an island in the Pacific (based on a true story).

Paterson, Katherine. *Bridge to Terabithia.* (New York: HarperCollins, 1977). A classic work of fiction on the subject of coping with the death of a friend.

————. *The Sign of the Chrysanthemum.* (New York: HarperCollins, 1973). When his mother dies, Muna must travel to twelfth-century Japan to find his father, a samurai warrior. Only then will he become a man.

Sperry, Armstrong. *Call It Courage.* (New York: Aladdin–Macmillan, 1940). Mafatu, a Polynesian boy, determines to conquer his fear of the sea by setting off in a canoe alone.

Taylor, Mildred. *Roll of Thunder, Hear My Cry.* (New York: Bantam, 1976). A bitter, memorable, and moving story of a close-knit African-American family struggling to survive in Mississippi during the Depression. See also the sequel, *Let the Circle Be Unbroken.*

Voigt, Cynthia. *Homecoming.* (New York: Atheneum, 1981). An amazing story of three children, abandoned by their mother in a shopping mall, who set out on a journey of 200 miles to find the home of their aunt. The children undergo a second loss and rejection before persuading a relative, through their hard work and good character, to take them in. See also the sequel, *Dicey's Song.*

Index

649.1   Ellis, Elizabeth
E11   M.
              Raising a
            responsible
            child

GAYLORD R